Getting Anger Under Control

NEIL T. ANDERSON AND RICH MILLER

HARVEST HOUSE PUBLISHERS
Eugene, Oregon 97402

Cover by Terry Dugan Design, Minneapolis, Minnesota

GETTING ANGER UNDER CONTROL

Copyright © 2002 by Neil T. Anderson and Rich Miller
Published by Harvest House Publishers
Eugene, Oregon 97402

Library of Congress Cataloging-in-Publication Data
Anderson, Neil T., 1942–
    Getting anger under control / Neil T. Anderson and Rich Miller.
       p. cm.
    Includes bibliographical references.
    ISBN 0-7369-0349-6
       I. Miller, Rich, 1954–   II. Title.
BV4627.A5 A53 2002
248.4—dc21   2001051575

04 05 06 07 08 09 / BC-VS / 10 9 8 7 6 5

A Word of Dedication

The terrorist attack of September 11, 2001, on the World Trade Center and the Pentagon, occurred as we were doing the final editing of this book. The shock of this terrible tragedy was felt deeply by us as well as by people all around the world. Americans responded in disbelief and wondered how this could happen to us, a peace-loving nation. But what was intended to dishearten and destroy us took a different turn. It brought out a heroic spirit of brotherhood and revealed that the church is still the soul of America.

These deplorable acts of violence brought about a righteous indignation that caused our country to unite against godless terrorism. This act of war is evidence of the continuing battle between good and evil being fought on this planet. The battle is not between Christians and Muslims, nor is it between America and the Arab world. Sadly, however, some of our anger over this is not righteous and has brought out the worst of our bigotry and hatred.

We do not know at this writing what action our country is going to take to seek justice, but we pray that we *will* seek justice, not revenge. We also pray that our response will be made not out of pride, but out of humility. This is a time to humble ourselves, turn from our self-centered ways, and pray. We could be on the verge of a worldwide conflict, or we could be witnessing the beginning of a worldwide revival. Maybe both. But if a revival is coming, "Lord, let it begin with us!"

This book is dedicated to the policemen and firemen who gave their lives that others could live. It is dedicated to the innocent victims on the commercial airplanes used as weapons of war. It is dedicated to the memory of the mothers and fathers, brothers and sisters who lost their lives that tragic morning in New York, Pennsylvania, and Washington, D.C. Finally, it is dedicated to all those serving in the armed forces who face the prospect of dying for their country, for the cause of justice and freedom.

Freedom has always come with a price; it cost the life of Jesus in order that we might be alive and free in Him.

> *We know love by this, that He laid down His life for us;*
> *and we ought to lay down our lives for the brethren.*
> —1 John 3:16

Neil and Rich
September 2001

Contents

A Note from the Authors

In relating true stories and testimonies throughout the book, we have changed names to protect individual identity and privacy.

For ease of reading we have usually not distinguished ourselves from each other in authorship or experiences, preferring to use "I" and "we" as opposed to "I (Rich)" or "I (Neil)." The exceptions are illustrations referring to family.

An Anger Epidemic

~

The world has a serious and growing problem with anger, and America is no exception. A recent *U.S. News* poll revealed that "a vast majority of Americans feel their country has reached an ill-mannered watershed. Nine out of 10 Americans think incivility is a serious problem, and nearly half think it is extremely serious. Seventy-eight percent say the problem has worsened in the last 10 years."[1]

In the U.S. workplace, more than 2 million people each year are victims of crime, with 75 percent of those cases being simple assaults. Workers aged 35 to 49 are the most common targets, with 37 percent of them per year becoming victims of workplace violence. From 1994 to 1996, businesses ranked violence in the workplace as their number one concern.[2]

Why Are We So Angry?

Why have our offices and places of business become hotbeds for anger? Leslie Charles, in her book *Why Is Everyone So Cranky?* writes, "People say work isn't fun like it used to be. They don't have time. They are always behind the eight ball. They are always put on the spot. They're asked to move in one direction, then told to completely switch and move in another direction."[3]

A recent newspaper article painted this picture of a white-collar worker:

> You're stuck in traffic, making you late to work for the third time in a week. Walking in the door, you pass by a co-worker you cannot stand, who offers you a fake smile and a "you're late" comment. You keep walking, but the anger that is simmering below the surface begins

7

to move to the top. Upon reaching your desk, you notice a stack of work waiting that your boss wants done "ASAP." You think about having a cup of coffee, then notice someone took the last drop and didn't bother refilling the pot. About now, it feels like the top of your head may come off. You are truly cranky, and it's not even 9 A.M.[4]

A recent Gallup poll found that 49 percent of those surveyed generally experience anger at work, with one out of six becoming so angry that he or she felt like hitting another person.[5] Adding to this, an Internet survey conducted by *Access Atlanta* discovered that 67 percent of those responding had become so angry at work that they had thought about slapping a co-worker.

Escaping a hostile work environment by retreating to the peace and safety of our homes doesn't appear to be an answer. Experts in the field of domestic violence believe that the true incidence of "partner violence" is around 4 million occurrences annually. Thirty percent of American women report that their husband or boyfriend has, at one time or another, physically abused them.[6] In fact, of the $450 billion cost of crime each year, about one-third is accounted for by domestic violence and child abuse. In 1995, for instance, nearly 1 million cases of child abuse were confirmed by child and protective services.[7] And that doesn't include the millions of incidents of angry outbursts, hateful words, and vicious looks, as well as the countless unreported cases of neglect and abuse.

If the character of a nation can be measured by its treatment of the young, the infirm, and the elderly, then America would not be judged well. Reported cases of elder abuse rose 106 percent from 1986 to 1994, according to the National Center of Elder Abuse. Total incidents range from 1 to 2 million cases annually, though perhaps only 1 in 14 cases is actually reported to any public agency.[8] Whether they are manifested in overt violence and abuse or covert hostility and neglect, it's clear that anger, impatience, frustration, disrespect, and incivility have become a part of the American personality. Whether it is road rage, airplane rage, grocery-store rage, or rage at sporting events, rage is suddenly "the rage." And too many of us feel our anger is justified. In a recent *USA Today* article, an elementary school teacher probably spoke for many people when she said,

> If you have been sitting in traffic on freeways that have been clogged year after year, rage might seem rational. There are, what, more than 260 million of us now? Our roads were not built to accommodate that. The grocery-store parking lots are filled. It is hard to get into the bank. The airport tells you to come 90 minutes before your flight. Parking is at a premium. Overcrowding has become part of society at large and that contributes to a sense that "anything goes."[9]

Does it? Do we have a right to be angry?

Do We Have Good Reason to Be Angry?

Almost every day a new twist on anger hits the newsstands. A Florida high-school baseball coach breaks an umpire's jaw over a disputed call. Two shoppers exchange blows over who deserves the first spot in a checkout lane that just opened. In California, an angry driver yanks a pet dog out of the vehicle that bumped his car and throws the animal into the oncoming traffic. The dog dies, and the man is sentenced to three years in jail. A Reading, Massachusetts, youth hockey coach is beaten unconscious by an irate parent. The coach, Michael Costin, dies two days later. The parent pleads "not guilty" to manslaughter charges. A 15-year-old boy gets fed up with being put down by his classmates and opens fire on them in his suburban San Diego high school. Two are dead, 13 wounded.

Are we justified in turning our society into an instant replay of *The Jerry Springer Show*? (Ironically, one day after we had written this, a warrant was issued for the arrest of Ralf Panitz for the murder of his ex-wife. The two of them had verbally assaulted each other on *The Jerry Springer Show* earlier in the week).[10] We may shake our heads as the walls of propriety come crashing down and public outbursts of anger become the norm, but anger is nothing new. And neither is the feeling of being justified in it.

Nearly 2800 years ago, the reluctant prophet Jonah sat in his self-made bleachers outside the city of Nineveh, hoping for a performance of God's judgment. If nothing else, Jonah was prepared for a full-scale pity party, and the only invited guests were "me, myself, and I." He was upset because the people of Nineveh had repented at his preaching, and the prophet knew that God (unlike Jonah himself!) was "slow to anger and abundant in lovingkindness, and one who relents concerning calamity" (Jonah 4:2). Jonah wanted the city destroyed, but God seemed bent on sparing its residents if they would repent. So Jonah was angry.

The Lord asked Jonah a question, one which we need to ask ourselves: "Do you have good reason to be angry?" (Jonah 4:4). Jonah tried to ignore the issue that God was putting His finger on, so the Lord decided to give the prophet an object lesson. Here's the rest of the story:

> So the LORD God appointed a plant and it grew up over Jonah to be a shade over his head to deliver him from his discomfort. And Jonah was extremely happy about the plant. But God appointed a worm when dawn came the next day and it attacked the plant and it withered. When the sun came up God appointed a scorching east wind, and the sun beat down on Jonah's head so that he became faint and begged with all his soul to die, saying, "Death is better to me than life." Then God said to Jonah, "Do you have good reason to be angry about the plant?" And he said, "I have good reason to be angry, even to death." Then the LORD said, "You had compassion on the plant for which you did not work and which

you did not cause to grow, which came up overnight and perished overnight. Should I not have compassion on Nineveh, the great city in which there are more than 120,000 persons who do not know the difference between their right and left hand?" (Jonah 4:6-11).

As with most people today, Jonah's moods were based on circumstances. When God "appointed" the plant for shade, Jonah was happy. When God "appointed" the worm and the scorching wind, he was angry and miserable. When things were going his way, Jonah's anger was under control. But it didn't take much to set it off again.

Jonah was understandably angry with the Ninevites because of their evil deeds that warranted God's judgment. But he was unwilling to exercise grace and mercy toward them even when they repented. The prophet was aggravated with God because He chose to forgive them. Finally, he was furious with God because the Lord took away his personal beach umbrella and turned up the thermostat. Jonah was an angry man, and he was convinced he had a right to be angry, even if it killed him.

The Roots of Anger

God revealed that Jonah cared more about his own comfort and the well-being of a plant than he did about the souls of people. Like Jonah, many believers today are stuck in their anger and, subsequently, are miserable. One mother wrote to us,

> While you are at it, you might think about writing a book for angry teenagers. My 16-year-old daughter's anger has over the years slowly turned her mind away from Christ and toward the pop culture. Her situation is an ironic one that exists, I believe, in many homes where Christian school, church, and family values have been predominant. For her, the situation posed a dilemma. If she chose Christ, she would never "fit in." If she chose pop culture,

she jeopardized her relationships at home and with this "distant" God who "doesn't care anyway because He doesn't give me what I want." So she got stuck in angry defiance. At home, she acts out her anger. At school, she's decided to get rougher and tougher so that she won't be hurt.

Looking back, I see that I was clueless about the roots of anger and the consequences of wrong thinking. On the outside, it seemed like we were on top of the situation. Yet there were critical stages of anger that we didn't have the tools to see or confront. Now we are doing some major parent intervention in her life. Hopefully it isn't too late. There is no question that her anger has nearly destroyed her relationship with her father and me, caused her to form unhealthy social interactions with peers, and seriously damaged her relationship with God. This is all a pressure cooker for us but, ironically, to the unwary eye she seems like such a "good" kid from a "good" family. "Good" kids can have deeply rooted anger that destroys.

The apostle Paul warned that in the last days "difficult," "terrible" (NIV), or "perilous" (KJV) times would come (2 Timothy 3:1). An alternate translation in the New King James Version says "times of stress" will come. The sorry litany of life lived with a root of self-centered anger reads like today's headlines:

> People will be lovers of themselves, lovers of money, boastful, proud, abusive, disobedient to parents, ungrateful, unholy, without love, unforgiving, slanderous, without self-control, brutal, not lovers of the good, treacherous, rash, conceited, lovers of pleasure rather than lovers of God (2 Timothy 3:2-4 NIV).

USA Today puts it this way: "Leading social scientists say the nation is in the middle of an anger epidemic that, in its mildest forms, is unsettling and, at its worst, turns deadly. The epidemic rattles both those who study social trends and parents who fear the country is at a cultural precipice."[11] One parent expressed it well by saying, "We have lost some of the glue holding our society [together]. We have lost our respect for others. The example we are setting for our kids is terrible."[12] This undercurrent of hostility and lack of respect in our country was captured in an article by Alan Sipress, writing for the *Washington Post*:

> Road rage has come to this. Amid the hectic lives of many Washingtonians, there is no longer time for death. Once, motorists would pull aside and permit funeral corteges to pass. Now, drivers regularly cut them off at intersections rather than allow them to continue through red lights, and weave in and out of processions instead of pausing, funeral directors and police say. The actions are often accompanied by honking, cursing and vile gestures.[13]

Apparently this symptomatic shift away from respect and common courtesy toward self-centered anger has taken place in just the last five to ten years. As one man put it, "How you treat your dead says something about how civilized you are. The traditions of the past have been lost, and clearly the respect that should be extended to funeral processions is no longer there."[14]

Simple respect for the living is no longer there either. Drivers who tailgate, cut off, and even attack other drivers are not seeing the others as neighbors to be loved as oneself. They have become opponents, obstacles, and even enemies.

Although aggravating circumstances certainly make anger in America worse, the Bible makes it clear that the root problem lies within the human heart:

> When He [Jesus] had called all the multitude to Himself, He said to them, "Hear Me, everyone, and understand: There is nothing that enters a man from outside which can defile him; but the things which come out of him, those are the things that defile a man....For

from within, out of the heart of men, proceed evil thoughts, adulteries, fornications, murders, thefts, covetousness, wickedness..." (Mark 7:14-15,21-22 NKJV).

Anger Divides and Kills

Anger is a heart disease that can kill. In our one-to-one ministry to people, almost without exception each individual is having problems with unresolved anger. From our observation, the problem of bitterness and unforgiveness could very well be the most rampant, debilitating problem in the body of Christ today. The anger epidemic in America has viciously infected the church as well.

Our adversary, the devil, seeks to divide and conquer. He will try to divide a human heart, for a double-minded man is unstable in all his ways (James 1:8). He will attack a marriage, a family, or a church because a "house divided against itself will not stand" (Matthew 12:25). Even people groups and nations are fair game for Satan's strategies, for "any kingdom divided against itself is laid waste" (Luke 11:17).

Paul's admonition to the Ephesian church stands in sharp contrast to the spirit of resentment, hostility, and rage so evident in human cultures. He writes this to them:

> Laying aside falsehood, speak truth each one of you with his neighbor, for we are members of one another. Be angry, and yet do not sin; do not let the sun go down on your anger, and do not give the devil an opportunity.... Let no unwholesome word proceed from your mouth, but only such a word as is good for edification according to the need of the moment, so that it will give grace to those who hear. Do not grieve the Holy Spirit of God, by whom you were sealed for the day of redemption. Let all bitterness and wrath and anger and clamor and slander be put away from you, along with all malice. Be kind to one another, tenderhearted, forgiving each other, just as

God in Christ also has forgiven you (Ephesians 4:25-27, 29-32).

Every evening the sun will set on the unresolved anger of millions of people. This anger poisons the soul and rots the culture. The devil is delighted, and the Holy Spirit of God is grieved. Here is a typical personal story of a man struggling with habitual, unresolved anger:

> I have struggled with anger all my life, since I was a little boy. My peers always picked on me and my dad constantly criticized everything I did. I have come a long way. However it seems that there is still some stronghold in my mind over this area. I get really upset if I am mistreated or disrespected by people, especially family members. I don't hold on to grudges for as long as I used to, but there still appears to be some block in the process of forgiveness. I react so quickly with outbursts of anger that I don't even realize where they come from or the reason behind them. My wife tells me if I'm mad to "get happy," as if we have direct control over our feelings like that. I know that the problem is in my mind, but the negative thoughts appear to be so buried that I don't even know they are there. Pray that God would reveal the root causes of this bondage to me.

By the grace of God, this book is our attempt to do just that—to examine the phenomenon of anger, to expose its roots, and to provide a handle on how to allow Jesus to liberate you from it's controlling influence.

Anger Can Be Resolved

Anger will never completely disappear from our lives this side of heaven. Nor should it. There is a time and a place for anger under control. Anger is our servant when we live a liberated life in Christ. But anger is the master of a defeated life. If we desire to be angry and *not* sin, then we need to be like Christ and be angry *at* sin.

We need to get beyond "anger management," which is merely a means of keeping one's anger from erupting in behavior destructive to self or others. The goal is to *resolve* the personal and spiritual issues *behind* the anger and discover the fruit of the Spirit, which is "love, joy, peace, patience, kindness, goodness, faithfulness, gentleness, self-control" (Galatians 5:22-23). Those who are alive and free in Christ don't *manage* destructive behavior, they *overcome* it. "Do not be overcome by evil, but overcome evil with good," as Paul wrote in Romans 12:21.

Sure sounds good, doesn't it? Maybe to you it sounds too good to be true. You may have struggled with anger all your life, without much success in overcoming its mastery over you. Or you may be living with a "rage-aholic" or an explosive child. Perhaps your body bears the scars of anger out of control. Or at the very least, your soul does.

We want to offer you hope. Jeremiah 32:17 (NIV) declares, "Ah, Sovereign LORD, you have made the heavens and the earth by your great power and outstretched arm. Nothing is too hard for you." If God can create and control such a vast universe, is He not also able to control your anger and empower you to deal with the anger of those around you?

There is no reason to feel you are a hopeless case, an exception to the rule. Paul writes, "May the God of hope fill you with all joy and peace in believing, so that you will abound in hope by the power of the Holy Spirit" (Romans 15:13).

What Do You Truly Want?

On the other hand, maybe the opposite is true. Perhaps you like your anger. It gets you what you want when you want it. You learned to control people with angry tantrums as a child, and the technique is still working. You've just become more sophisticated. Instead of stomping your feet, you raise your voice (a lot!) and level your gaze and make threats. People are afraid of you, and you like that surge of power and control. Or perhaps you think that anger is a means of protecting yourself against further abuse.

True, anger may temporarily get you what you want. But fleshly anger will never get you what you really need or desire, because "the anger of man does not achieve the righteousness of God," as James tells us (1:20). Some of the most insecure people on earth are angry controllers and abusers. Using anger and sex as bludgeons to oppress and manipulate others reveals a sickness of the soul that only Christ can overcome.

So, whether you were given this book (which may have made you angry already!) or you picked it up on your own, we have good news for you. Jesus Christ came to set you free from the control of anger. He came that you might have life and have it more abundantly (John 10:10). He has promised us a peace, but it's not like the peace the world gives—based on peaceful circumstances (John 14:27). It is a peace of mind and heart running so deep and strong that it goes beyond human understanding (Philippians 4:6-7).

Negative circumstances that would drive a natural person up a wall can be overcome by the indwelling Prince of Peace. Such a powerful peace can reign in our lives that the apostle Paul describes it as "the God of peace" being with us (Philippians 4:9). The presence of God fills our lives with love, patience, and kindness when before there was only hostility, resentment, and rage. We trust that, deep down, this is what you truly want in life.

Let Yourself Be Molded by God

In the pages that follow, we'll first take a look at anger in general and how our body, soul, and spirit work together. We'll then examine the battle for our minds and find out how we can keep from being controlled by our emotions through choosing to believe and focus on the truth. We'll see how we have developed mental strongholds and examine various flesh patterns* of anger. Then we'll look at the grace of God, which offers us forgiveness and new life in Christ. The journey to freedom from our past begins as we learn how to forgive from our hearts.

Next we'll learn how to let the gentle and humble Jesus live in and through us in the power of the Holy Spirit. It is not enough just to know what to do—we must have the power to do it. That spiritual energy only comes from the Spirit of God. And in the final chapters we'll summarize what we've learned, by sharing how to overcome strongholds of anger.

Is it truly possible to be free from controlling anger? The answer to that question is a resounding "Yes!" Will it be a painless process? Probably not. Is it worth it? Absolutely, though you are going to have to come to that conclusion yourself.

One day God told the prophet Jeremiah to go down to the house of the potter. There He promised to speak to him. So Jeremiah did as he was told and saw the potter molding something on the wheel. "But the vessel that he was making of clay was spoiled in the hand of the potter; so he remade it into another vessel, as it pleased the potter to make" (Jeremiah 18:4).

What was the moral of the story? Why had God wanted Jeremiah to see this man skillfully at work at his craft? "Then the word of the LORD came to me saying, 'Can I not, O house of Israel, deal with you as this potter does?' declares the LORD. 'Behold, like the clay in the potter's hand, so are you in My hand'" (Jeremiah 18:5-6).

This passage is echoed in Paul's second letter to Timothy, where he writes,

> Now in a large house there are not only gold and silver vessels, but also vessels of wood and of earthenware, and some to honor and some to dishonor. Therefore, if a man cleanses himself from these things, he will be a vessel for honor, sanctified, useful to the Master, prepared for every good work (2 Timothy 2:20-21).

---

*Throughout the book we use the term "flesh pattern" to mean any habit we have developed to try to cope with life and get our needs met while relying on our own human resources rather than on Christ. In essence, a flesh pattern is self-sufficiency.

There is no greater honor, no greater privilege, and no greater joy than to allow the Master to mold us as He pleases. To be set apart, useful to the Master, is what we were made for. But first, a man must cleanse himself of all that dishonors, including the anger that simmers or boils in the heart.

Will you join us as we pray about this?

> *Dear heavenly Father, You are a holy God, and You call me to be holy, set apart for Your use. Like You, I have the capacity for anger. But unlike You, I also have the capacity for using that anger wrongly. You have called me to freedom, but have told me not to use my freedom as an opportunity for the flesh. Rather I am to serve others in love. Please open my eyes to understand the source of my anger and the bitterness of my soul. Free me from my past, that it may no longer have any hold over me. Fill me with your Holy Spirit, that I may live a righteous life of patience, gentleness, and self-control. I thank You that You are indeed gracious and merciful, slow to anger, and abounding in lovingkindness and truth. In the name of the gentle and humble Jesus I pray, amen.*

PART ONE

How Anger Works in You

1

Anger—A Matter of Life and Death

Anger:
an acid that can do more harm
to the vessel in which it is stored
than to anything on which it is poured.

~

J im was trying to wrap up another busy day at the office. His son was having a Little League game at 5:30, and he'd promised him he would be there since demands at work had prevented him from being at the last three games. Jim was a highly motivated insurance salesman who had won the salesperson-of-the-year award for three straight years. His desire to climb the corporate ladder was often in conflict with his Christian convictions about being a good husband and father, but it wasn't hard to rationalize his work ethic. Achievement awards, higher salaries, and greater commissions had made it possible for his family to have a higher standard of living and afford better vacations.

Late-afternoon calls were irritating him as he rushed to get out the door. *Why do people always call at the last minute?* he wondered. He glanced at his watch as he merged into the rush-hour traffic. Just enough time to make it if the freeways would cooperate. As he tried to work his way into the fast lane, he was abruptly cut off by another car. "Stupid jerk! Where are the cops when you need them?" The traffic slowed to a crawl, and Jim found himself stuck behind a large truck that blocked his view and made his lane slower than those on either side. As he tightened his grip on the steering wheel he angrily said out loud, "Trucks shouldn't be allowed to drive anywhere other than the right lane!"

The Body's Response to Anger

What was going on inside Jim's body in response to all these frustrating circumstances? The thoughts and feelings running wild in Jim's left cerebral cortex had already sent a signal deeper in the brain to nerve cells in the hypothalamus. The activated emergency system of the hypothalamus had stimulated sympathetic nerves to constrict the arteries carrying blood to Jim's skin, kidneys, and intestines. At the same time, the brain had sent a signal to the adrenal glands to pump large doses of adrenaline and cortisol into his bloodstream. As he sat behind the truck, Jim's muscles tightened, his heart beat faster, and his blood pressure rose. In such a state his blood would have clotted more rapidly in case of injury. Muscles at the outlet of his stomach were squeezing down so tightly that nothing could leave his digestive tract. This caused spasms, which resulted in abdominal pains. The blood was directed away from his skin, making it feel cool and clammy and toward the muscles to facilitate a "fight or flight" response.

As the angry thoughts continued, Jim's increased heart rate had already pumped far more blood than was needed just to sit in the car. His body was prepared to spring into action, but there was nowhere to go. He was tempted to let off some steam by rolling down the window and telling somebody what he thought of them, or by leaning on the horn, but he knew that wouldn't do any good. The adrenaline that had been released stimulated Jim's fat cells to empty their content into his bloodstream. This would provide additional energy in the event the situation required immediate action. But instead Jim just sat there, fuming at the traffic while his liver converted the fat into cholesterol. He had no one to fight and nowhere to take flight to. He felt trapped.

Over time the cholesterol formed from the unused fat in his bloodstream will accumulate, forming into a plaque in his arteries that begins to block the flow of blood. If Jim's struggle with anger continues, one day the flow of blood could be entirely cut off to a portion of his heart. Then Jim would become a statistic—one of the 500,000 Americans each year who suffer from a heart attack. One such person was the famous psychologist, John Hunter, who "knew what anger could do to his heart: 'The first scoundrel that gets me angry will kill me.' Some time later, at a medical meeting, a speaker made assertions that incensed Hunter. As he stood up and bitterly attacked the speaker, his anger caused such a contraction of blood vessels in his heart that he fell dead."[1]

Anger kills in other ways, too. Tragically, all too often anger gets the best of people and brings out the worst in them, especially when jealousy enters the mix. Proverbs 27:4 says, "Wrath is fierce and anger is a flood, but who can stand before jealousy?" Whether the weapon of choice is a car or an airplane, an explosive or a firearm, a germ or a chemical, the threat of violence has our nation on edge. And such fear often manifests itself in fury. In fact, an undercurrent of hostility is becoming more evident in America and around the world. Too many people are at the boiling point, and who knows when the slightest provocation will set them off into a deadly rage? Or who knows when the calculated hostility of terrorists will erupt into mass destruction either here or abroad?

Either way, anger can kill.

The Role That Personality Plays

In my first pastorate, I was given a book by one of the more successful members of our church. He said, "You ought to read this book, because I think you may need it." The book was *Type A Behavior and Your Heart* by Meyer Friedman and Ray Rosenman. This highly motivated IBM engineer went on to explain that he had a type A personality and he suspected that I did too. After reading the book, I did see some aspects of my personality that were type A. (I also gave a message a few weeks later entitled "Jesus Was Type B.")

Friedman and Rosenman were cardiologists who began to notice that certain personality types were more prone to have heart problems. Those who burnt the candle at both ends, climbed the stairs two steps at a time, took little time off, and were driven to accomplish their goals were classified as type A. They are the task-oriented high achievers of this world, and they are driven to accomplish their goals. Type B individuals are more laid-back, less driven, and probably more relational.[2]

These observations have made a profound effect on our society. Not only have these classifications of type A and type B personalities become very well-known, but the authors started a flood of research into psychosomatic illnesses. Before the publication of their work, stress was not considered to be a major contributor to heart disease, cancer, and other major illnesses. Today, stress is considered to be a major cause of life-threatening illnesses.

Redford and Virginia Williams, in their book *Anger Kills*, adapted the work of Friedman and Rosenman to the problem of anger. In their research, they show how those with a hostile personality are more prone to coronary heart disease. For many years, researchers, therapists, and schools of higher education have used the MMPI (Minnesota Multiphasic Personality Inventory) to assess clients and students. Since many of these test results have been kept, they could be compared many years later with the physical health of those who took the test. The Williamses, along with other colleagues, isolated certain responses from the MMPI that reflected in the answerer a cynical distrust of others, the frequent experience of angry feelings, and the overt expression of cynicism in aggressive behavior. They summarize their findings as follows—

1. Hostile people—those with high levels of cynicism, anger, and aggression—are at a higher risk of developing life-threatening illnesses than are their less hostile counterparts.

2. By driving others away, or by not perceiving the support they could be deriving from their social contacts, hostile people may be depriving themselves of the health-enhancing, stress-buffering benefits of social support.

3. A quicker activation of their flight-or-fight response, in combination with a relatively weak calming response from the parasympathetic nervous system, is a biologic mechanism that probably contributes to the health problems that afflict hostile people.

4. Hostile people also are more prone to engage in a number of risky behaviors—eating more, drinking more alcohol, smoking—that could damage their health.[3]

The Body, the Mind, and Anger

People do die from psychosomatic illnesses, which indicates that more is going on in our body than just a response to life on the physical plane. We must also reckon with the non-physical—our soul. To understand how the body and the soul interact, let's consider how God created us in His image. See the following diagram:

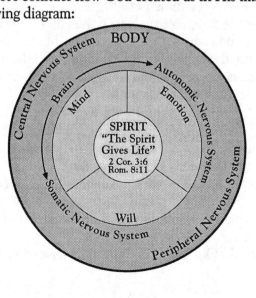

In the original creation, God formed Adam and Eve from the dust of the earth and breathed into them the breath of life. This union of divine breath and earthly dust is what constituted the physical and spiritual life that Adam and Eve both possessed. Every human being is composed of both an inner person and an outer person. In other words, we are both material and immaterial. Our outer person, or material part, is our physical body. Through our body's five senses we relate to the world around us. The inner person, or immaterial part, consists of our soul and spirit. Being created in the image of God, we have the capacity to think, feel, and choose (soul) and commune with God (spirit).

Because we are fearfully and wonderfully made, it only makes sense that God would have created the outer person to work together with the inner person—for example, the brain and mind. Their correlation is obvious, but they are fundamentally different. Our brains are like organic computers, and they will return to dust when we physically die. At that time, if we are born-again believers, we will be present with the Lord; but we will not be there mindless because the mind is part of the soul, the inner person.

Using the computer analogy, if the brain is the hardware, then the mind is the software. In our earthly life, neither the software nor the hardware is any good without the other. And as we explain later, the brain cannot function any way other than how it has been programmed.

The brain is the center of the central nervous system, which also includes the spinal cord. Branching off from the central nervous system is a peripheral nervous system that has two distinct channels. One channel is the somatic nervous system. That system is what regulates all our muscular and skeletal movements. It is that which we have volitional control over. In other words, provided we have adequate physical health, we can mentally choose to move our limbs, to smile and to speak. Obviously, the somatic nervous system takes orders from our will. We don't do anything without first thinking it. The thought–action response may be so rapid that we are hardly aware of the sequence, but it is always there. (Though involuntary muscular movements do occur when the system breaks down, as is the case with Parkinson's disease.)

The other channel is the autonomic nervous system, which regulates all our glands and obviously works together with our emotions. We don't have direct volitional control of the functioning of our glands. In the same way, we don't have direct volitional control of our emotions, including the feelings of anger. We cannot will ourselves to like people we have an emotional hatred for. We *can* choose to do the loving thing for them even though we don't like them; but we cannot simply tell ourselves to stop being angry, because we cannot directly manage our emotions that way. When we acknowledge that we are angry, however, we do have control over how we are going to express it. We can keep our behavior within limits, because that is something we have volitional control over. And we *do* have control of what we will think and believe, and that is what controls what we do and how we feel.

Controlling What We Think

We can do a similar thing when we talk to angry people. Telling them that they shouldn't be angry will only produce guilt or defensiveness (rationalization) in them or bring retaliation from them. But we can encourage them to manage their behavior. For instance, we can say, "I know you are angry right now, but you don't have to take it out on others or yourself. Why don't you walk away and come back when you have cooled down, and we can discuss it later?" However, you will have as much success telling them to stop being angry as they will have if they try to keep their autonomic nervous system from functioning.

It is important to realize that what is causing the autonomic nervous system to respond this way is not the brain; nor is it the brain that is causing us to feel angry. It is the *mind* and the way it has been programmed. Neither do the circumstances of life or other people make us angry. It is our *perception* of those people and events and *how we interpret them* that determine whether we will lose our temper or not. And that is a function of our mind and how its been programmed.

Let's apply that reasoning to the problem of stress. When the pressures of life begin to mount, our bodies try to adapt. Our adrenal glands excrete hormones into our bloodstream, enabling us to rise to the challenge. But if the pressure persists too long, then stress becomes distress, and our system breaks down and we become sick. But why do some people respond positively to stress while others get sick? Is it because some people have better adrenal glands than others? It's true that some are physically able to handle more than others, but that is not the primary difference. The primary difference is found in the mind, not the body.

Beliefs and Anger

Suppose two partners in a business are confronted with a setback. They have just lost a contract they thought would bring them to a new level of prosperity. One partner, a nonbeliever, sees this as a financial crisis. He had believed that this new contract would make him successful. Many of his personal goals were going to be realized, but now his dreams are dashed. He responds in anger to all who try to console him and calls his lawyer to see if he can sue the company who broke the contract.

The other partner is a Christian who deeply believes that real success lies in becoming the person God created him to be. He believes that God will supply all his needs. Therefore, this loss has very little impact on him. He experiences some disappointment, but he doesn't get angry because he sees this temporary reversal as an opportunity to trust in God. One of these two partners is stressed out and angry, while the other partner is experiencing very little stress and anger. Can faith in God have that kind of an effect on us? Clearly so, because in our example the difference is in the two partners' belief systems, not in their physical capacity. From the wisdom literature we read, "As he thinks within himself, so he is" (Proverbs 23:7). How we behave flows from the reservoir of what we believe.

What Are You Thinking?

Anger doesn't happen in a vacuum. Anger, like all of our emotions, is primarily a product of our thought life. Suppose you are busy shopping one day, when another person suddenly knocks you down and falls on top of you. You have no idea why the person has done that. If your initial thought is that the person is careless or rude, you will likely get angry. Your nervous system will respond immediately, enabling your body to react in a flight-or-fight response. If your external senses are telling you that the person is a thief who is armed, your adrenaline rush will help equip you to flee or protect yourself. If your external senses pick up that it was just some kids playing without supervision, you will be inclined to push them off you, dust yourself off, and reprimand them for their carelessness. Whatever the case, your anger is a natural response to how your mind interprets the data that is being picked up by your five senses.

Suppose your initial thought is directed toward the other person and not yourself. You may be wondering what has happened to this person who has fallen and is now lying on top of you. You may initially be angry, or at least startled, until your external senses give you some important new data. Now you realize this person is in trouble, and your anger quickly turns to sympathy, and that causes you to cry out for help. Then upon further examination, you realize that the person is simply drunk and has passed out. Now you are angry, and you push the person off with a strength you never knew you had. So how you feel is dependent upon the data you receive and how your mind interprets that data.

Feelings Follow Beliefs

This brings up another important concept. If what we believe does not conform to truth, then what we feel does not conform to reality. Suppose a man angrily bursts through the door of his boss's office and says, "I demand to know why you did it!" His startled boss cannot understand why the man is angry. Unknown to the boss, a rumor had been circulating that some recent promotions might have to be rescinded, and the man assumed his was one of them. As it turned out, the rumors were totally false, but the employee was angry because he believed them to be true. Once the boss got him simmered down, he was able to convince the disgruntled employee that no such thing had happened. Now the man is no longer angry with his boss, but chances are he may be a little angry with himself—and with the people who circulated the rumor.

It is not the events themselves that trigger our physiological responses. Nor is it our adrenal glands themselves that initiate the release of adrenaline. Rather, external events are picked up by our five senses and sent as a signal to our brains. The mind then interprets the data and choices are made—and that is what determines the signal that is sent from the brain and central nervous system to the peripheral nervous system. The brain cannot function any other way than in the way it has been programmed by the mind. That is why we are transformed by the renewing of our minds (Romans 12:2).

Programming for Renewal

How our minds have been programmed is revealed by our belief system, which reflects our values and attitudes about life. Let's take another look at Jim, the successful salesman. He held certain beliefs about himself, about life, and about what he valued. Chances are his sense of worth was largely tied into his career: He believed he would be a successful person if he did well on the job and a failure if he didn't. He also had beliefs about himself: He was a salesman and a good one. But he was also a father and he held certain Christian values about being a good parent. That afternoon he didn't want to go back on his word and miss his son's game, but neither did he want to miss a couple of late-afternoon calls that could affect his sales. Was he a salesman first, or a father first?

Jim made choices that afternoon that had a profound effect on how he felt. He could have written the time of his son's game on his calendar and made it just as important as any business appointment. Then he could have left earlier and avoided all the traffic. His secretary could simply have told his callers that he had an important meeting that he could not miss, but that he would do his best to get back to them tomorrow. It wasn't really the stalled traffic that made him angry; the anger was Jim's own emotional response to the cumulative effect of the wrong choices he had made that day.

When I attended my first doctoral class years ago, I was the only professing Christian enrolled. The instructor was an ex-nun who liked to display her liberation from the church. I think she was especially delighted to have a "reverend" in her class whom she could occasionally put on the spot. I saw this as a challenge to my faith that I was delighted to accept.

Near the end of the semester, we were asked to share with the class the topic of our term papers. I said I was doing a paper on managing our anger. Another doctoral student protested, "You can't do a paper on managing your anger." I asked her, "Why not?" "Because you don't get angry." Apparently, she would have responded in anger to some of the targeting that I was getting in the class. She couldn't believe that I would choose to do a paper on anger, and she reminded me of this several times. I assured her that I do at times get angry.

Our differences became clearer as the semester came to an end. She and her brother, who also attended the class, were members of a cult. And the differences between our belief systems became more and more evident as they were tested under fire.

What we believe does affect how we respond to the circumstances of life. If our identity and security are centered in our eternal relationship with God, then the things of life that are temporal have less of an impact on us. As we are conformed to the image of God, we will become a little less type A and a little more like Jesus.

If this is your desire, we invite you to join us in prayer about it.

> *Dear heavenly Father, thank You that I am indeed fearfully and wonderfully made by You. It is amazing how You have caused my spirit, soul, and body to be so intertwined and interconnected. But that truth brings a sobering warning to me as well. I can see how my perceptions or misperceptions of reality have negatively affected my emotions. And how when I lose my temper it hurts me physically even as it hurts others emotionally. Only You, Lord Jesus, giving me Your life through my spirit, can conquer this struggle that I have. But I want You to win so that I might become more like You. I pray for this now in Your name, Jesus, amen.*

Goals and Desires

Be not angry that you cannot make others
as you wish them to be,
since you cannot make yourself
as you wish to be.

—THOMAS À KEMPIS

∾

It was a peaceful evening and time for dinner at the Miller household. As usual, my wife, Shirley, had put together a feast. I was ready to relax, enjoy the meal, and perhaps impart some profound thoughts to my family. But suddenly the tired, angry shrieks of my then one-year-old son Brian shattered the idyllic home atmosphere.

Upset at his lousy timing, I marched over to where Brian was sitting, roughly picked him up, and shouted "No!" right in his face. Now my son was not only upset but also frightened, and so he cried even louder. And I got even angrier.

Fuming, I put him back down and stalked off to the dinner table to begin eating. After a moment I noticed that Shirley was not eating. There was no way she could eat with Brian feeling so bad! She walked over to the living room where he was sitting, gently calmed him down, and brought him into the kitchen for dinner. The meal was finished without further incident.

An hour or so later, I was vegging out in front of the TV, and our daughter Michelle (then three years old) strolled into the den. I barely noticed her out of the corner of my eye, being so absorbed in the show.

"Daddy, you shouldn't get mad at Brian like that," she stated firmly.

Basically ignoring her, I muttered something like, "Yeah right, honey. Okay." Now those who have daughters know that there is no created being on earth who can be as simultaneously sweet and bossy as a three-year-old little girl! Michelle was not about to give up.

"Daddy! You shouldn't get mad at Brian like that!" Her tone of voice was more insistent, and it got my attention—and so did the Spirit of God. Convicted of my sinful anger, I said to Michelle, "You're right, honey. Daddy was wrong. I shouldn't get mad at Brian like that. I'll try not to do it again, okay?"

Satisfied that she'd made her point, she nodded her approval, said "Okay!" and strutted triumphantly out of the room.

Looking at My Anger

But the Lord was just beginning His work on me. Prompted by my own sorrow for being nasty to Brian, I prayed, "Lord, why did I get so angry with Brian?" All I wanted was a nice quiet dinner with all my children behaving properly, as they should. But Brian didn't cooperate, and I got mad when the events of the evening weren't going my way. The Lord reminded me that the fruit of the Spirit is *self*-control, not spouse or child control. By angrily trying to control others so I could fulfill my own purpose or satisfy my own desire for comfort, I was not acting in love.

That wasn't all the Lord wanted to speak to me about. So I prayerfully wondered, *Why did I get even angrier when I told Brian "No!" resulting in him crying even louder?* The Lord then convicted me of the false belief that I could persuade anybody of my point of view and get them to do what I thought was right. That is not only arrogant but futile as well, especially with an irrational, screaming one-year-old!

Humbled, I confessed my sin and renounced (verbally rejected) the false beliefs and consequent anger. I had believed that my success as a father and sense of worth as a person were dependent upon other people—people whom I had no right or ability to control. According to Jesus, the joy of living does not come from getting our way, but from doing the will of our heavenly Father: "If you keep my commandments, you will abide in My love; just as I have kept my Father's commandments and abide in His love. These things I have spoken to you so that My joy may be in you, and that your joy may be made full" (John 15:10-11).

Defining Anger

We can all look back at times when we responded poorly to life's situations and succumbed to anger. We have seen that our personalities and temperaments have something to do with how we respond. Some people are more relational and naturally laid-back. Others are more task-oriented and driven. Most of us are somewhere in between. According to Dr. J.R. Averill, 90 percent of people stuff their anger inside while responding outwardly in a passive, submissive manner.[1] This "silent majority" actually harbors the most anger but does little about it.[2] But the expression of anger is not just related to our temperaments, it is also related to what we believe right now as we react to others and the situations of life. According to the *Baker Encyclopedia of Psychology*, anger is:

> an intense emotional reaction, sometimes directly expressed in overt behavior and sometimes remaining a largely unexpressed feeling....Being angry is an emotional readiness to aggress.[3]

Webster's New World Dictionary gives this definition of anger:

> A feeling that may result from injury, mistreatment, opposition, etc.; it usually shows itself in a desire to hit

out at something or someone else; wrath; indignation; rage; ire.

The two Greek New Testament words most often translated as "anger" and "wrath" are *orge* and *thumos* respectively. *Vine's Expository Dictionary* gives an explanation of the difference between the two words:

> *Thumos*, wrath (not translated "anger"), is to be distinguished from *orge* in this respect, that *thumos* indicates a more agitated condition of the feelings, an outburst of wrath from inward indignation, while *orge* suggests a more settled or abiding condition of mind, frequently with a view to taking revenge. *Orge* is less sudden in its rise than *thumos* but more lasting in its nature....*Thumos* may issue in revenge, though it does not necessarily include it. It is characteristic that it quickly blazes up and quickly subsides, though that is not necessarily implied in each case.[4]

In the New Testament, the Greek word *thumos* is used 18 times, seven times in the book of Revelation in reference to God's wrath. Every other time *thumos* is used in the New Testament, it indicates a sinful human behavior.[5] In fact, *thumos*—translated "outbursts of anger," "outbursts of wrath" (NKJV), "fits of rage" (NIV)—is one of the deeds of the flesh listed in Galatians 5:20.

We are warned by the apostle Paul in Ephesians 4:31 to "get rid of all...rage [*thumos*] and anger [*orge*]" (NIV). Although anger is a natural human emotion, it is clear that we as believers in Christ have no business harboring fleshly anger in our hearts. Otherwise, why would Paul be so adamant about our need to get rid of *all* of it?

What Makes Us Angry?

Why do people get angry anyway? Some get angry because they see the injustices of life. Such righteous indignation is justified, and is similar to the wrath of God, which is spoken of more times in Scripture than is the anger of mankind. Godly anger becomes a powerful motivator to correct social injustices. Others get angry because life is not going their way and they are not getting what they want. This reveals flesh patterns, defense mechanisms, or mental and spiritual strongholds that are the result of living independently of God in a fallen world. (We'll discuss these things in more detail in chapters 4 and 5.) This kind of anger has become a settled part of such people's character and will surface at the slightest provocation. That is especially true of those who are caught in the bondage of bitterness. For these people, anger is the manifestation of deeper issues that have never been resolved in Christ. These include *rejection, guilt, shame, fear, embarrassment, confusion, frustration, humiliation, failure, and feeling trapped, used, controlled, betrayed, or misunderstood.*

Physical conditions such as *acute or chronic pain, weariness, and sickness* leave us emotionally depleted and less able to control our anger. Many times individuals who are suffering will try to medicate themselves. The use and misuse of alcohol, prescription drugs, and street drugs to try to numb the pain of life is rampant. But all too often their use opens a Pandora's box of volatile emotions and violent anger.

It is characteristic of the human soul to try and rid itself of pain. If I am angry because I feel trapped or controlled in a relationship, I am going to express that anger—somewhere, somehow. It may be toward the controller, an innocent bystander, or myself. If I am struggling with anger over guilt in my own life and am not willing to take it to the cross, then I am a prime candidate for angrily blaming others. Unresolved anger will find a victim. "An angry man stirs up strife, and a hot-tempered man abounds in transgression" (Proverbs 29:22).

Roots of Anger in Childhood

Children have been described as the world's best observers but the world's worst interpreters. They are, therefore, most vulnerable to picking up and packing in the anger of their parents (who likely did the same when *they* were children). The fruit of parents' anger contains seeds of rejection that are often sown in their children's early years. And many children will not wait until adulthood to express their anger.

In far too many cases more bitter seeds of rejection are sown throughout adolescence until the young person is overwhelmed by a world that is hostile and cruel. In recent days we have seen these bitter seeds bear tragic, deadly fruit as adolescents have exploded in violence.

We will discuss in chapter 10 the effect of the "world system" on anger, focusing especially on the current climate in American society. But for a young child, his or her "world" is primarily the home. Those who grow up in an environment where they are fed a steady diet of *overt* rejection are getting the message loud and clear: *You are worthless, inadequate, stupid, hopeless, dirty, and unwanted.* They are unloved and they know it. That rejection will produce a deep-seated anger or rage in the rejected child's heart.

But rejection can also be *covert*, hidden behind the walls of a seemingly healthy family environment. Bill Gillham, in his book *Lifetime Guarantee*, explains the difference between overt and covert rejection:

> In the case of the person who is being overtly rejected, all the cards are up on the table, and by the teen years most children see very well that they are being rejected. In the case of covert rejection, however, most kids never discern what's happening to them. It simply seeps over their personalities like a slowly gathering fog they can't identify, much less verbalize to someone else. The *emotional results are the same* for both types of rejection, though, so the covertly rejected child might say, "I *feel* as if they don't love me," whereas the overtly rejected child might say, "I *know* nobody loves me."[6]

Gillham then goes on to explain numerous ways in which covert rejection can show up. One is perfectionism: parents imposing their unrealistic expectations of themselves on their children. Children trapped in this system learn that they are just not good enough. Ignoring your children and not spending time with them sends the message that they are worth *less* than other people and things. No wonder they come to view themselves as worthless! Comparing children unfavorably to others or ridiculing them can cause them to think they are unlovable, unacceptable, and unworthy. Apart from the grace of God, those soul-labels can mark them for the rest of their lives. Overindulgence can cause children to be angry at a world that will not bow its knee at their demand when they grow up. Overprotection can communicate to children that they are weak and ill-prepared to face the world.

Probably the most rampant source of covert rejection, however, is performance-based acceptance. This is acceptance with strings attached. It is conditional love expressed as, "We love you when..." or "if...." It is the motivating force behind many driven people. It is the frown that creases the face of a mom who sees the Bs and ignores the As on her children's report cards. It is the proud slap on the back from the dad when his son scores the touchdown and the look of disgust when he fumbles. It is the joy in parents' eyes when their children declare their decision to enter the medical profession and the disapproval expressed when they choose to pursue a career in music.[7]

However it is expressed, performance-based acceptance is not truly acceptance at all. It is rejection, and like all rejection, it can cause a child to feel angry, worthless, and unwanted. In reaction, some will strive to gain the acceptance of others and prove that they are worthy. They are driven to beat the system and in the process often become angry controllers. Others will rebel against the system in deep anger and bitterness. They would have you believe they don't want or need your love and acceptance, but in reality they desperately need it. Our characters are most affected by the presence or absence of unconditional love and acceptance in our homes— and this primarily in the early years of our development.

Blocked Goals

In the Bible there are numerous cases where family and friends provoked men and women to anger. Here are a few examples.

- Miriam and Aaron were angry with Moses out of envy (Numbers 12).

- Esau was angry with Jacob because he was tricked out of his father's blessing (Genesis 27:41-46).

- Jacob became angry with Rachel because she had expectations of him he felt powerless to fulfill (Genesis 30:2).

- Jacob also was mad at his uncle, Laban, for treating him unfairly (Genesis 31:36).

- Potiphar was angry at Joseph because he believed he had been betrayed by a friend whom he trusted (Genesis 39:19).

- Balaam became furious with his donkey because the animal refused to obey him and move forward (Numbers 22:27).

In each of the cases, these people's anger was based on something or someone they had no right or ability to control. Consciously or subconsciously, we all have certain expectations of others and of ourselves, with the hope that the circumstances of life will allow us to carry out our life plan. But sometimes others don't cooperate, and the circumstances are not always favorable. If we believe that our identity and sense of worth is dependent upon the cooperation of other people and upon favorable circumstances, then we will likely try to control them. When we discover that we can't, then those people or circumstances are blocking us from our goals, and we get angry. If any outcome we desire is uncertain, we feel anxious; and if our goal seems impossible to reach, we get depressed.[8]

Goals and Desires

There are no goals for our lives that can be blocked or be uncertain or impossible if they're given to us by God. With Him all things are possible (Matthew 19:26), and we can do all things through Christ who strengthens us (Philippians 4:13). If God wants it done, it can be done—and whatever God has required us to do, we can do by His grace. The question then is, What is included in, and excluded from, "all things"? To answer that question, we need to distinguish between a godly *desire* and a godly *goal*.

"A godly goal is any specific orientation that reflects God's purpose for our lives and is not dependent on people or circumstances beyond our right or ability to control."[9] God's goal for our lives is to become the person He created us to be. Paul said, "This is the will of God, your sanctification" (1 Thessalonians 4:3). Nobody—nothing—on planet Earth can keep us from becoming the person God created us to be. The only ones who can interfere with that goal is ourselves. But if we falsely believe that who we are, and our purpose for being here, are dependent upon other people or favorable circumstances, we will experience a lot of anger, anxiety, and depression, because other people will not always cooperate with our wishes, and the circumstances of life will not always be favorable. And of course we never have the absolute right or ability to control others or the circumstances of life.

Now contrast a godly *goal* with a godly *desire*, which is any specific result that *does depend* on the cooperation of other people, the success of events, or favorable circumstances that we have no right or ability to control.[10] Godly desires will become a problem for us if we raise them to the level of goals.

For example, a cashier in the grocery store has to check the price of an item the person in front of you is buying. You're in a hurry to get home and fix dinner, but the cashier seems to be moving at the speed of a glacier. You're frustrated with the delay and start to get angry. That "slowpoke" is blocking your goal of getting in and out of there fast! But the cashier is not determining who you *are*. How you respond will reveal your flesh patterns and your belief system. Patience is a fruit of the Spirit, and if you were walking by the Spirit, it would become evident. In this case you have a godly desire (fixing dinner on time), but it has been elevated to a goal that is driving you into impatience and anger.

Suppose you're cruising down the interstate, excited about getting home to your family. Suddenly, up ahead you see the dreaded sight of the brake lights of hundreds of cars, indicating a traffic jam. With no place to turn off and make a detour around it, you slam your hand on the steering wheel in anger. Another blocked goal! Now it may be that your desire to get to a certain place on time is blocked, but God's goal for you to be conformed to His image is not being blocked—it is being tested. Will you elevate your godly desire (getting home to be with the family) to the level of a consuming goal? If so, anger will most assuredly master you, and the fruit of the Spirit will be suppressed.

Suppose your goal as a parent is to have a loving, harmonious, happy, Christlike family. Who can block that goal? Every other member of the family can, and they all will at some time. That is a legitimate godly desire, but there is no way you can control every member of your family to make it happen, and if you try, there will be a lot of angry people in your household. However, it *is* a godly goal to become the spouse and parent God created you to be, and nobody can block that goal but you.

Threats to Our Goals

As we've seen, consciously or unconsciously we develop goals in our lives and proceed to live according to a plan to achieve those goals. When something or someone comes along and prevents us from achieving our plans, we get mad. We see that person or event as making life more difficult for ourselves, so we react in anger.

The intensity with which we react to a particular situation and the duration of our anger over it indicate how threatening that event seems to us. In other words, how important a goal in our lives is, is shown by how long and strong our anger is when that goal is blocked. Think about how you'd feel if you got a flat tire; then think about how you'd feel if you were told by your boss and colleagues that you were a complete failure on your job. The flat tire may disrupt your plans and prevent you from getting to a certain place on time. But you can always change the tire, or call AAA and they will change it for you. Annoying as it may be, you will probably get over it in a short time. But a stinging reproach to your professional competence or a disruption of your career goals strikes a deeper chord. The anger you would feel toward those who made such an attack on you or prevented your promotion would likely cause a few sleepless nights and could even throw you into a tailspin of doubt, debilitating introspection, and even depression. Some people might even respond in angry violence.

We have a choice. We can respond according to our old flesh patterns by having an outburst of anger, or we can respond by faith in the power of the Holy Spirit. The fruit of the Spirit is love, and love is exhibited in joy, peace, and patience. Instead of getting depressed when a goal seems impossible, we can have the joy of the Lord. Instead of getting anxious when a goal appears to be uncertain, we can have the peace of God that passes all understanding. Instead of anger, we can learn to be patient with people and grow through the testing and trials of life.

The Role of Trials and Disappointments

If the difficulties of life make you angry, then consider Paul's words in Romans 5:3-5: "We also exult in our tribulations, knowing that tribulation brings about perseverance; and perseverance, proven character; and proven character, hope; and hope does not disappoint, because the love of God has been poured out within our hearts through the Holy Spirit who was given to us." The inevitable pressures and stresses of life serve to reveal *wrong* goals, but they make possible *God's* goal for our life, which is proven character. There is no crisis in life that we cannot grow through.

When your children are not behaving properly, they are not making you angry. They are helping you conform to the image of God. When they are misbehaving, they need you to be the parent God created you to be, and you need to become that kind of a parent. If a traffic accident has blocked your lane, maybe you should pray for those who are injured instead of getting angry because your desire to get someplace is being blocked.

A suit salesman attended one of our conferences and shared his experience:

> Your conference has had a profound impact on my life. I was a suit salesman. No, I was an angry suit salesman. I would get so mad if a customer walked away without buying a suit when I was sure he was going to make a purchase. We had these sales meetings where we were challenged to set a goal for the number of suits we wanted to sell that week. Prizes were offered if we met or beat our goals. I wanted to be the salesperson of the year and win a trip to Hawaii. To make matters worse, my boss is Jewish and I have been a horrible witness to him. He had to pull

me aside a number of times when I got angry and tell me to settle down.

I realized this week that I had the wrong goal. My goal is not to sell a certain number of suits. My goal is to be the suit salesman that God has called me to be. Rather than trying to manipulate and persuade a customer to buy a suit, I began to think of what the customer really needed. I actually talked a customer out of buying a suit that I knew he wouldn't be satisfied with. This simple truth has had such a profound impact on my countenance that my boss pulled me aside last night and asked, "Are you all right?" This newfound freedom I feel must have had some effect on my customers, because I sold more suits last week than I ever have before.

What if a godly desire isn't met? We will feel disappointed. But let's face it, life will not always go our way, and people will not always respond to us as they should, but that is not what determines who we are. God has already determined who we are. As His children, we are in the process of being conformed to His image—and nobody or nothing can keep that from happening but we ourselves. Our disappointments can and should be stepping-stones to greater maturity, as the following poem expresses:

> "Disappointment—His appointment,"
>   Change one letter, then I see
>
> That the thwarting of my purpose
>   Is God's better choice for me.
>
> His appointment must be blessing,
>   Tho' it may come in disguise,
>
> For the end from the beginning
>   Open to His wisdom lies.
>
>
> "Disappointment—His appointment,"
>   No good thing will He withhold,

From denials oft we gather
    Treasures of His love untold.

Well He knows each broken purpose
    Leads to fuller, deeper trust,

And the end of all His dealings
    Proves our God is wise and just.

"Disappointment—His Appointment,"
    Lord, I take it, then, as such,

Like clay in hands of a potter,
    Yielding wholly to Thy touch.

All my life's plan is Thy molding;
    Not one single choice be mine;

Let me answer, unrepining—
    "Father, not my will, but thine."

                —Edith Lillian Young[11]

Let's pray together:

Dear heavenly Father, I have lived my life too often driven by goals that should have stayed as mere desires. And I have been deceived into believing that my identity and value as a person are based on my being right, being respected, being understood, and being in control. I have tried so hard to get my needs met and "win" because I thought that it was up to me. Thank You for forgiving me for my foolish pride and the anger that has been the result. I choose to give up all ungodly goals, and I ask You to show me Your purposes for my life. I thank You that I can trust You to take care of me and make my character like the Lord Jesus. And it's in His name I pray, amen.

Be Angry
but Don't Sin

*He that would be angry and sin not
must not be angry with anything but sin.*

—THOMAS SECKER

≈

When I walked into Byron's office I felt like making a U-turn and heading out of town. His wife, Marilyn, and teenage daughter, Meredith, were there as well. You could cut the anger and tension in that room with a knife. I was glad no one actually had one! The conflict I had come to address was caused by Meredith being bound and determined to marry Jonathan, a new Christian about eight years her senior. Her father, Byron, steadfast in his embracing of biblical principles, was bound and determined to do everything he could to stop her...or die trying. It was a classic case of the irresistible force meeting the immovable object. Marilyn, a godly woman, was being ripped apart, torn between submitting to her husband and not wanting to alienate her daughter. Her story is gut-wrenching.

> As a family we were in the test of our lives. Mostly responding as things were hurled at us—flaming arrows! Byron was really angry and could not control it. I became angry with him for driving Meredith away. I thought I could be the one to keep these two strong-willed, emotional, stubborn people I loved so much from destroying each other. I could not! So much damage, so many inappropriate

actions—ANGRY—so many destructive words—ANGER.
I remember screaming at Byron at the top of my voice,
"Why won't you stop this!" This was the last time Meredith
asked if she could come home. Byron's answer—"Leave
Jonathan!"

Meredith was screaming at him, too. I can't believe this
memory, such an explosion of emotion. I remember
before Meredith left home, after we found out she was still
seeing Jonathan. My husband dared Jonathan to come and
face us. Byron lost it with Meredith while Jonathan was on
his way over to our house. He got physical with her. The
first time ever. Totally out of control. I was petrified. I
remember feeling desperate. I couldn't figure out how to
defuse Byron. I knew he was going to have a heart attack.
I could see his heart beating through his shirt. There was
no color in his lips. His eyes were not his. Help, God!
Meredith was traumatized! I really wondered what would
happen to Jonathan when he drove up. Help, God!

Fortunately, God intervened. In my meeting with the
family, each person was able to freely express his or her feelings and anger. Through a process of God's healing, Byron
came to accept Jonathan and Meredith's marriage. First,
though, we had to help Byron through a very painful process
of giving up a godly desire that had deteriorated into an
ungodly goal.

Learning from Our Trials

James 1 and Romans 5 teach us that trials are designed to
produce endurance, prove character (like Christ's), and hope.
Through trials we can become *better*...or we can become *bitter*.
In other words, trials are one of God's main tools to accomplish His goals in our lives.

As we began to discuss in the previous chapter, when we
refuse to accept God's goals as our own, we end up viewing
tough times as tests of God's love for us rather than as tests of
our own character. We angrily cry out to God, or lash out at
others rather than being able to give thanks (1 Thessalonians

5:18). If we allow our anger to turn to bitterness we can "[come] short of the grace of God" (Hebrews 12:15), thus severely hindering the process of becoming like Jesus.

At this point you might be saying, "So what do you expect me to do if I get fired—thank God or something?" As a matter of fact, that's exactly what we are saying. To do otherwise is to invite anger, anxiety, and depression to take control, rather than the Spirit of God. Thanksgiving demonstrates faith and is a powerful anger-defuser. It demonstrates that you have adopted God's goal for your life (becoming like Christ) when you can pray like this:

> *Dear heavenly Father, I am upset with what has just happened to me. I don't understand it and I don't like it. But I am choosing right now to thank You that You love me and have promised to take care of me. I choose to believe that this situation or these people are not keeping me from being the person You created me to be. I refuse to allow my anger to control me. Instead I choose to walk by faith, and I invite Your Holy Spirit to fill me. I thank You that You will use even this setback to make me more like Jesus. That is what I want most of all. I know You will give me Your peace and wisdom to know what to do. In Jesus' name I pray, amen.*

Instead of just giving in to anger or feeling ashamed of it, let it act as a "warning light" to indicate the probable presence of a selfish or worldly goal rather than a godly one. By allowing anger to be your diagnostic tool, you can learn from your mistakes rather than simply repeating them. That's what I was trying to do when I asked the Lord why I was so angry with Brian (see the previous chapter). Believe me, the Lord is far more motivated to answer those kinds of questions than we are to ask them!

When Goals Become Idols

The bottom line is that wrong goals may simply be good desires that have become too important to us, something we feel we can't or don't want to live without. When this happens, that goal becomes our god—an idol. An idol is anything that we look to before or in the place of God to meet our needs or satisfy our desires. (In contrast, the martyred missionary Jim Elliot wrote, "He is no fool who gives what he cannot keep to gain what he cannot lose.")

Take, for example, the desires to be noticed, or to be appreciated, or to be respected. Certainly there is nothing wrong with those desires. There would be something wrong with someone who cared nothing about the perspective and opinion of others. But what happens when those legitimate desires become driving goals? We will sin by striving to get our own way and have our need for approval met through people rather than God.

If we are deceived into believing we need the approval of other people in order for our own needs to be met and to be happy, we will be driven to gain that approval. The more difficult it is to obtain the acceptance and respect of others, the harder we'll push. But trying to control or manipulate other people will not meet our needs. We'll just become angrier as we encounter negative circumstances and people who fail to meet our "expectations." If we do not know that we are already loved, accepted, and approved by God, far too many of us will try to get those needs met through other people. The apostle Paul wrote in Galatians 1:10, "Am I now seeking the favor of men, or of God? Or am I striving to please men? If I were still trying to please men, I would not be a bond-servant of Christ." People-pleasers are bond servants of other people, not of Christ.

Some Kinds of Anger Are Normal and Right

This issue becomes especially acute when we experience rejection from a loved one, such as a parent, child, or spouse. These instances are the most emotionally volatile. The closer the relationship, the more painful the wounding and the greater potential for anger. In our experience, when we have encouraged people to make a list of who they need to forgive, the first people mentioned are mom and dad, 95 percent of the time. It is normal to hurt and to experience anger when someone we love does not love us in return. C.S. Lewis wrote, "Anger is the fluid that love bleeds when you cut it."[1] Not all anger is the result of wrong goals being blocked. Sometimes we experience anger because we have genuinely been hurt.

Everybody has an inherent sense of justice, that is, what he or she perceives to be right or wrong. Observe what happens when one person's idea of justice doesn't agree with another person's idea of right and wrong. If both have strong convictions it will inevitably lead to a heated if not angry exchange. You can observe this on many television talk shows where people with opposing views are brought together. Such public debates usually lead to an angry exchange.

Righteous Anger

Anger also comes in response to a perceived violation of one's rights or to a perceived abdication of responsibility by another person. When someone's rights are violated, we call that *abuse*. When someone fails to properly care and provide for those they are responsible for, we call that *neglect*. We get angry when we perceive others or ourselves being abused or neglected. If we are judging correctly, then our anger is righteous. Anger is legitimate and justified when actual abuse or neglect has taken place.

For example, you are in the mall and you see an adult fiercely dragging a child by the arm and calling her cruel names because she accidentally broke something in a store. You immediately feel moral outrage and indignation over the damage being done to that child. That is righteous anger, and it ought to prompt you to take action on behalf of that child. That is a true case of abuse, and therefore your anger is legitimate, as long as the Spirit of God leads any subsequent action you take. The righteous person *should* be angry when he or she encounters political corruption, racial prejudice, abortion, pornography, child or elder abuse and neglect, wife-battering, and other human-rights violations.

Righteous anger consists in getting angry at the things that anger God, and then seeking a proper remedy to correct the wrong. Jesus demonstrated these things when He cleansed the temple, crying out, "It is written, 'My house shall be called a house of prayer'; but you are making it a robbers' den" (Matthew 21:13). Jesus was legitimately angry at the defamation of God's glory in His temple, and He did something about it. However, if you want to get angry and not sin, then get angry the way Christ did. Get angry at sin. Jesus forcefully put a stop to the sinful behavior, but He did not hurt the sinners.

On one Sabbath, Jesus entered the synagogue and saw a man with a withered hand. Hoping to accuse Jesus, His enemies watched to see if He would do anything. When Jesus asked them, "Is it lawful to do good or to do harm on the Sabbath, to save a life or to kill?" (Mark 3:4), they remained silent.

The Lord looked "around at them with anger, grieved at their hardness of heart," and proceeded to heal the man anyway (3:5). Jesus was filled with indignation at the Pharisees, who valued their religious traditions so much and human life so little. The Pharisees showed total neglect of the disabled man's need for mercy and healing. So Jesus became angry in accordance with the righteous anger of God. That anger moved Him to do what was right.

Righteous Anger Should Lead to Action

Unfortunately, not all of our anger is as righteous as the Lord Jesus' was. Far too often we wrongly judge others and react angrily when they fail to live up to our expectations. These flesh patterns reveal a faulty belief system, and violate the commandment to "judge not, that you be not judged."

Righteous anger that does not result in righteous action may lead to cynicism and a sour spirit. Righteous indignation should lead us to do something constructive—to forgive, pray, alleviate suffering or oppression, crusade for justice, and so on. When we simply stew in our indignation, we develop a bitter spirit. Psalm 37:8 warns us to "cease from anger and forsake wrath; do not fret, it leads only to evildoing."

Righteous indignation should result in *assertive anger*. This is the anger we experience and express when people invade our personal space, threaten our rights, or violate the emotional or physical boundaries of ourselves and others. As opposed to hostile or aggressive anger that seeks to do harm, assertive anger is designed to firmly say "This far and no farther!" and then escort out those who have crossed the line. This is not a selfish or unloving thing to do at all—rather, the opposite is true. When we set limits on what we allow others to do by exercising assertive anger, the door remains open for love. If we fail to take action, however, we will find ourselves growing increasingly irritable, drained, and resentful.

There are frequent opportunities to express assertive anger toward those who knowingly or unknowingly take advantage of others. In so doing we need to speak the truth in love (Ephesians 4:15) and have the other person's best interest at heart. The goal is not to get even but to correct that which is wrong so that all are built up. Here are some examples of assertive anger from *The Anger Workbook*.[2]

- An overworked church member can politely but firmly say no to a request to do even more projects.

- A parent can state guidelines for discipline without resorting to debate or condescension toward the child.

- When swamped with more responsibilities than he or she can manage, a person can request help from friends.

- A tired mom can tell her family she will take a 30-minute break with no interruptions.

- Spouses can talk about their differences, offering helpful suggestions without raising their voices or repeating their messages incessantly.

- A family member may choose to pursue an independent activity instead of succumbing to the persistent demands of extended family.

I once counseled a man whose mother kept calling him on the phone and mercilessly belittling him. Every time he would hang up the phone, he'd be devastated. But he felt guilty if he hung up on her. Later he would feel angry and would deeply resent her accusations. It was demoralizing to both him and his wife.

I suggested that he not answer the phone when it rang. I encouraged his wife to act as "secretary" to screen his calls and even check the answering-machine messages when they returned home. Then I encouraged the husband to call his mother and politely inform her that he would speak to her only so long as she remained civil. The moment she went off into one of her tirades, he would politely hang up. What a relief for them when they were given a workable plan to use assertive anger for their own safety and sanity!

Mastering Our Anger

The whole line of reasoning we've been following may be new to some of God's people. Many Christians have been taught all their lives that any and all anger is evil. This is simply not the case. Ephesians 4:26 says, "Be angry, and yet do not sin." The apostle might have been quoting Psalm 4:4, which commands, "Tremble, and do not sin." In other words, we may have an initial reaction of anger toward what we perceive to be wrong, but we don't have to behave sinfully as a result. Remember that we have no control over our autonomic nervous system, but we do have volitional control over what we think and do.

Cain reacted in anger when God rejected him and his sacrifice of crops while accepting his brother, Abel, and his sacrifice of an animal. This first biblical incident of anger is worth a look.

> So Cain became very angry and his countenance fell. Then the LORD said to Cain, "Why are you angry? And why has your countenance fallen? If you do well, will not your countenance be lifted up? And if you do not do well, sin is crouching at the door; and its desire is for you, but you must master it" (Genesis 4:5-7).

Cain either never understood God's direction for the proper way to worship Him, or he willfully disobeyed. This perceived rejection by God made him angry. Dr. Gary Chapman describes how Cain's body likely responded to his angry assessment of the situation:

> The body gets in on the experience of anger. The body's nervous system "gets the adrenaline flowing." Depending upon the level of anger any or all of the following may happen physically. The adrenal glands release two hormones: epinephrine (adrenaline) and norepinephrine (noradrenaline). These two chemicals seem to give people the arousal, the tenseness, the excitement, the heat of anger. "These hormones in turn stimulate changes in heart rate, blood pressure, lung function, and digestive tract activity which further add to the general arousal feelings people have when they are angry." It is these physiological changes that give people the feeling of being overwhelmed by anger and unable to control it.[3]

Cain was experiencing anger in reaction to what he perceived to be rejection. He was not right with God, but he still had the chance to make it right. His anger had not reached the point of sin. Notice God's warning: "If you do not do well, sin is crouching at the door; and its desire is for you, but you must master it" (Genesis 4:7). The fact that sin was at the door and had not yet come in shows that Cain was in grave danger of sinning, but that he had not yet crossed that line.

We Can Control Our Anger

The intense physiological reactions produced by our adrenal glands can deceive us into thinking our anger is beyond control and that we have to give in to it. But that is simply not true. When we find ourselves emotionally overcome, sin is crouching at the door, and its desire is for us. But we must master it, and that is *our* responsibility, according to God. If we don't, not only we but also those around us will be the worse for it.

It is a poor excuse to say "That's just the way I am" or "Temper just runs in our family." It is sinful to wink at anger and proudly declare it to be part of our ethnic heritage. Turning to God and choosing the truth can control volatile anger. So when does the emotion of anger become sin? When, as God warned Cain, *we do not do well.* Cain had the opportunity to offer an acceptable sacrifice to God. Had he done so, his anger would have been gone and so would its physical effects (his countenance would have been lifted up).

When the emotion of anger becomes wrath or rage (*thumos*), or fleshly hostility (*orge*), it has become sin. It has become a controlling force that will cause us to behave wrongly. In Cain's case, it resulted in the murder of his brother, an act that put him in league with the evil one (1 John 3:11-12). This act of murder was the end result of Cain's uncontrolled anger. In reality, Cain had murdered Abel in his heart before he carried out the deed with his hands. In Matthew 5:21-22, Jesus teaches that the battle has to be won in our hearts.

> You have heard that the ancients were told, "You shall not commit murder" and "Whoever commits murder shall be liable to the court." But I say to you that everyone who is angry with his brother shall be guilty before the court; and whoever shall say to his brother, "You good-for-nothing," shall be guilty before the supreme court; and whoever shall say, "You fool," shall be guilty enough to go into the fiery hell.

Maintaining Control by Thinking Righteously

To maintain control over our emotions, we have to assume responsibility for our thoughts. The anger is there because we have mentally processed the data our physical senses have picked up. We do have the capacity to choose what we are going to do with that information, and by *choosing the truth* we will manage our emotional response of anger. Often when we see another person emotionally overcome, we want to grab hold of the person and say, "Think. Put this in perspective. Get hold of yourself." And the only way to maintain control is by thinking righteously.

When our initial response is anger, then our thought process should be as follows:

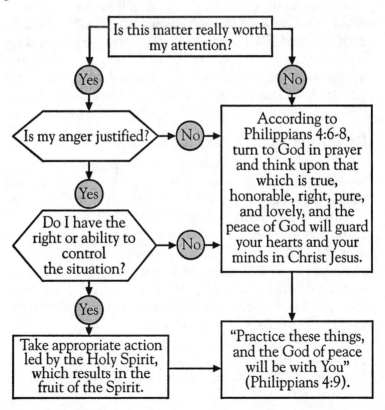

Anger that leads to unrighteous deeds is sinful and destructive, but anger that motivates us to righteous deeds is good. It is constructive. It is the fulfillment of Romans 12:21, which says, "Do not be overcome by evil, but overcome evil with good." However, allowing anger to fester and boil within our heart is the same as letting the sun go down on our anger, which gives the devil an opportunity (Ephesians 4:27) to operate his "divide and conquer" and "search and destroy" mission (1 Peter 5:8). Such anger results in angry words that grieve the Holy Spirit (Ephesians 4:29-30). It decays into "bitterness and wrath and anger...along with all malice" (Ephesians 4:31).

To win this battle for our mind we have to practice "threshold thinking." As soon as a thought steps into the door of our mind, we must take that thought captive to the obedience of Christ (2 Corinthians 10:5). If what we are thinking is not in accord with the Word of God, then we must choose not to set our mind on it. Choose rather to think on the things that are true, right, pure, honorable, and so on (Philippians 4:8).

Be Wary of the Powers of Darkness

We can't blame everything on the responses of our flesh, however. The battle for our mind may have a spiritual base outside ourselves, as Paul clearly warned us about. "The Spirit explicitly says that in later times some will fall away from the faith, paying attention to deceitful spirits and doctrines of demons" (1 Timothy 4:1). "I am afraid that, as the serpent deceived Eve by his craftiness, your minds will be led astray from the simplicity and purity of devotion to Christ" (2 Corinthians 11:3). We have seen the evidence of this all over the world in hundreds of counseling sessions.

The role that the powers of darkness can play in anger out of control is obvious in Scripture. For instance, after David's victory over the Philistines, a women's choir sang, "Saul has slain his thousands, and David his ten thousands" (1 Samuel 18:7). Saul "became very angry" and "looked at David with suspicion from that day on" (verses 8 and 9). It is clear that Saul was a very insecure man, who felt extremely threatened when anyone took the limelight away from him.

On the following day an evil spirit came upon Saul and incited him to try to murder David (verses 10-11). The attempt failed, but Saul came to dread David (verse 15) and became obsessed with trying to kill him.

This connection between the devil and murder should not surprise us, since Jesus Himself described Satan as "a murderer from the beginning" (John 8:44). He is a liar, and he uses his lies to deceive us into thinking that other people are the enemy rather than he himself.

Two things need to be said at this point, however. First, unlike in the case of King Saul, who lived under the old covenant, the Spirit of God will not leave us and be replaced by an evil spirit. Hebrews 13:5 promises that God will never desert us or forsake us. Second, not all angry people attempt murder, though they may experience more murderous thoughts than they care to admit.

Having said this, we still dare not minimize the risk of coming under a measure of demonic influence when we allow anger to fester in our hearts. Paul commanded in Ephesians 4:26-27,

> Be angry, and yet do not sin; do not let the sun go down
> on your anger, and do not give the devil an opportunity.

The Greek word translated "opportunity" is *topos*, meaning a "place" or "ground." It refers to a jurisdiction, place of control, or military beachhead from which an enemy can launch his operations. Clearly, unresolved anger in our lives gives the devil the opportunity to oppress us. The remainder of Ephesians chapter 4 gives us some indications of what the results of that oppression might be. They include theft, destructive words that grieve the Spirit of God, bitterness, rage (*thumos*), anger (*orge*), clamor (or brawling—NIV), slander, and malice (verses 28-31).

If you have given the devil a place in your life by believing lies or willfully sinning, then you must resolve those issues through genuine repentance. You must submit to God and resist the devil (James 4:7). That is the purpose of the "Steps to Freedom in Christ" located in the back of this book. Once you have resolved your personal and spiritual conflicts, then "the peace of God, which surpasses all comprehension, will guard your hearts and your minds in Christ Jesus" (Philippians 4:7).

As we will explain in a later chapter, one of the reasons for going through the Steps to Freedom is to cultivate a heart of being "kind to one another, tenderhearted, forgiving each other, just as God in Christ also has forgiven" us (Ephesians 4:32). For now, let us turn to the only One who can enable us to be angry and yet not sin.

> *Dear heavenly Father, I accept the fact that anger is an emotion given by You. I now realize that it is part of being created in Your image. I understand that it can motivate me to do righteous deeds and establish justice or, in my flesh, turn me toward evil. And I am sobered to realize that I can open myself up to demonic attack by harboring anger in my heart. I confess to You that much of my anger is petty, self-centered, and fleshly. Most times I have not allowed it to be a window into my soul, but have used it as a hammer to harm others. Thank You for Your forgiveness. Continue to open my eyes to the true nature of the anger in my life. I want to be like Jesus, learning to "be angry, yet...not sin." In Jesus' name I pray, amen.*

Mental Strongholds

*For many years I have observed that the moralist
typically substitutes anger for perception. He
hopes that many people will mistake his irritation
for insight.*

—MARSHALL MCLUHAN

∼

Jesse was an angry man, though if you met him you would
not have guessed that was his problem. Like many men, he
had learned to camouflage it effectively. He had channeled
his anger into a driven work ethic that had served him well
during 11 years in the NFL. Nearing the end of his career,
however, he was almost at the end of his rope.

When I met him, his body was hobbled due to injuries.
Worse yet, his family life was falling apart and his spiritual life
was anemic. His eight-year-old son spent much of his time in
conversations with the Mighty Morphin' Power Rangers, and
his wife was very bitter. Jesse was a believer in Christ, but was
having a lot of trouble connecting intimately with the Lord.
Despite the high salary he was making, I would not have
wanted to spend one day in his cleats.

I met with Jesse on his day off. Not finding anything particularly traumatic in Jesse's past, I began to inquire about his
relationship with his mom and dad. He shrugged, saying that
he would have liked his dad to have been at home more, but
that was about it. Having discipled athletes in the past, I knew
that some of them had been frustrated with their parents'

noninvolvement in their athletic careers. I felt led to ask, "Jesse, have your parents been involved much in your football career?"

The eyes of this 250-pound man opened wide with shock. He looked like he'd been shot with a gun. "That's it," he said angrily. "Through six years of junior and senior high school, four years in college and eleven years in the pros, my parents have never come to one of my games!"

Instead of facing his anger, Jesse had channeled it into sports. His success had helped net him a healthy bank account, but also an impoverished soul. He was an insecure and driven man. He confessed to me that even if he caught ten passes in a row, he would be terrified of dropping the eleventh one. Frustrated and angry at his inability to gain attention and approval from his mom and dad, Jesse had subconsciously come to view God as distant and uninterested as well.

I assured him that God was not like that. Looking him straight in the eye with all the compassion I could muster, I said, "Jesse, God is the Father you have always needed and wanted, and He has never missed one of your games!" In a flood of emotion, Jesse began to let out 21 years of anger and hurt as he forgave his mom and dad. At one point he retreated to the next room to try to regain his composure. Jesse had come to understand that he no longer had to try to perform to impress God. God's love was and is unconditional.

That Sunday night I happened to be watching ESPN, and I saw video footage of Jesse catching a touchdown pass. So I made a telephone call to congratulate him. His response was that of a man set free from 21 years of anger and drivenness. He said, "After 20 years of playing football, that was the first game in my entire life where I enjoyed myself!"

The Human Condition

The tragedy of unmet needs and the resulting anger and pain, as Jesse experienced, has been played out to one degree or another in each of the six billion people on planet Earth. But that is not how God intended it to be.

God created Adam and Eve in His image, and therefore they had *dignity* (Genesis 1:26-27). They had *joy and intimacy with the Lord* as "God blessed them" and spoke to them personally (1:28). He also generously provided beauty and pleasure for their enjoyment (2:9). In addition, Adam and Eve felt *secure* in the Father's provision of their need for food (1:29) and companionship (2:18). They also felt *acceptance* from one another, because "the man and his wife were both naked and were not ashamed" (2:25). They had nothing to hide and nothing to cover up. Finally, they experienced a deep sense of *significance* because God had given them dominion over all the earth (1:28)!

Every single human need was perfectly met by God's provision of Himself, human companionship, and the Garden of Eden. Since there were no unmet needs, no frustrations, no blocked goals, and no sense of injustice, there was no anger. Adam and Eve lived in perfect peace with God and each other.

Suddenly paradise was shattered. They ate the fruit from the tree of the knowledge of good and evil, which God had expressly forbidden them to do (Genesis 2:17). Sin entered into their world when Eve believed the serpent's lie that there was something wonderful to be had outside of God's will. Eve was deceived, and Adam chose to sin (1 Timothy 2:14); and "through the one man's disobedience the many were made sinners" (Romans 5:19).

Immediately, Adam and Eve felt fear, shame, and guilt. They crudely covered their physical nakedness with fig leaves and foolishly sought to hide from God's presence among the trees of the garden (Genesis 3:7-8). They spiritually died when their sin separated them from God. And they and their descendants would now have to experience every kind of

physical and emotional distress that ultimately leads to physical death.

Adam and Eve had entered into this world both physically and spiritually alive. Physical life (*bios* in the Greek) is
the union of the soul and spirit with the body. Spiritual life
(*zoe* in the Greek) is the union of the spirit with God. God
had warned them that "in the day that you eat from [the fruit
of the tree of the knowledge of good and evil] you will surely
die" (Genesis 2:17). Did Adam and Eve die physically on the
day they ate? No, they remained physically alive for hundreds
of years, although physical death would ultimately be a con-
sequence of their sin as well. However, they did die spiritually
the moment they sinned. Their spirits were no longer in union
with God. That's why they felt such alienation from the One
who had been their closest Friend just minutes before!

As a result of their sin, we have all entered this world
physically alive but spiritually dead. Since in our physical life
we are all descendants of Adam, you could say that apart from
Christ we are all part of the "Adam's Family." We are *in Adam*
(1 Corinthians 15:22). Paul's words in Ephesians 2:1-3 provide a precise and accurate description of our condition apart
from Christ:

> You were dead in your trespasses and sins, in which
> you formerly walked according to the course of this
> world, according to the prince of the power of the air, of
> the spirit that is now working in the sons of disobedi-
> ence. Among them we too all formerly lived in the lusts
> of our flesh, indulging the desires of the flesh and of the
> mind, and were by nature children of wrath, even as the
> rest.

The Formation of "Mental Strongholds"

Apart from Christ, we are people dominated by the world,
the flesh, and the devil. Without Christ, our body can physically function in union with our soul (our intellect, emotions,

and will), but we are spiritually dead, cut off from God. Having neither the presence of God in our lives nor the knowledge of His ways, we learn to live our lives independent of God. During the early and formative years of our lives we develop mental strongholds, which are similar to what psychologists call defense mechanisms. Others have called them flesh patterns. We have to learn how to cope, succeed, and survive with only our own limited strengths and resources.

The attitudes we form about ourselves and the world around us are assimilated from the environment in which we are raised. Most of this assimilation comes through our prevailing experiences in the homes we are raised in, the schools we go to, the friends we choose, the church we attend or don't attend. (It is important to realize that two children can be raised in essentially the same environment but can choose to respond differently. Even at the earliest ages we choose to evaluate our experiences and respond accordingly.)

Strongholds are also formed through traumatic experiences such as a death in the home, the separation or divorce of parents, or abuse by others. These damaging experiences are burned into our minds, causing us to have strong feelings and attitudes toward God, others, and ourselves. These deeply imbedded emotions from the past can be triggered by present events. For instance, if you were deeply wounded earlier in life, and you now see another person being treated in the same way you were, you are probably going to react angrily.

However, childhood traumas are not what keeps us in bondage to our past. Rather, we are in bondage to the *lies we have believed* as a result of the trauma. That is why *truth* sets us free. At the time of the trauma, you mentally processed what was happening and chose how you were going to respond to it. This mental action established a belief about people and the world you live in, such as "God doesn't love me"; "I'm no good"; "I can never trust anyone"; "All men are perverts"; "I have to be self-sufficient"; and so on.

Little children are especially vulnerable to faulty processing of traumatic events. Imagine a dad coming home from work and angrily beating his son for not cleaning his room. What message will be going through that little boy's mind? He will not be thinking, "Boy, dad really needs help for his anger problem." Instead he will tell himself, "There must really be something wrong with *me*." That kind of destructive message can lodge deep in a child's heart, becoming an unconscious driving mechanism even into adulthood.

In order to survive with such negative beliefs, people adopt certain ways of defending themselves, such as lying, blaming, denying, rationalizing, withdrawing, fighting, and so on. Many will hold on to their anger, which they falsely believe will protect them from further abuse.

Life in the Flesh

We simply cannot regain by our own human effort what was lost in paradise—dignity, joy, intimacy, security, acceptance, and significance. In reality, that is trying to find life apart from Life Himself, the Lord Jesus. Even our best efforts at self-reformation will fail, and we will remain a product of our past. Even our most noble efforts at life apart from Christ will be hopelessly tainted by our own sin, because we are separated from God. If that makes you angry, then consider Paul's words in Titus 1:15-16:

> To the pure, all things are pure; but to those who are defiled and unbelieving, nothing is pure; but both their mind and their conscience are defiled. They profess to know God, but by their deeds they deny Him, being detestable and disobedient and worthless for any good deed.

Apart from Christ, *we have no choice but to live according to our own flesh*. Steve McVey, in his excellent book *Grace Walk*, puts it this way:

We have all learned to rely on our own strategies for getting our needs met. The Bible calls this mechanism for servicing our own needs the *flesh*. Every person has developed his flesh-life in order to get what he wants out of life as much of the time as possible. Don't think of flesh as skin, but as personal *techniques* for meeting your own perceived needs, apart from Christ....Walking after the flesh is simply relying on your own ability instead of on God's resources.[1]

Although there is never any excuse for living in sin and selfishness, the truth of the matter is that someone who rejects Christ has no other alternative! He or she must cope somehow in the flesh or give up on life. The following story is a vivid example of the angry, self-protective life of the flesh.

I grew up with a rage-aholic father. There was constant tension, verbal abuse, and anger expressed freely, throughout my childhood. Not only by my parents but by me as well. I did not realize there was anything wrong with this type of lifestyle because it was all that had been modeled to me by the adults in my life. Through counseling I came to understand that—being raised in a dysfunctional home—I had developed wrong patterns of living. I came to realize that I had adapted to the anger and rage around me by forming my own dysfunctional coping mechanisms. I had built strong walls of protection around me, had a tough countenance and hard exterior. I would only let certain people "in" and I was very guarded around people because it was very difficult for me to trust anyone. I discovered that my "safe" emotion was anger, so every emotion I experienced was expressed in anger of some sort. I was also very codependent, insecure, and performance-oriented, I feared rejection, craved approval and affirmation, was a perfectionist, and feared failure and disappointment. All of these areas were manifestations of the internalized anger I had experienced growing up.

Selfish to the Core

This "birth defect" of life in the flesh that is inherent in all of us is sinful and idolatrous to its very core. It is sinful because the essence of sin is living life independent of God's presence and power, trying our level best to milk all the love, life, liberty, and pursuit of happiness we can out of the world, rather than trusting God as our Source. And it is idolatrous because it places something other than God—that is, ourself—at the center of our life.

The apostle Paul cuts to the heart of this congenital problem in Romans 8:5-8:

> Those who are according to the flesh set their minds on the things of the flesh, but those who are according to the Spirit, the things of the Spirit. For the mind set on the flesh is death, but the mind set on the Spirit is life and peace, because the mind set on the flesh is hostile toward God; for it does not subject itself to the law of God, for it is not even able to do so; and those who are in the flesh cannot please God.

Because the flesh's entire purpose for existence is to preserve, protect, and provide for the sinful self, it is by nature selfish. Self-protective, demanding, self-reliant, controlling, self-serving, and self-promoting, the flesh experiences the almost continual threat of angry conflict with others. Why? Because one selfish, fleshly person is going to be in conflict with every other selfish, fleshly person he or she encounters. Angry interactions are unavoidable if I am trying to get my own needs met my way and you stand in my way (or vice versa). The apostle James gives this explanation:

> What is the source of quarrels and conflicts among you? Is not the source your pleasures that wage war in your members? You lust and do not have; so you commit murder. You are envious and cannot obtain; so you fight and quarrel. You do not have because you do not ask. You ask and do not receive, because you ask with wrong

motives, so that you may spend it on your pleasures (James 4:1-3).

We're No Longer a Product of Our Past

A person without Christ can live only according to his or her own fleshly nature. But as children of God, we have experienced a miraculous transformation. Paul explained this in 2 Corinthians 5:17, "If anyone is in Christ, he is a new creation; old things have passed away; behold, all things have become new" (NKJV). As believers we are no longer simply a product of our past. We are now primarily a product of the work of Christ on the cross, and through His resurrection we have new life in Him. Because of this transformation, we can and should no longer live for ourselves, but for Him who died and rose again for us (2 Corinthians 5:15). We are now the temple of the Holy Spirit, who lives in us and who wants to empower us to walk in the newness of life that we have in Christ (1 Corinthians 6:19; Romans 6:4; 8:13).

Then why do I as a new believer still think and feel much the same as I did before salvation, and why do I still struggle with a lot of the same anger and bitterness? Because everything that was programmed into my mind before salvation is still there. God did not create our mental computers with an automatic "clear" or "delete" button. That is why Paul wrote in Romans 12:2, "Do not be conformed to this world, but be transformed by the renewing of your mind, so that you may prove what the will of God is, that which is good and acceptable and perfect." As believers we can continue to be conformed to this world if we keep doing what we have always done. But now that we are in Christ, we have the mind of Christ within us (1 Corinthians 2:16), and the Holy Spirit will lead us into all truth. This doesn't happen instantly, but as we allow our minds to be renewed by the truth of God's word, we will see mental strongholds and defense mechanisms fade away.

Good News—in Christ

Perhaps you are reading this book and the Spirit of God is making it clear to you that you have never humbled yourself and received Jesus Christ as your Savior and Lord. To you, this talk about a "new life" in Christ sounds good, even great, but in all honesty it is foreign to your experience. To be blunt, you have lived your life first and foremost for yourself. You have been your own god, and you have become angry with other people because they have refused to treat you in the way you felt you deserved. (It is a small step from worshiping yourself to expecting others to pay homage as well.)

Are your efforts to justify your anger being exposed for what they are? Are you aware that what seemed to be a normal life is not normal at all in God's eyes? Have you existed by your own strength and resources, for your own gain, and thus damaged others and hurt yourself as well? Worst of all, have you offended God, the Holy One? Are you seeing that you have never experienced a new, abundant life in Christ? Are you tired of being controlled by sinful thoughts, feelings, and actions? Do you honestly and sincerely want out?

If that is the spiritual state in which you find yourself today, then we've got good news. In fact, that's what the word "gospel" means. Good news!

The holy God who created you also loves you deeply and wants to begin a relationship with you through His Son, Jesus Christ. But first you must realize and admit that sin has separated you from God, as Isaiah 59:1-2 says:

> Behold, the LORD's hand is not so short that it cannot save; nor is His ear so dull that it cannot hear. But your iniquities have made a separation between you and your God, and your sins have hidden His face from you so that He does not hear.

In the Old Testament, the word *iniquity* means "perversity or moral evil."[2] In the New Testament, the word means "injustice, dishonesty or lawlessness."³ Every angry, cruel word, hateful attitude, or vengeful act is iniquity, and iniquity has separated us from the love of God.

But God, knowing our sinful state and desiring to reconcile us to Himself, took the most loving action possible. He sacrificed His Son, the Lord Jesus, and poured out His anger upon Him rather than upon us. The prophet Isaiah also told us about God's cure for our sin and iniquity that would be provided through the coming Messiah when he wrote these words:

> Surely our griefs He Himself bore, and our sorrows He carried; yet we ourselves esteemed Him stricken, smitten of God, and afflicted. But He was pierced through for our transgressions, He was crushed for our iniquities; the chastening for our well-being fell upon Him, and by His scourging we are healed. All of us like sheep have gone astray, each of us has turned to his own way; but the LORD has caused the iniquity of us all to fall on Him (Isaiah 53:4-6).

Now Is the Time

Today is the acceptable day, the Bible says. Today is the day of salvation (2 Corinthians 6:2). Today, if you hear God's voice, don't harden your heart (Hebrews 3:15)! The Lord Jesus Christ, "holy, innocent, undefiled, separated from sinners and exalted above the heavens" (Hebrews 7:26), literally became sin for us "so that we might become the righteousness of God in Him" (2 Corinthians 5:21).

Are you willing to make the great exchange—your sin for Christ's righteousness? Will you receive the free gift of God, which is eternal life in Christ Jesus our Lord, or will you continue to suffer the wages of sin, which is death (Romans 6:23)? If your heart is hungry for God and for the forgiveness, righteousness, and new life that only come from Him, then we encourage you to pray with us.

Dear heavenly Father, I have sinned against You. I have lived for myself by myself, and in so doing I have been controlled by my flesh. I have hurt others and offended You. I now repent and turn away from this life of sin, and I open my heart to Your Son, the Lord Jesus Christ. Thank You that He took all the punishment for my sin and shed His precious blood on the cross for my forgiveness. And because He rose from the dead, I can now experience a new life—His life in me. I receive You, Lord Jesus, as my Savior and Lord, not on the basis of any good deeds or actions that I have done, but as a free and undeserved gift of Your grace. Thank You, Jesus, for making me a child of God and a new creation in You. In Your name I pray, amen.

The Process of Transformation

As believers in Christ, we now have the very power of God within us to enable us to walk in a manner worthy of our calling (Ephesians 4:1). When the apostle Paul wrote, "Now to Him who is able to do far more abundantly beyond all that we ask or think, according to the power that works within us," he was describing that power.

Do you doubt God's capacity to change you? Are you skeptical that the anger in your heart or in the hearts of those you know and love can ever be transformed into patience, gentleness, and kindness? Take courage! The greatest transformations that *we* can imagine merely scratch the surface of what God can do in His power!

Some people will find a miraculous deliverance from the power of controlling anger and rage at the moment of salvation. With most believers in Christ, however, it will take time for their minds to be renewed; it will take time for them to learn to overcome their flesh through walking by the Spirit. But bondage to anger need not and should not follow us to the grave. Second Corinthians 10:3-5 ought to be a great source of hope to every Christian struggling with controlling anger:

> Though we walk in the flesh, we do not war according to the flesh, for the weapons of our warfare are not of the flesh, but divinely powerful for the destruction of fortresses. We are destroying speculations and every lofty thing raised up against the knowledge of God, and we are taking every thought captive to the obedience of Christ.

Another Look at Mental Strongholds

As we talked about earlier in this chapter, the "fortresses," or mental strongholds, that Paul writes about are deeply ingrained patterns of belief that cause us to react emotionally and behaviorally contrary to God's will and Word. They are mental habit patterns of thought—flesh patterns—burned into our minds over time or by the intensity of traumatic experiences. Feeling and acting in accordance with these memory traces is like driving a truck in a pasture along the same route for many years. You won't even have to steer the truck after awhile because deep ruts have been made—and any attempt to steer out of the ruts will be met with resistance.

In the book *Freedom from Addiction*, which Mike and Julia Quarles coauthored with Neil, Mike explains how a stronghold of anger formed early in his life. Mike's father was a raging, abusive alcoholic, and his mother was extremely overprotective. Here's a part of Mike's story:

> As a child, I didn't introduce myself by saying "Hi, I'm Mike Quarles. I'm unaccepted, inadequate, insecure and guilty. Something is wrong with me." In the recesses of my soul, however, those feelings were there. Like everyone, I longed to have my basic needs of love, acceptance and approval met. I developed my own patterns

in how to deal with life, solve my problems, become a successful person and meet my needs.

I don't remember any love between my mom and dad. In the house they fought violently in an ongoing war. Scattered into the arguments were a few moments of peace and calmness. Several times my dad turned over the kitchen table, scattering food across our floor and breaking dishes. I could not bring my friends home to such a miserable situation. Using any excuse, I stayed away from home as much as possible. In some of my most vivid childhood memories, I remember lying in bed at night and listening to my mom and dad in one of their violent arguments. Once my dad chased everyone out of the house with a loaded shotgun. I lived in fear that one morning I would find one of my parents had killed the other one.

Today as I look back, I'm convinced it's a miracle no one died a violent death. My brother is two years younger and my sister four years younger than I am. As children, we responded to our home life in a predictable manner. As the oldest, I learned to fight and rebel against our alcoholic father and his abusive authority. My brother became the people pleaser and did anything to placate Dad. My sister learned to withdraw, hide and stay out of the way. Of course, we adopted these same patterns for dealing with stress in our adult lives.[4]

God's Power at Work

The good news is that no matter how strong these fortresses may be, God's power is greater. We can indeed watch the stubborn "walls of Jericho" in our own souls come crashing down. Parts of our personality that we thought would not and could not ever change can be truly transformed by the power of Christ. In Him, the person enslaved to anger and rage can find the power to steer out of those ruts and instead be guided "in the paths of righteousness for His name's sake" (Psalm 23:3).

Mike Quarles found his freedom in Christ, and he is no longer an angry, driven man. It is now his privilege and ours to help others find their freedom in Christ and to show them from the Scriptures how Christ can meet our needs for acceptance, security, and significance, as follows:

In Christ

I am Accepted:

John 1:12	I am God's child
John 15:15	I am Christ's friend
Romans 5:1	I have been justified
1 Corinthians 6:17	I am united with the Lord, and I am one with Him in spirit
1 Corinthians 6:20	I have been bought with a price—I belong to God
1 Corinthians 12:27	I am a member of Christ's body
Ephesians 1:1	I am a saint—a holy one
Ephesians 1:5	I have been adopted as God's child
Ephesians 2:18	I have direct access to God through the Holy Spirit
Colossians 1:14	I have been redeemed and forgiven of all my sins
Colossians 2:10	I am complete in Christ

I am secure:

Romans 8:1-2	I am free forever from condemnation
Romans 8:28	I am assured that all things work together for good
Romans 8:31-34	I am free from any condemning charges against me
Romans 8:35-39	I cannot be separated from the love of God

2 Corinthians 1:21-22	I have been established, anointed, and sealed by God
Colossians 3:3	I am hidden with Christ in God
Philippians 1:6	I am confident that the good work that God has begun in me will be perfected
Philippians 3:20	I am a citizen of heaven
2 Timothy 1:7	I have not been given a spirit of fear, but of power, love, and a sound mind
Hebrews 4:16	I can find grace and mercy in time of need
1 John 5:18	I am born of God, and the evil one cannot touch me

I am significant:

Matthew 5:13	I am the salt of the earth and the light of the world
John 15:1,5	I am a branch of the true vine, Jesus, a channel of His life
John 15:16	I have been chosen and appointed by God to bear fruit
Acts 1:8	I am a personal, Spirit-empowered witness of Christ's
1 Corinthians 3:16	I am God's temple
2 Corinthians 5:17	I am a minister of reconciliation for God
2 Corinthians 6:1	I am God's co-worker
Ephesians 2:6	I am seated with Christ in the heavenly realm
Ephesians 2:10	I am God's workmanship, created for good works
Ephesians 3:12	I may approach God with freedom and confidence
Philippians 4:13	I can do all things through Christ who strengthens me![5]

Let's pray together:

Dear heavenly Father, I need Your power to destroy the fortresses of anger and rage in my life. I want to live out the truth of my new identity in Christ, but there are these "walled cities" in my soul. Too often I hide in these places, and that keeps me from knowing You as my "rock and my fortress and my deliverer" (Psalm 18:2). I retreat back into these false fortresses and try to defend myself rather than letting You be my Defender. Thank You for Your patience, Your forgiveness, and Your unconditional love. Please open my eyes to the specific strongholds of anger in my life and to the lies that keep those "walls" up. In Jesus' name I pray, amen.

Flesh Patterns of Anger

Anyone can become angry. That is easy. But to be angry with the right person, to the right degree, at the right time, for the right purpose and in the right way—that is not easy.

—ARISTOTLE

~

Evangelist D.L. Moody, the "Billy Graham" of the nineteenth century, had a sharp temper that he learned to control—usually. One evening Moody was conducting two evangelistic services back-to-back. After the first service, as Mr. Moody was standing near the door welcoming the new crowd, a man approached him and delivered a highly offensive insult of some sort. Moody never told what the insult was, but it must have been contemptible, for in a sudden fit of anger, Moody shoved the man and sent him tumbling down a short flight of steps.

The man was not badly harmed, but Moody's friends wondered how the evangelist could now possibly preach at the second service. "When I saw Moody give way to his temper," said one observer, "I said to myself, 'The meeting is killed.' The large number who have seen the whole thing will hardly be in condition to be influenced by anything more Mr. Moody can say tonight."

But Moody stood up, called the meeting to order, and with trembling voice spoke these words: "Friends, before beginning tonight I want to confess that I yielded just now to my temper, out in the hall, and have done wrong. Just as I was coming in here tonight, I lost my temper with a man, and I want to confess my wrong before you all, and if that man is present here whom I thrust away from me in anger, I want to ask his forgiveness and God's. Let us pray." Instead of being a lost cause, the meeting seemed unusually touched that night, with many people deeply and eternally impressed with the Gospel.[1]

We have all developed one or more flesh patterns, or strongholds, of anger. We may be aware of what our patterns are, and we may be finding great success in overcoming those aspects of the flesh through the liberating power of the Spirit, as Moody did that night. On the other hand, we may not be aware of our own flesh patterns and therefore have done little to overcome them. Many people in this condition just assume that this is the way they are—and others are just going to have to live with it as they have learned to live with it. Or we may be somewhere in the middle—uncomfortable with how we manage our anger, but lacking the insight to do anything about it.

Before we can experience the transforming power of God in the tearing down of strongholds, we need to understand what our own flesh patterns of anger are. In this chapter we will examine some of the more common manifestations of fleshly anger, with the desire that it will provide a helpful window into your soul.

The Anger Avoider

Ron and Pat Potter-Efron describe the first anger personality type we want to look at.

> *Anger avoiders* don't like anger much. Some avoiders are afraid of their anger, or the anger of others. Anger seems too scary to touch. They're scared of losing control if they get mad, of letting out the monster inside of them. Other avoiders think that it's bad to be angry.

They've learned sayings like "Only dogs get mad" and "Be nice, don't be angry." They hide from their anger because they want to be liked.[2]

People who are anger avoiders try to keep the peace at all costs. They want to be known as "nice" people. They feel very uncomfortable around anger and so will accommodate and appease whenever possible. When that's not possible, they will withdraw in fear. It is possible for a person to be so well-trained in avoiding and suppressing anger that such a person genuinely believes he or she simply has no anger. Such was the case with a dear friend of ours. He wrote of himself,

> After my wife passed away and I was in counseling, I was asked the question, "How much anger did you have?" I answered, "None." "You don't have *any* anger?" was the next question. "No, I don't have any anger," was my reply. "Well, how did it make you feel?" "I felt hurt, but I didn't have any anger!" They immediately went on to explain that if I felt hurt, then I had anger. They explained that when people feel hurt, they have anger. But I kept insisting, "No, I don't feel angry." Then they changed their questions: "Do you ever lose your temper?" "No!" "How do you feel about others getting angry and losing their temper?" "I don't appreciate it." "How do you feel about Christians getting angry?" "I don't believe they should!" After some time they explained to me that I was stuffing my anger. I had it but was just not acknowledging it. They pointed out that since I didn't believe in Christians being angry, I just kept denying mine and keeping the lid on it; and that's why I didn't feel it. I really didn't believe that I had anger.

This man, who had served as a pastor for decades, finally understood how far out of touch with his emotions he had become. In a fleshly effort to stay "in control," he had slammed the door shut on his emotional life. Sadly, this man who had believed the lie that he had to be in control, had himself become controlled by the lie. He was in bondage to his own emotional denial. His "after" testimony is refreshing and instructive:

> Since I have acknowledged my emotions and have allowed myself to accept how I feel, I am enjoying so many good feelings of joy. After they explained things to me, I came to see that when I stuffed my bad feelings I also stuffed my good ones. It's so freeing to be myself and experience the joy of walking in who I am in Christ—that I can have normal emotions, just like Jesus did when He lived upon earth.

We have seen extreme cases where ritual-abuse victims have been unable to express any emotions at all—including anger. These "zero-affect," or "flat-affect," individuals have been programmed to believe that if they express how they feel (cry, get angry), they or someone else will be hurt. They may have seen or experienced horrible torture when emotion was expressed, so their fear was once based in reality.

As in all cases of bondage, such an individual must renounce the lies that he or she has believed, and choose the truth. We will thoroughly examine this critical principle of freedom later in the book. Suffice it to say for now that in these cases, it will be necessary for the one in bondage to verbally exercise his or her authority in Christ. Statements such as, "I renounce the lie that I am not angry, but I declare that I am free to be angry and not sin" or "I renounce the lie that if I show anger or any other emotion, I or someone I love will be hurt or killed" can be immensely powerful and liberating.

Are you an anger avoider? Have you felt guilty when you have experienced even a twinge of anger? Have you believed that good Christians don't get angry? Have you been angry with yourself for not being assertive enough? In the past, have you hung up the phone and kicked yourself internally for pledging money to a cause you really had no interest in supporting? Have you beat yourself up inside for letting a more powerful personality persuade you to take on another task that you knew you had neither the time nor energy to tackle?

Realize that anger avoidance is a fleshly means of coping with the fear of anger, confrontation, disapproval, and rejection. If the Lord is opening up your eyes to this reality, don't get discouraged! Jesus can set you free to "be angry and yet... not sin" (Ephesians 4:26).

Anger Exploders

At the other end of the anger spectrum are the *anger exploders.* Since those who express anger too freely are capable of doing great damage to others, we need to examine this "style" of the flesh in depth. We begin with a personal story.

> I am currently working through the Freedom in Christ series with my pastor in a church congregational setting. Weekly I feel the bondage being broken and freedom settling in. I have always been a little bullheaded and am tempted to anger easily. My anger usually comes suddenly...and fiercely...scaring even me at times. Usually it is stress-oriented and a culmination of events that I hold within me until that last little insignificant incident lights the very short fuse. When the smoke clears I am left feeling desolate and humiliated.
>
> I have tried desperately for years to control this anger but at best have only learned to avoid stressful situations, and even that is not great. I would be so happy to be truly free from these fits of rage once and for all. I would love to know how to deal with anger the way Christ would have me to. It really wrecks my witness when I go off into rantings, and I end up tearful before the Lord when they do come. Please help me...I would truly love to be free from anger.

Anger exploders are like active volcanoes. There is always the threat of an eruption. If they had a seismograph attached to their emotions, they would find that continual tremors were taking place. They live in a continual state of agitation. Whereas calm people will normally be at a 0 or 1 on a 1-to-10 anger scale, anger exploders wake up in the morning registering 6 or 7. They are already angry! That's why they erupt in anger at the slightest provocation. They don't need to warm up to anger like most people; they are already hot!

Why is that? There can be a variety of reasons, both internal and external. We'll look at the environmental reasons why our nation is such a hotbed for anger in chapter 10. It's true that we live in a stressful society, but stress alone is not the problem.

Dominant Leaders

One reason that some people explode in anger is that, internally, they have hard-core type A personalities. Years ago, psychologist William Marston identified four behavioral styles into one of which he believed all people fall. John Geier and Dorothy Downey refined Marston's model and developed the *DiSC* test. This *DiSC* model identifies people as falling into one of these four categories: *dominant (D)*, *influencing (i)*, *steady (S)*, and *compliant (C)*.[3]

In their book *Understanding How Others Misunderstand You*, Ken Voges and Ron Braund describe the dominant personality:

> Because of the High D person's concentration on tasks and goals, he has a tendency to be insensitive to the feelings of others. Rarely is this deliberate neglect, but the intensity with which he strives to meet his objectives can cause him to consider emotional expressions as obstacles. The High D person is prone to see life as a battle during which any walls in his way must be torn down. Unfortunately, that approach is likely to result in emotional casualties along the way.[4]

High D's can become excellent leaders, like Joshua in the Bible, who overcame great obstacles in possessing the

Promised Land. With the right talent, they can become great athletes and coaches as well, being determined and strongly motivated by competition. But the same competitive fire that fuels a passionate Bill McCartney in the Spirit can also produce an angry Bobby Knight in the flesh. Bill McCartney left a successful football coaching career at the University of Colorado to found the Promise Keepers. Bobby Knight was fired from a successful basketball coaching career at Indiana University because he could not control his explosive temper.

Those who score high on the dominant scale are usually task-oriented leaders who are highly motivated to accomplish their goals. The apostle Paul would probably fit into this category. Paul describes his own drivenness before his conversion in Acts 26:9-11:

> I thought to myself that I had to do many things hostile to the name of Jesus of Nazareth. And this is just what I did in Jerusalem; not only did I lock up many of the saints in prisons, having received authority from the chief priests, but also when they were being put to death I cast my vote against them. And as I punished them often in all the synagogues, I tried to force them to blaspheme; and being furiously enraged at them, I kept pursuing them even to foreign cities.

Director or Dictator?

Anger exploders must admit to themselves that being competitive, determined, goal-setters does not give them license to angrily control or trample people. God is interested in accomplishing tasks, but never at the expense of people. James admonishes the impatient person, "My dear brothers, take note of this: Everyone should be quick to listen, slow to speak and slow to become angry, for man's anger does not bring about the righteous life that God desires" (James 1:19-20 NIV).

A year after Shirley and I (Rich) were married, we moved to Manila in the Philippines to oversee a new ministry to high-school students. Our daunting first task was to send follow-up material to over 52,000 students who had received Christ or indicated spiritual interest!

I immediately shifted from director to dictator. I drove myself, my wife, and my Filipino staff hard (and nearly crazy). I was impatient and insensitive, lashing out whenever they were unable or unwilling to perform up to my standards. I stepped on quite a few toes as I crusaded forward in my pursuit to finish the follow-up and establishing model ministries around the city.

One day I was reading in 1 Corinthians 13, and the Lord riveted my attention to verse 13, "But now abide faith, hope, love, these three; but the greatest of these is love." I sensed the Lord speaking to my mind and saying, "Rich, if someone were to look at your life, they would say that you believed the greatest of these is faith."

Now of course we are saved by faith, and we walk by faith—and without faith it's impossible to please God. This illustration in no way diminishes faith's importance to the Christian life. But I knew what the Lord was saying. In an effort to reach my goals, I was using, not loving, people. I broke down before the Lord, confessing my sin and asking that He somehow make me a compassionate person.

A Warning to Leaders

Christian leaders need to realize that teachers incur a stricter judgment (James 3:1). We dare not whip those sheep allotted to our charge in an effort to achieve our numerical goals, meet our budgets, or build our new, bigger, and better facilities.

Moses was the most humble man on earth (Numbers 12:3), and yet he was also a man given to angry outbursts. One day he made a terrible mistake in his anger, as Numbers 20:7-12 records:

> The LORD spoke to Moses, saying, "Take the rod; you and your brother Aaron assemble the congregation and speak to the rock before their eyes, that it may yield its water. You shall thus bring forth water for them out of the rock and let the congregation and their beasts drink." So Moses took the rod from before the LORD, just as He had commanded him; and Moses and Aaron gathered the assembly before the rock. And he said to them, "Listen now, you rebels; shall we bring forth water for you out of this rock?" Then Moses lifted up his hand and struck the rock twice with his rod; and water came forth abundantly, and the congregation and their beasts drank. But the LORD said to Moses and Aaron, "Because you have not believed Me, to treat Me as holy in the sight of the sons of Israel, therefore you shall not bring this assembly into the land which I have given them."

We believe there is a strong warning for dominant leaders in this passage. God is loving and kind and will take care of His people, even when human leaders fail. But if we trivialize the holy calling of God and try to control His people in anger, we may find the Lord rising up to oppose the very goals He once gave us. And in the end, we may only gaze with longing eyes upon the dreams we once strove so mightily to fulfill.

Exploding Because of Pain or Shame

Some people become anger exploders because of the accumulation of painful experiences in their lives. Abused and neglected victims who have not released their anger can become very angry, bitter people. Rather than forgiving their offenders, these people keep on "making a list and checking it twice" of all those who have hurt, betrayed, controlled, offended, or used them. And, as Matthew 18:34 warns, they are turned over to the torturers.

Convinced that everyone else is "out to get them," they suspiciously lash out in preemptive strikes—angrily hurting and rejecting others before they themselves suffer that painful fate. They live by the motto "Do unto others before others do unto you."

These hurting people desperately need warm, loving human relationships to help heal their wounds, but they sabotage relationships before other people become too close. Their attitudes, words, and demeanor can be so caustic, critical, and cruel that they drive away even the most well-meaning people. Using their anger like a shield of protection, they are unaware that their shield is becoming a coffin around their own hearts, choking off the flow of life-giving love from God and others.

People whose lives are centered around shame are often a similar type of anger exploder. Feeling unlovable, unworthy, shameful, and dirty, they stiff-arm the rest of the world, keeping them at a safe emotional distance. To allow people to get too close is too risky. Others might discover the skeletons in their closet and be as repulsed as they themselves are by what they see. Anger then becomes a sword forged out of self-loathing, used to ward off those who threaten to exhume the buried pain of past sin and shame. Professional counselors can all tell stories of how the wrath of shame-based clients was poured out on them when they got too close for comfort.

Anger Addicts

Some anger exploders are *anger addicts*. They get a rush out of the strong feelings that come from the surge of hormones into their bloodstream. The Potter-Efrons provide insight into this.

> Why, then, do some people seek it [anger] out? How could anyone get hooked on anger? The answer is the rush. The anger rush is the strong physical sensation that comes with getting really mad. The rush is the result of

the body's natural fight-or-flight response to danger. The surge of adrenaline. The faster heart rate. Quickened breathing. Tensed muscles. Anger activates the body. The adrenaline boost can help you feel strong. It injects excitement into a dull day. [5]

Like any addict, anger addicts build up a tolerance for the "drug." That means that more intensity is required in order to get the same high. The result can be deadly—on the road, in the home, or elsewhere.

The Anger Exploiter

Closely akin to the anger addict is the *anger exploiter*. This person enjoys the power that comes from anger and believes that, by using anger or the threat of anger, he or she can gain power over other people. Such a person gets more of an emotional than a physical rush from anger. It comes from creating fear in others and making others give them what they want. In fact, some anger exploiters never really get angry at all. They just act angry or threaten anger, knowing that others will come or go at their beck and call.

Anger exploiters are, in reality, simply grown-up toddlers throwing (or pretending to throw) temper tantrums. Chances are they were permitted to do so as children. Their parents, fearful of their children's rage, caved in to their demands. That stronghold was firmly established in the pre-school years and has just taken on a more sophisticated façade in the adult years.

Our son Luke came into our family by adoption at the tender age of four, with an already very advanced system of flesh patterns. Apparently, at the orphanage in Thailand where he had lived, the "squeaky wheel got the oil." When we picked him up, we asked his caregiver, through an interpreter, what Luke did when he didn't get his way.

"He screams," she said with a smirk on her face.

That turned out to be the understatement of the century! In his early days in our home, any denial of his "wants" or any reprimand to his behavior sent him into a 45-minute fit—yelling, screaming, crying, throwing things, stomping his feet, you name it. Since his bedroom door opened out, I had to brace my feet against his door to keep him there for a few minutes of "time-out." The door would literally bow outward as he put all his force against it! To be honest with you, at times his anger was pretty scary.

Turn the clock ahead 20 or 30 years and imagine what Luke would be like were it not for consistent, loving discipline. You would have a fully developed anger exploiter and probably a rage-aholic.

The Calculating Avenger

The ways in which flesh patterns or strongholds of anger manifest themselves are nearly as numerous as the people who employ them to cope. But there are a few more common ones that we should examine. One of the most dangerous of all strongholds of anger is the flesh pattern of the *calculating avenger*. Not prone to angry outbursts, he or she is the incarnation of seething, revengeful anger. This person invented the motto "I don't get mad, I get even." In actuality, this person does both.

The Bible contains some graphic examples of this kind of anger flesh pattern. King David's son Absalom waited two full years after his half-brother Amnon had raped his sister Tamar to carry out his plan of revenge on him.

This simmering, festering anger showed up in Absalom again when he plotted to overthrow the throne of David, his father. After three years in exile following the murder of Amnon, King David permitted Absalom to come back to Jerusalem to live. But David refused to see him for two more years, even though they lived minutes away from one another. Absalom's resentment over this went bone-deep.

Absalom secretly took revenge against David and stole the hearts of the people away from him (2 Samuel 15:6), conspiring to usurp his father's throne (15:10). His vehement disdain for his father was further evidenced by his sleeping with David's concubines (16:22).

Esau, the older twin brother of Jacob, displayed the heart of a calculating avenger in response to Jacob's deceitful theft of their father Isaac's blessing. Genesis 27:41 tells the story: "So Esau bore a grudge against Jacob because of the blessing with which his father had blessed him; and Esau said to himself, 'The days of mourning for my father are near; then I will kill my brother Jacob.'"

Fortunately for both brothers, the story had a happy ending. Jacob escaped from Esau, and the two were eventually reconciled, many years later. Esau never took the revenge he first threatened. In the upcoming chapter on forgiveness, we will explain why taking revenge is useless and wrong. For now, just allow Romans 12:17-21 to renew your mind to the truth.

> Never pay back evil for evil to anyone. Respect what is right in the sight of all men. If possible, so far as it depends on you, be at peace with all men. Never take your own revenge, beloved, but leave room for the wrath of God, for it is written, "Vengeance is Mine, I will repay," says the Lord. "But if your enemy is hungry, feed him, and if he is thirsty, give him a drink; for in so doing you will heap burning coals on his head." Do not be overcome by evil, but overcome evil with good.

The Grump

The *grump*, though certainly not the scariest person to live with, may exhibit the most annoying anger style of them all. Like a persistent mosquito on a hot summer night, the grump is always buzzing around a listening ear with a whole truckload of complaints. Griping, grousing, and fuming, the grouchy grump seems only to be "happy" when unhappy. If things are going well, the grump quickly recalls a time when things were not, totally convinced that bad times lie just ahead.

No amount of rational argument will keep a grump quiet for long nor improve his sour disposition. The reason for this is that the grump feels that life has dealt him a bad hand. Whether he is disgruntled at God, others, himself, or all of them, he is an angry man. He has been hurt. Perhaps he had long ago gotten his hopes up and they were demolished. Maybe this happened time and time again, until it became safer to give up hope and just expect the worst. Angry, griping pessimism has become his shield against further pain.

Apart from genuine repentance toward God and forgiveness toward those who have given him a raw deal, a grump will just worsen with age. Years of functioning in this self-protective mode will most likely produce a cynical, sarcastic, bitter person. Unable to truly enjoy life or experience joy for long, the grump feels justified in his angry, pessimistic view of life. In fact, he would call himself a "realist," at times feeling smugly superior to those with a more "shallow," optimistic view of life.

The Critical Perfectionist

Similar to the *grump* is the *critical perfectionist*. Struggling to live up to unrealistic and unkind personal standards and expectations, this person feels like a failure. The baffling reality of such individuals is that the rest of the world is usually amazed at how much they accomplish and how well they do it!

But critical perfectionists battle with shame and self-loathing even as they are driven to do things better, faster, harder, smarter. Unable to quiet the angry taskmaster inside their heads, they pour out their venom on those around them. The unfortunate victims may be spouses, children, employees, or even co-workers in the church.

These people unconsciously act on the principle "Since I feel bad, at least I can drag others down with me." And they are capable of uttering cruel, cutting, and destructive words. Motives are judged, behavior exactingly critiqued, successes demeaned, and failures magnified in a tragic lose–lose situation.

The father of a high-school student I was discipling was a critical perfectionist. He also happened to be an angry exploder, too, but it was the former that was the most demoralizing. Convinced that his boys really couldn't do anything right, one day he dared them to wash his truck. If, after the job was done, he was unable to find a place they had missed, the man would give his sons $25.

They should have known better. A critical perfectionist will always find something wrong. But instead, they worked and worked, trying to show their dad they could live up to his high expectations. They couldn't (nobody could!), and with a smug sense of glee, he gave them no money. This was just one in a series of angry, demeaning events in the life of his eldest son, who one night gave up and tried to take his life with his Boy Scout knife. Fortunately, the restraining hand of God spared his life. Soon after, the redeeming grace of God saved his soul, though the residual effects of an angry, critical father have continued to plague him.

The Passive–Aggressive

Finally, we can't neglect to mention the passive–aggressive person, labeled the *anger sneak* by the Potter-Efrons. You will recognize this flesh pattern immediately as you read their description.

> Anger sneaks can be angry without ever having to admit it. They never attack directly. They can't be accused of aggression. They can honestly say, "I don't understand why you're so upset. I haven't done anything." And they haven't either. They haven't mowed

the grass as they said they would (you were almost certain they promised, but maybe they didn't, you can't be 100 percent sure). They haven't filled out that application for work that's been sitting on the counter for weeks. They haven't suggested love-making for months. They haven't watched the kids so you could get a break. They haven't...[6]

Anger sneaks despise being told what to do. They abhor being bothered, directed, or guided by anyone else. They just want to be left alone, and they are upset with anyone who "disturbs the peace."

Les Carter and Frank Minirth give a clear diagnosis of the passive–aggressive anger sneak in *The Anger Workbook*.

Passive aggression is caused by a need to have control with the least amount of vulnerability. This form of anger is different from suppression in that the person knows he or she is angry (in contrast to suppressed anger, which is denied). But because this person assumes it is too risky to be open, he or she frustrates others by subtle sabotage. The need for control is evidence of a strong competitive spirit. Whereas healthy relationships do not keep score regarding right and wrong, the passive aggressive person is out to win. Like the openly aggressive person, the passive aggressive person is engaged in a battle for superiority. But this person has cleverly realized that too much honesty about personal differences lessens his or her ability to maintain an upper hand. In contrast, sly forms of handling anger tend to keep him or her in the driver's seat.[7]

There is an inherent fear factor in the anger sneak's modus operandi, and an element of pride. The fear of anger, confrontation, and potential rejection drives this person to an "end-around" rather than direct approach to expressing anger. The smug sense of superiority that grows out of having outwitted his or her opponent gives the anger sneak a feeling of power. The whole episode becomes a sort of game to be won.

The prize? Being left alone while leaving the other person frustrated and worn out.

Becoming Free from Bondage to Anger

Has the Lord used this chapter to expose strongholds of anger in your life? If so, don't be discouraged, be encouraged! The Lord is bringing these areas of sin to the surface so that you can be free from bondage to the flesh.

Dr. Lee LeFebre sums up the flesh as "everything we are apart from Christ."[8] God did not miraculously eradicate all our flesh patterns when we came to know Christ, but by His grace we can be free from their controlling influence. To become free will require a firm commitment to righteousness and a fierce hatred of evil. No casual, half-hearted effort will do. A.W. Tozer writes,

> The ancient curse will not go out painlessly; the tough old miser within us will not lie down and die in obedience to our command. He must be torn out of our heart like a plant from the soil; he must be extracted in agony and blood like a tooth from the jaw. He must be expelled from our soul by violence, as Christ expelled the money changers from the temple. And we shall need to steel ourselves against his piteous begging, and to recognize it as springing out of self-pity, one of the most reprehensible sins of the human heart.[9]

Will you join us in prayer?

Dear heavenly Father, Your word is living and active, sharper than a two-edged sword. It divides even between my soul and spirit and judges the thoughts and intentions of my heart. In the past I have sometimes winked at my fleshly anger, while at other times I have been painfully aware of its presence and power to hurt. In either case, I have not taken a radical stand against my unhealthy flesh patterns, thus allowing unrighteous anger a continued presence in my heart. No more! I want my heart to be pure, Lord, because only the pure in heart will see You. And that is what I want more than anything else. So, having seen my flesh for what it is, I choose not to turn away and hide or forget. I choose instead to acknowledge You, Lord, inviting the full expression of Your holy power to tear down these strongholds. In Jesus' mighty name I pray, amen.

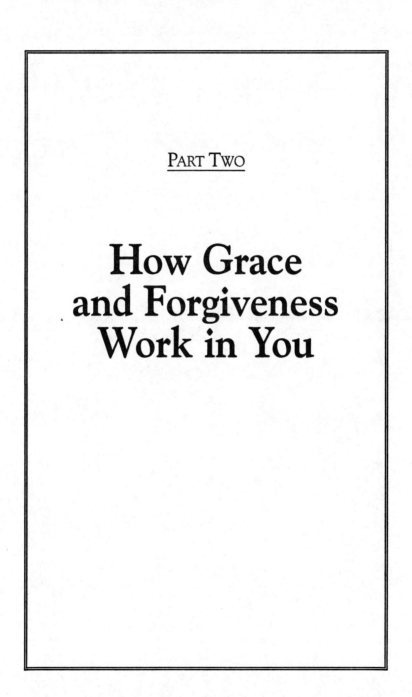

PART TWO

How Grace
and Forgiveness
Work in You

Amazing Grace

There, but for the grace of God, goes John Bradford.
—JOHN BRADFORD

~

It was Christmas Eve 1972. I (Rich) had just finished my first semester in college, a highly motivated freshman meteorology student at Penn State University (a "Weather Channel geek" in the making). It was great to have finals over and to just be able to relax and enjoy the festive holiday season back home in Levittown, Pennsylvania.

But something was wrong. The usual "magic" of Christmas was missing. As a family we always trimmed the tree on Christmas Eve, and so I helped do that, but my heart wasn't in it. Maybe the problem was that I was growing up, having snipped the umbilical cord of day-to-day life at home by going off to school. Or maybe it was the fact that everyone else in the house was busy wrapping presents or cooking. I wasn't alone, but I felt intensely lonely.

I wandered around the house reading the decorative Christmas literature that my mom always put out. Most of it was Currier & Ives kind of stuff about snow, Santa Claus, and so on. But one book of carols caught my attention—and some words within it touched my heart: "To save us all from Satan's power when we were gone astray...O tidings of comfort and joy!"

Six months earlier, my older brother, Tom, had mustered up the courage to share the gospel with me. Considering what a cynical, intellectual agnostic–evolutionist I was, that was no small matter. Though I wasn't convinced that there even *was* a God, I told Tom, "You know, for some reason I know that one day I'll make this decision [to trust Christ as Savior and Lord]." But I wasn't close to being ready at that time.

Bravely, my brother and one of his fraternity brothers would visit me from time to time in my dorm room that fall. I would throw out every "intellectual" objection that I could think of, enjoying the sense of power it gave me to keep them off balance. In retrospect, I can't remember a word they said in response. What I do remember was their love and patience with me and the fact that they just kept on visiting. They had a quality of life that I could not fake and could not shake from my mind.

All the truth and love that I had been confronted with since the summer came flooding back into my mind as I walked back to my room that Christmas Eve. Having an extremely nominal church background (I decided to pass it off as irrelevant around age 12), this was all very new and very unsettling.

Without realizing what I was doing, I found myself talking to God, complaining about how commercialized the Christmas season had become. "This is supposed to be about the coming of Jesus to earth to save us, and we have turned it into a money-making operation!" I said to the God I suddenly believed in.

I was stunned. I couldn't believe what I was doing. "I'm starting to sound like my brother!" I told myself. Within minutes I found myself deeply convicted of my sinfulness. I had been angry with the world, angry with my parents, angry with my brother, angry with myself, and even angry with God. In my anger I had lashed out with a vengeance but had only found myself increasingly isolated and alone. The emptiness in my heart I felt that December 24 was so acute I couldn't stand it.

Crying out to Jesus to forgive me and somehow create in me the capacity to love like my brother, I put my sinful life into the hands of a gracious, merciful God. I cannot describe the release that took place at that moment except to say that the crushing load I felt was gone and the bitter filth of my soul was cleansed. Instantly.

I was amazed! I went running around the house so excited, knowing that something incredible had happened inside of me. What it all meant I didn't know. But I did know it was real and that—unlike my childhood "belief" in Santa Claus—I would never "grow up" and discover it to be a lie. I am now approaching my twenty-ninth spiritual birthday, and my heart is still full of the reality of the amazing grace of Jesus Christ. The fullness has even matured over the years!

Why Grace?

So why a chapter on the grace of God in a book about anger? Because it is the grace of God that has made us new creations in Christ. We need His presence in our lives to be the kind of people He created us to be. As an aerospace engineer, I (Neil) was a type A individual who scored high on the dominant scale before I knew Christ. Now I am no longer driven to achieve. I am called to serve others and the dominance in my personality has dramatically decreased.

It is only by the grace of God that we can be freed from our past. God doesn't fix our past; He sets us free from it, along with the anger that has festered for years because of neglect and past abuses. By the grace of God we are transformed by the renewing of our minds.

Perhaps you can't recall a time when you did *not* believe in Jesus, and so you could be tempted to believe that your conversion to Christ was not so dramatic. Rich's two oldest children, Michelle and Brian, came to Christ at age three. They were not delivered out of hard-core drug addiction, sexual immorality, or crime! But they were just as radically changed inside as Rich was. And they were just as in need of the grace of God as was their father. And so are you.

Our Condition Before Grace

Before we can begin to truly appreciate all that God has graciously done for us in Christ, we need to be reminded again of our condition apart from Him. Writing to his Gentile audience in Ephesus, Paul described their "B.C." days like this: "Remember that you were at that time separate from Christ, excluded from the commonwealth of Israel, and strangers to the covenants of promise, having no hope and without God in the world" (Ephesians 2:12).

Whether a lost person senses this alienation from God or not, that separation from Him is very real. There are many people in our world who are dangerously ignorant of the cancer that grows in their physical bodies. Because they experience no symptoms, they are deluded into thinking all is well. But if they do not discover their true condition soon enough, they will perish. God, through Hosea the prophet, cried out, saying, "My people are destroyed for lack of knowledge" (Hosea 4:6). Clearly there is no more perilous ignorance than that of an unbeliever who is unaware of his or her true spiritual plight.

Romans 5:6-8 tells us the truth regarding the human race's critical condition and Christ's cure: "While we were still *helpless*, at the right time Christ died for the *ungodly*. For one will hardly die for a righteous man; though perhaps for the good man someone would dare even to die. But God demonstrates His own love toward us, in that while we were yet *sinners*, Christ died for us" (emphasis added).

We were helpless—totally incapable of saving ourselves. We were ungodly—completely unlike God in our character. We were sinners by nature—twisted and bent toward self-centeredness and evil. That is God's diagnosis of an individual without Christ. That is who we were in Adam. Not a pretty picture, is it? As Isaiah 64:6 says, "All of us have become like one who is unclean, and all our righteous deeds are like a filthy garment; and all of us wither like a leaf, and our iniquities, like the wind, take us away."

The God of All Grace Intervenes

But God. Did you catch those two words in Romans 5:6-8? What a word of hope! What a message of deliverance! Like the bugle blast from the U.S. Army racing to save the imperiled settlers, those words signal the arrival, at just the right time, of the cavalry from Calvary!

"*But God* demonstrates His own love toward us, in that while we were yet sinners, Christ died for us" (Romans 5:8, emphasis added). God wanted to do something that would be so arresting that we would never doubt His love again. So He paid the ultimate price of death for us guilty, helpless sinners so that we could become forgiven sons and saints.

In Ephesians 2, Paul describes our spiritually dead condition apart from Christ, ending his diagnosis with the words, "[we] were by nature children of wrath, even as the rest" (Ephesians 2:3). With no hope of changing ourselves, without Christ we were all by nature (who we were in the core of our beings) doomed to experience God's wrath.

But God. There it is again! Ephesians 2:4-5 continues, "*But God*, being rich in mercy, because of His great love with which He loved us, even when we were dead in our transgressions, made us alive together with Christ (by grace you have been saved)" (emphasis added).

In my (Rich's) training as a lifeguard, we were equipped to handle most water accidents. We knew what to do when a spinal injury might have taken place. We were ready to handle a frantic, thrashing victim, and we were trained to perform CPR on someone in need of resuscitation.

Only once in my lifeguarding career did I actually have to save someone. It was a little boy who was a visitor to the pool where I worked. He could not swim and knew it, but still he wandered out into the deep end. When I noticed him, he was desperately trying to keep his head above water. Though he was in only five-foot-deep water, that was sufficient for him to drown in since he was only four feet tall! Others were around him, but were apparently oblivious to the danger he was in.

I jumped into the water, went over to where he was, reached out to him, and let him put his arms around my neck. Without any fanfare and without many others knowing what was going on, I carried him out of the pool to safety and onto a lounge chair.

What might the "testimony" of that little boy have been? Maybe something like this:

> I did something really dumb. I knew I couldn't swim, but I went out in the deep water anyway. I guess my pride got the better of me. Anyway, when I realized that my feet couldn't touch bottom, I got really scared. I tried as best I could to keep from drowning, but I was helpless to save myself. But the lifeguard came to my rescue! He saved my life! He brought me out of the water that was too deep for me and took me safely to the side.

God's Attitude Is Full of Grace

You may recall Jesus' parables of the lost sheep, the lost coin, and the prodigal son, in Luke 15, but you may have forgotten the context in which Jesus told them: "All the tax collectors and the sinners were coming near Him to listen to Him. Both the Pharisees and the scribes began to grumble, saying, 'This man receives sinners and eats with them. So He told them this parable, saying…'" (Luke 15:1-3).

In the first parable, the shepherd leaves the 99 sheep that have stayed with him in order to find the one that has strayed and is lost. When he finds the lost sheep, he lays it on his shoulders with great joy. And he calls his friends together and they have a party, just because he found that one sheep!

We might chime in with our logic, "Well, that was a pretty risky thing to do! After all, what's the big difference between having 99 or 100 sheep? One sheep is only 1 percent of his assets. It would have been smarter to take the loss and move on rather than risk the 99 by leaving them!" But the shepherd had no such thoughts. His love for the one was so intense that it never occurred to him not to look for it *until he found it!*

Likewise, the woman who had lost one of her ten coins lit a lamp and swept the house, searching carefully until she found it (Luke 15:8). And she too called her friends together to celebrate the lost coin she had found!

Finally, the brokenhearted father, while giving his prodigal son the freedom to leave, kept his eyes glued to the road coming back home, always watching and waiting for his son. Consider again the father's reaction to his son's return. Let the words of Jesus in Luke 15:20-24 have a fresh impact on you.

> While he was still a long way off, his father saw him, and felt compassion for him, and ran and embraced him and kissed him. And the son said to him, "Father, I have sinned against heaven and in your sight; I am no longer worthy to be called your son." *But the father* said to his slaves, "Quickly bring out the best robe and put it on him, and put a ring on his hand and sandals on his feet; and bring the fattened calf, kill it, and let us eat and celebrate; for this son of mine was dead and has come to life again; he was lost and has been found." And they began to celebrate (emphasis added).

In the video *Becoming a Contagious Christian*, Bill Hybels makes three points about these parables. His first point is that Jesus told these stories so that we would know how much God loves lost people. Second, he observes that lost people matter so much to God that it warrants an all-out search to find them. And third, when one lost person receives the Lord, there is an incredible celebration in heaven![1]

Grace and Celebration

Can you put yourself in the prodigal's place for a moment? Can you see yourself squandering the good things God has given you, wasting your life in sin, desperately trying to survive? Then can you picture yourself coming to your senses and repenting, running to your Father? Filled with guilt for what you've done and shame for what you've become, can you hear yourself confessing your sin to Him?

*But the father...*Once again, words of hope pour from the mouth of our gracious God! See the Father running to meet you, not wanting to miss one second of fellowship with you! See the compassion in His eyes! Feel the deep love in His warm, firm embrace, the joy in His kiss upon your cheek!

Can you feel your dignity and sense of worth being restored as He ignores your request to be made a servant? You are His son! There is no thought in the Father's heart that you would be anything but His son! Can you feel your heart burst with gratitude as He puts the robe and ring of honor on you and the sandals upon your tired, dusty feet? Welcome home!

Then the festive music and joyful dancing starts—the feast begins and the fattened calf is served. Smell the aroma! Taste the delicious food! See the eyes of your friends and your Father light up as you enter the room, and see the stunned look on your own face, because it's all for you! Child of God, it is a party in your honor!

Does this imagery surprise or even offend you? Is it hard for you to imagine having a party with God? Does it seem somehow "beneath" Him to revel and celebrate with such abandon? (Is it perhaps uncomfortably reminiscent of some of the ancient Greek myths about the riotous lives of their gods?)

The late Henri Nouwen, stunned by Rembrandt's painting *The Return of the Prodigal Son*, wrote about this side of God in his book by the same name.

> There is no doubt that the father [in the parable] wants a lavish feast. Killing the calf that had been fattened up for a special occasion shows how much the father wanted to pull out all the stops and offer his son a party such as had never been celebrated before. His exuberant joy is obvious. After having given his order to make everything ready, he exclaims: "We will celebrate by having a feast, because this son of mine was dead and has come back to life; he was lost and is found," and immediately they begin to celebrate....I realize that I am not used to the image of God throwing a big party. It seems to contradict the solemnity and seriousness I have always attached to God. But when I think about the ways in which Jesus describes God's Kingdom, a joyful banquet is often at its center.[2]

Isn't that true? Jesus talked about people coming from the four corners of the earth to "recline at the table in the kingdom of God" (Luke 13:29). And told us that "the kingdom of heaven may be compared to a king who gave a wedding feast for his son" (Matthew 22:2). That theme is echoed in the book of Revelation when an angel declares to John, "Blessed are those who are invited to the marriage supper of the Lamb" (Revelation 19:9). In fact, the Bible says that God saved us and has us sitting right next to Him in heaven so that He can love on us and love on us some more, forever (Ephesians 2:4-7)!

This is God's free gift of love and kindness: From death to life. From lost to found. From disgrace to grace.

Dr. J.I. Packer, in his book *Knowing God*, wrote this about grace:

> The grace of God is love freely shown towards guilty sinners, contrary to their merit and indeed in defiance of

their demerit. It is God showing goodness to persons who deserve only severity, and had no reason to expect anything but severity....It is surely clear that, once a man is convinced that his state and need are as described, the New Testament gospel of grace cannot but sweep him off his feet with wonder and joy. For it tells how our Judge has become our Savior.[3]

The Truth About Our God of Grace

The tragedy for so many believers in Christ, however, is that in their own perception their Savior has become their Judge. Having once known grace, they now experience guilt. Having once danced in the freedom of forgiveness, they now labor under a yoke of slavery to the law, seeking desperately to please a seemingly unpleasable God. In their guilt they are angry—with God, at themselves, at the church, at preachers, at—you fill in the blanks. Who wouldn't be angry? After all, what is more frustrating than being expected to do the impossible?

Let's try to make some sense out of all this. First of all, assuming you are a child of God, what do you think Jesus' first words might be if He were to appear to you personally? "Shape up or ship out!" "Get your act together!" "Try harder!" "Why didn't you witness to that person today...or yesterday...or...?"

While not wanting to put words in God's mouth, we believe that Jesus would say something like this: "Grace and peace to you from God the Father." These words (or a similar greeting) begin 15 of the New Testament letters to churches and individuals. That greeting is not just the first-century version of "Hi, how are you?" It is a blessing from God, reminding the recipients of those God-breathed letters of their right standing before Him. They were standing in God's gracious presence and were at peace with Him, and nothing could change that.

What an encouragement to know that, despite sins in their midst (yes, Paul greeted even the fleshly Corinthian church with "grace and peace to you"—twice!) and trials and perils in their lives (see Peter's letters), they were forgiven, accepted, and affirmed. Completely. Irrevocably. Eternally.

Why is there so often an intense battle in our minds to believe that truth? We believe it is because the enemy of our souls knows that we will be unable to grow spiritually or bear fruit if we do not truly believe we are forgiven children of God. Listen to Peter's words about God's work:

> By [His own glory and excellence, God] has granted to us His precious and magnificent promises, so that by them you may become partakers of the divine nature, having escaped the corruption that is in the world by lust. Now for this very reason also, applying all diligence, in your faith supply moral excellence, and in your moral excellence, knowledge, and in your knowledge, self-control, and in your self-control, perseverance, and in your perseverance, godliness, and in your godliness, brotherly kindness, and in your brotherly kindness, love. For if these qualities are yours and are increasing, they render you neither useless nor unfruitful in the true knowledge of our Lord Jesus Christ. *For he who lacks these qualities is blind or short-sighted, having forgotten his purification from his former sins* (2 Peter 1:4-9, emphasis added).

Did you catch the impact of Peter's message? He declared that it is a real and present danger to lose sight of the forgiveness we have in Christ! And if we do, then we will not develop spiritual disciplines, we will not grow, and we will not bear fruit.

Remembering His Grace

Perhaps the condition that Peter describes is the one you find yourself in today. If so, God wants you to be reminded of your purification from your former sins. He wants you to know

His grace and peace once again. He wants you to know that you are indeed forgiven and are a new creation in Christ. Consider the following Scriptures:

> Who is a God like you, who pardons sin and forgives the transgression of the remnant of his inheritance? You do not stay angry forever but delight to show mercy. You will again have compassion on us; you will tread our sins underfoot and hurl all our iniquities into the depths of the sea (Micah 7:18-19 NIV).

> The Lord is compassionate and gracious, slow to anger, abounding in love. He will not always accuse, nor will he harbor his anger forever; he does not treat us as our sins deserve or repay us according to our iniquities. For as high as the heavens are above the earth, so great is his love for those who fear him; as far as the east is from the west, so far has he removed our transgressions from us (Psalm 103:8-12 NIV).

> He was pierced through for our transgressions, He was crushed for our iniquities; the chastening for our well-being fell upon Him, and by His scourging we are healed. All of us like sheep have gone astray, each of us has turned to his own way; but the LORD has caused the iniquity of us all to fall on Him (Isaiah 53:5-6).

> "This is the covenant that I will make with them after those days, says the LORD: I will put My laws upon their heart, and on their mind I will write them," He then says, "And their sins and their lawless deeds I will remember no more." Now where there is forgiveness of these things, there is no longer any offering for sin (Hebrews 10:16-18).

> When you were dead in your transgressions and the uncircumcision of your flesh, He made you alive together with Him, having forgiven us all our transgressions,

having canceled out the certificate of debt consisting of decrees against us, which was hostile to us; and He has taken it out of the way, having nailed it to the cross (Colossians 2:13-15).

"Come now, and let us reason together," says the LORD, "though your sins are as scarlet, they will be as white as snow; though they are red like crimson, they will be like wool" (Isaiah 1:18).

"I have wiped out your transgressions like a thick cloud, and your sins like a heavy mist. Return to Me, for I have redeemed you" (Isaiah 44:22).

The imagery that God has given us in the Scriptures of His forgiveness could not be more vivid. He forgives and remembers our sins no more. He laid every last one of them on Christ and nailed them to the cross with Him. God has holy amnesia when it comes to all our wrongdoing. He has driven our sins away like the breeze blowing away the morning fog.

Child of God, you are forgiven! You are free! You are alive in Christ!

"Paid in Full"

Do yourself a favor. Take out a piece of paper and write down every wrong thing whose guilt still haunts you. The things you should have done but didn't. The things you shouldn't have done but did. Write down every bit of anger that you still harbor against God, yourself, and others.

Then write the words "PAID IN FULL" in red letters across that paper. That is the literal translation of the heart cry of Jesus on the cross when He said, *"Tetelestai!"* Often rendered "It is finished!" (see John 19:30), it is our Lord's exclamation point to His sacrificial death that paid the complete penalty of death for our sins.

It is over.

Now take that paper and do something with it that will stay in your memory. Trample on it. Rip it to shreds. Burn it. Tie it around a rock, go out in your boat, and throw it into the deepest part of a lake. Whatever you do, know that you are only acting out symbolically what God in Christ has already done for you, by grace, forever.

Please join us in this prayer:

Dear heavenly Father, grace and truth came through Your Son, Jesus Christ. And I have received of His fullness, grace upon grace. I don't want to be like the nine ungrateful lepers who were healed but never came back to express their gratitude to Jesus. So I say "Thank You, Lord!" for the grace and mercy You lavished upon me in Christ. Make today a landmark day for me so that I will never forget the forgiveness that is mine in Him. Give me discernment to recognize the accuser's lies, by which he seeks to drag me again into the gutter of guilt. I renounce all his deception and choose to believe the truth of what You have done for me. Heal my damaged emotions, Lord. In Jesus' name I pray, amen.

7

Grace for Life

*All the dealings of God with the soul of the believer
are in order to bring it into oneness with Himself.*

—HANNAH WHITALL SMITH

❧

I had the privilege of being present with my brave wife, Shirley, during the birth of our three biological children. With Michelle, she decided to go with a totally natural childbirth. Once was enough for that—for both of us—so with Brian she decided to go with an epidural. He arrived so quickly, however, that she had to go natural again. By the time Shirley was pregnant with Emily, she was ready to start having epidurals in the seventh month—just to make sure!

In addition to the pain their mother experienced as they came into this world, each of the three had one more thing in common. Even after they were born, they were still connected to Shirley by their umbilical cords.

Remarkably, children in the womb are so united with their mothers by that cord that what affects mom affects baby. In the case of nutrition, this is a blessing. In the case of crack and other harmful substances, it is a tragedy. Though mother and child are separate individuals, you can accurately say that the baby is in the mother and the mother in the child.

Grace Is "in Christ"

What a picture this is of the union that has taken place, by grace, between the Lord Jesus Christ and us! In fact, for

115

every verse in Scripture in which Christ is said to be in us, there are ten verses stating that we are "in Christ"! There is a spiritual umbilical cord that links us with our Lord, a cord that was not cut at the new birth and that will never be severed. David Needham comments on this in his book *Alive for the First Time*: "In that moment when God gave both life and birth to you, *he never severed the umbilical cord*. Enveloped in the Savior, identified with everything Jesus is and did—including the cross and the resurrection—you are always, ever 'in him.' But Jesus is also 'in you.' "[1]

You see, God's amazing grace did not stop with simply saving us from hell and preparing a place for us in heaven. There are countless spiritual treasures that were brought out and bestowed on us at the moment of our salvation. All of them are ours because we are joint heirs with Jesus and spiritually alive "in Christ." You likely are familiar with some of them, but maybe you've never before thought of them as antidotes to anger.

Recall the discussion in chapter 4 in which we explained that all of Adam and Eve's deepest needs were met by God in the Garden of Eden. But they were on their own to meet those needs after they chose to sin. In the flesh they were futilely seeking to regain "paradise lost." Only in Christ can our deep spiritual needs of life, identity, intimacy with God, dignity, acceptance, security, and significance be met. Our contention is that if any believer in Jesus truly grasps the reality, on a deep heart level, of how those needs are fully met in Christ, most of his or her struggles with fleshly anger will melt away.

It is easy, in a materialistic society, to believe that "the good life" comes from what we possess. Jesus laid that idea to rest when He said in Luke 12:15, "Beware, and be on your guard against every form of greed; for not even when one has an abundance does his life consist of his possessions."

The truth is this: Jesus is the "resurrection and *the life*" (John 11:25, emphasis added) and "the way, and the truth, and *the life*" (John 14:6, emphasis added). He came that we might have life and have it more abundantly (John 10:10). Jesus actually is our *life!* No longer do we need to try and find life through the world or the flesh, because life is a *person*—the Lord Jesus Christ—who lives in us and we in Him.

The "Old You" Is Dead

The apostle Paul made it clear that when our minds are set on Christ, who is our life, then we will be empowered to put to death the deeds of death.

> If you have been raised up with Christ, keep seeking the things above, where Christ is, seated at the right hand of God. Set your mind on the things above, not on the things that are on earth. For you have died and your life is hidden with Christ in God. When Christ, who is our life, is revealed, then you also will be revealed with Him in glory. Therefore consider the members of your earthly body as dead to immorality, impurity, passion, evil desire, and greed, which amounts to idolatry. For it is because of these things that the wrath of God will come upon the sons of disobedience, and in them you also once walked, when you were living in them. But now you also, put them all aside: anger, wrath, malice, slander, and abusive speech from your mouth (Colossians 3:1-8).

The thrust of Paul's argument is simple and powerful. The old you (the you without Christ) is *dead*, the new you is *alive in Christ*. In fact, Christ is your life and the source of life. In Christ you already have all you need. It is futile to try making a name and life for yourself by what you can gain on earth through your own strength and resources. Everything you accumulate on earth you will someday lose. But what you gain in Christ can never be taken away from you. As you discover your life, identity, acceptance, significance, and security in Christ, you will experience increasing victory in your struggle with anger. Why? Because fleshly, controlling anger stems from living our lives independently of God.

The Path to Freedom from the Flesh

Knowing who we are in Christ is the biblical path to liberation from the control of the flesh. Paul wrote: "I have been crucified with Christ; and it is no longer I who live, but Christ lives in me; and the life which I now live in the flesh [body] I live by faith in the Son of God, who loved me and gave Himself up for me" (Galatians 2:20). By the grace of God, the old fleshly you *is* dead, and the new you *is* alive in Christ Jesus. Paul wrote, "How shall we who died to sin still live in it?" (Romans 6:2).

Romans 6:4-7 is God's Emancipation Proclamation from sin's control.

> We have been buried with Him through baptism into death, so that as Christ was raised from the dead through the glory of the Father, so we too might walk in newness of life. For if we have become united with Him in the likeness of His death, certainly we shall also be in the likeness of His resurrection, knowing this, that our old self was crucified with Him, in order that our body of sin might be done away with, so that we would no longer be slaves to sin; for he who has died is freed from sin.

In a later chapter we will explain more of the "how to" of walking in our new life in Christ and overcoming fleshly anger. But for now, rejoice that you are alive in Christ and your spirit is eternally in union with Him! (1 Corinthians 6:17) Your struggle with identity is also over, because "as many as received Him, to them He gave the right to become children of God" (John 1:12). "See how great a love the Father has bestowed on us, that we would be called children of God; and such we are" (1 John 3:1).

True Dignity Is "in Christ"

Besides our need for identity, another need that is fully met in Christ is our need for *dignity*. How many times do we experience defensive anger because someone says or does something that attacks our dignity as a person?

Recently I was speaking in another town, and a young man named Jeremy told me about his spiritual struggles and of his strong need and desire to seek help from his youth pastor. Jeremy's mother told me that he had gone rapidly downhill spiritually after an incident involving his baseball team. Unfortunately, the youth pastor had been asked to resign and had left town without counseling him. Jeremy was angry with the pastor for not taking the time to meet with him, but he was really angry at his team's coach for criticizing him. He felt a loss of dignity.

The coach had promoted him to varsity, and Jeremy had been flying high. But then, in a crucial situation, he had struck out. The coach pulled him out and callously said, "I guess you weren't ready." That rejection, his loss of dignity, and his consequent anger had sent Jeremy into a spiritual tailspin. What remedy can be applied to such a wound? How can Jeremy look at himself in the mirror, and his coach in the eye, again?

One thing is clear. Jeremy's hope does not lie in his coach's recanting and restoring him to favor on the team. That is a false hope because that would still make his dignity dependent upon his ability to perform as a player, as well as his ability to please his coach. He would still be set up for future rejection if he were to fail again.

Not long ago a woman called my office. Her husband was in the process of divorcing her. Apparently, for over 20 years this man had systematically sought to dismantle his wife's sanity. Any time she presented an opinion contrary to his, she would be met by weeks of silence or by violent outbursts of verbal abuse. Any effort she would make to exercise her authority over the children would be undermined. If she refused to give money to one of their adult children who was acting irresponsibly, her husband would bail the child out, making his wife look bad in the process.

This man had managed to surround himself with other Christian men who had an authoritarian view of headship in the home. She was told to "just submit" (translation: become a passive doormat) even by a well-meaning pastor who was totally unaware of the emotional (and at times physical) abuse that was taking place behind those placid suburban walls.

This woman's husband had even spread false rumors about her having an affair in order to justify his separation and divorce from her. To make matters worse, the couple had been involved in significant public ministry together and had a reputation for having a good marriage, when in reality they didn't. This abused and neglected woman was angry and was struggling to overcome her bitterness.

Restoring Dignity

What help is available for such a woman, whose husband may not ever see his desperate need for help? How can her dignity as a human being and a woman be restored? How can she find the truth to set her free from more than 20 years of living with an oppressive husband? The abuse was made all the more painful because it was periodically interrupted by times of sweet harmony in their home. But hope would disappear again as Dr. Jekyll would by transformed back into Mr. Hyde.

Like Jeremy, this woman's hope does not ultimately lie in her husband's repentance and recovery, although that would be wonderful. She has no right or ability to control him—but these things are not determining who she is, nor are they necessary for her to be alive and free in Christ. Nobody can keep her from being the wife and mother that God has created her to be. This is because her primary identity is not found in her relationship with her husband or with any other human being.

Only through relationship with God as His children can this beleaguered woman, can Jeremy, can the rest of us, find our identity and dignity restored.

And the desperate quest for dignity is not limited to America. In many Asian cultures that lack a Christian base, an individual would rather die than "lose face"; and to shame someone publicly could put one's own life at serious risk. Only the truth can set us free from such bondage.

Regardless of what any person thinks of us, we are deeply loved by God. King David addressed perhaps the most painful of all possibilities when he said, "My father and my mother have forsaken me, but the LORD will take me up" (Psalm 27:10).

That same David, as we observed earlier, knew intense rejection from his "boss," King Saul. Saul tried repeatedly to hunt down and kill him because David had made such a name for himself. Regardless, David was able to write (and even more important, live out) the truth that "even though I walk through the valley of the shadow of death, I fear no evil, for You are with me" (Psalm 23:4). Even if a spouse or a child should turn against us, God never will. King David knew this kind of pain as his wife Michal mocked his exuberant worship of God and his son Absalom cunningly usurped his throne.

What God Says About Our Dignity

In stark contrast to the opinions of other people and their attacks on our personal worth and dignity, listen to what God says is true about His children:

> You are a chosen race, a royal priesthood, a holy nation, a people for God's own possession, so that you may proclaim the excellencies of Him who has called you out of darkness into His marvelous light; for you once were not a people, but now you are the people of God; you had not received mercy, but now you have received mercy (1 Peter 2:9-10).

It is impossible for other people to take those realities away from you, no matter what they say or what they do. God knows who you are because He looks upon the heart, while the inhabitants of this fallen world can only look upon the appearance. Knowing that you are unconditionally loved and accepted by God is what makes it possible to overcome your anger and walk by the Spirit when the world lets you down.

True Dignity Brings Intimacy

Having received life and the restoration of our value and dignity through Christ, we are now free to enjoy the immensely satisfying joy of *intimacy with God*. The psalmist Asaph knew the value of that closeness to God. He wrote in one of his psalms,

> I am continually with You; You have taken hold of my right hand. With Your counsel You will guide me, and afterward receive me to glory. Whom have I in heaven but You? And besides You, I desire nothing on earth. My flesh and my heart may fail, but God is the strength of my heart and my portion forever....As for me, the nearness of God is my good; I have made the Lord GOD my refuge, that I may tell of all Your works (Psalm 73:23-26,28).

King David wrote, "You will make known to me the path of life; in Your presence is fullness of joy; in Your right hand there are pleasures forever" (Psalm 16:11). If your relationship with God is the source of supreme joy in life, there is far less reason to be angry. David, a man after God's own heart, wrote in Psalm 27:4, "One thing I have asked from the LORD, that I shall seek: that I may dwell in the house of the LORD all the days of my life, to behold the beauty of the LORD and to meditate in His temple." When you make the passionate pursuit of God the primary driving force in your life, you will never be disappointed (1 Peter 2:6).

True Acceptance and Security Are "in Christ"

With God, *security* and *acceptance* go hand in hand. Once you know you are accepted by Him, you can rest assured that He will take care of you, and that brings a deep sense of security. By His grace, He has both accepted you and made you secure in Christ! Romans 15:7 says, "Accept one another, just as Christ also accepted us to the glory of God." We are "accepted in the beloved" (Ephesians 1:6 KJV).

To be accepted means to be received and welcomed as you are, with no strings attached. It is the act of unconditional love and grace by which God treats His former enemies as His very best friends. Because they are! Here are Jesus' words in John 15:15: "No longer do I call you slaves, for the slave does not know what his master is doing; but I have called you friends, for all things that I have heard from My Father I have made known to you." This friendship carries with it the responsibility of obedience (John 15:14), but it is predicated on the fact that in Christ God has graciously chosen us to be united with Him.

An Invitation to God's Table

Fifteen years after the death of King Saul and his son Jonathan, King David inquired as to whether there was any surviving relative of that family to whom he could show kindness (2 Samuel 9:1). The 20-year-old crippled son of Jonathan, Mephibosheth, was brought trembling before the king. In those days disabled people were rejected by society and were not even allowed to enter the house of God, but David demonstrated the grace of God. "David said to him, 'Do not fear, for I will surely show kindness to you for the sake of your father Jonathan, and will restore to you all the land of your grandfather Saul; and you shall eat at my table regularly'" (2 Samuel 9:7).

Mephibosheth had every natural reason to fear David. The king could have seen the young man as a threat to his throne and had him slain. But he didn't. Unknown to Mephibosheth, David and Jonathan had made a covenant years before that each would care for the other's family (1 Samuel 18:1-4; 20:42). Mephibosheth was the beneficiary of David's grace, in the name of Jonathan his father.

Mephibosheth couldn't believe David would treat him with such kindness. He saw himself as a "dead dog," unworthy of such royal treatment (2 Samuel 9:8). Indeed, what David had bestowed on him was the highest honor, for in being invited to eat at the king's table he was being regarded as one of the king's sons!

Too many Christians are like Mephibosheth. Trembling before the God who loves them, they are afraid that the hammer of judgment will fall on them if they make one little mistake. Child of God, the hammer has already fallen on Christ! He has already died once for all our sins (Romans 6:10). As children of God, we are no longer sinners in the hands of an angry God, we are saints in the hands of a loving God who has called us to come before His presence with our hearts sprinkled clean (Hebrews 10:19-25) and with confidence and boldness (Ephesians 3:12).

Today, the King invites you to eat at His table of blessing. And what a spread He has provided! Every spiritual blessing in the heavenly places is yours to feast upon in Christ (Ephesians 1:1-14). You are a saint, a holy one (verse 1), a recipient of His grace and peace (verse 2), chosen before time began to be holy and blameless before Him (verse 4). You have been lovingly adopted into His family because of His kindness (verses 5-6), redeemed and forgiven by His lavish grace (verse 7), and given a wonderful inheritance, sealed and pledged by the gift of the Holy Spirit (verses 11-14). Receive the unconditional love and acceptance of God with joy!

Acceptance by Grace

Mephibosheth's position of blessing and honor before the king was not based on his works, but on grace. He was crippled!

He likely needed help just getting to the king's table. So it is with us. By God's gracious acceptance of us in Christ we are saved and by that same grace alone we stand (Romans 5:2).

For anyone who has angrily tried to protect themselves from being rejected, it seems too good to be true. For anyone who has tried so hard to look great, do good, dress right, perform well, achieve more, and earn much, the truth of God's unconditional love and acceptance in Christ can be the most wonderful news imaginable. In contrast to the vain American quest for the perfect body, the God who created us in our mother's wombs (see Psalm 139:13-16) offers the perfect love. And He accepts us completely and unconditionally in Christ—bags and sags included!

There is no degree you can obtain, no salary you can gain, no position of power you can hold, no level of health, fitness, or beauty you can reach that will cause God to love and accept you one bit more than He does right now. Nor is there anything that you as a child of God can do to cause Him to love and accept you less. God loves us because He is love. It is His nature to love us. Though He hates our sin, He loves *us*—before we sin, after we sin, even while we are sinning.

Our Security Comes from the Eternal God

Our personal sense of security must not be based on temporal things that we have no right or ability to control, because our security comes from an eternal relationship with God that cannot be shaken, according to the apostle Paul:

> If God is for us, who is against us? He who did not spare His own Son, but delivered Him over for us all, how will He not also with Him freely give us all things?...For I am convinced that neither death, nor life, nor angels, nor principalities, nor things present, nor things to come, nor powers, nor height, nor depth, nor

any other created thing, will be able to separate us from the love of God, which is in Christ Jesus our Lord (Romans 8:31-32,38-39).

Security Through Our Adoption by God

About two years ago my wife, Shirley, our three kids—Michelle, Brian, and Emily—and I took a trip to Thailand. Although we did some vacationing while there, that wasn't the main purpose of the trip. Our main reason for traveling halfway around the world was to adopt Luke.

Luke was four years old and likely had no idea what was going on when we picked him up from the orphanage. But he willingly walked hand in hand with us down the sidewalk, into the waiting minivan, and off to a totally new life.

Suddenly Luke was living in a new country and had become part of a new family who spoke a new language and practiced a new faith. He now wears new clothes, has had to learn to eat new food (no problem!), sleep in a new bed, and play with new toys in a new house. He goes to a new school, has new friends and new neighbors in a new neighborhood with a new, cold climate, where new plants and new animals live. Everything was and is new!

Everything except much of Luke's behavior, that is. He still lives much of the time as if he were still in the orphanage. Though he is now almost seven years old, he still has to wear a diaper, hoards food, hasn't learned to share, yells and screams when upset, and exhibits a host of other not-so-endearing behaviors. But none of that alters the fact that he is our son and always will be. Much of his behavior is still un-Miller, but by identity and position he is legally a Miller by adoption. He was no accident—we chose him.

When Luke's adoption was finalized, we received from the Superior Court of Gwinnett County, State of Georgia, a document entitled "Final Judgment and Decree of Adoption." Here is an excerpt from that document:

IT IS HEREBY ORDERED, ADJUDGED, and DECREED that the Petition for Adoption is granted and that this Final Judgment and Decree of Adoption be entered. The Court hereby terminates all the rights of the biological parents to said child, and the Court hereby declares the child to be the adopted child of the Petitioners, capable of inheriting their respective estates according to law, and that the name of said child shall hereafter be known as Joshua Luke Saibua Miller.

Child of God, your final judgment and decree of adoption has been entered into the Lamb's book of life in the courts of heaven! All the rights of your former spiritual father, Satan, have been terminated! You are now a child of the true and living God and a co-heir with Christ!

Everything is *new* for you, too! Paul wrote, "If anyone is in Christ, he is a new creature; the old things passed away; behold, new things have come" (2 Corinthians 5:17). You, too, have to learn a new language, practice a new faith, and relate to new family members. You have new garments of righteousness, and you can eat from the bread of life and drink from the fountain of many waters. And you, too, will one day receive a new name (Revelation 2:17).

Even when you act as if you are back in the domain of darkness and soil your soul, God the Father gladly cleans you up and restores you to health and wholeness through Christ and His shed blood.

Resting in the Secureness of Our Identity

Our son Luke is not afraid we'll give him up, and you ought never to fear God's rejection. Remember, there was nothing but the gracious love of God that moved Him to choose you in the first place. Therefore, there is nothing in you that can make Him change His mind, because God does not change (Malachi 3:6).

Luke is not concerned about whether his needs for food, clothing, shelter, and love will be met. And neither should you be. God has promised to supply all your needs according to His riches in glory in Christ Jesus (Philippians 4:19). So many people are angry because they have never known that or haven't believed it to be true. We must learn to rest in the secure relationship we have with the Father as His precious children! He is faithful. He is responsible. And He cares for you (1 Peter 5:7). You are secure in Him!

Dr. Packer's exuberance over understanding his identity in Christ is contagious.

> Meanwhile, the immediate message to our hearts…is surely this: Do I, as a Christian, understand myself? Do I know my own real identity? My own real destiny? *I am a child of God. God is my Father; heaven is my home; every day is one day nearer. My Savior is my brother; every Christian is my brother, too.* Say it over and over to yourself the first thing in the morning, last thing at night, as you wait for the bus, any time when your mind is free, and ask that you may be enabled to live as one who knows it is all utterly and completely true. For this is the Christian's secret of—a happy life?—yes, certainly, but we have something both higher and profounder to say. This is the Christian's secret of a *Christian* life, and of a *God-honoring* life; and these are the aspects of the situation that really matter. May this secret become fully yours, and fully mine.[3]

Won't you right now release all your needs and wants into the hands of your all-powerful, all-wise, all-loving heavenly Father? Won't you release to Him all your anger over not getting the acceptance, security, approval, respect, and rewards that you think you deserve from people?

Let Paul's words bring comfort and healing to you:

> You have not received a spirit of slavery leading to fear again, but you have received a spirit of adoption as

sons by which we cry out, "Abba! Father!" The Spirit Himself testifies with our spirit that we are children of God, and if children, heirs also, heirs of God and fellow heirs with Christ, if indeed we suffer with Him so that we may also be glorified with Him (Romans 8:15-17).

True Significance Is "in Christ"

Finally, how many people, even Christians, operate with a constant low-grade fever of frustration because they feel what they do in life is meaningless? For the believer, this is an unnecessary burden to bear, because in Christ our lives have great *significance*.

Christian, you are the salt of the earth and light of the world (Matthew 5:13-14)! Whatever your calling or vocation, you can "let your light shine before men in such a way that they may see your good works, and glorify your Father who is in heaven" (Matthew 5:16). To live in a way that points people to the true God is supremely important, whether you do it as a businessman or blue-collar worker, minister or mother.

My wife, Shirley, had spent 14 years in very fruitful full-time ministry with teens and their adult leaders before Michelle came along. Then came Brian and Emily and Luke as well. Changing diapers, cleaning up spills, nursing in the middle of the night, and staying home with sick kids while her husband travels and speaks can seem mundane and wearisome by comparison. But she is still in full-time ministry. Despite the lasting impact she made on the teenagers she formerly worked with, the investment she is making in our children is of great, eternal significance. Their future spouses and children will one day rise up and call Shirley blessed.

No matter what you do for a living, will you allow God to inject into the everyday a new sense of the eternal? Significance is related to time. What is forgotten in time is of little significance, but what is remembered for all eternity is of great significance. That is why there are no insignificant children of God. We shall live with our heavenly Father for all eternity. Significance comes from faithfully living in the will of God and by letting your light shine.

Be All You Are Called to Be

Are you angry because you feel like you are living an insignificant life? All God is asking from you is that you be the person He has called you to be and that you fulfill the ministry He has given you.

> All these things are from God, who reconciled us to Himself through Christ and gave us the ministry of reconciliation, namely, that God was in Christ reconciling the world to Himself, not counting their trespasses against them, and He has committed to us the word of reconciliation. Therefore, we are ambassadors for Christ, as though God were making an appeal through us; we beg you on behalf of Christ, be reconciled to God. He made Him who knew no sin to be sin on our behalf, so that we might become the righteousness of God in Him (2 Corinthians 5:18-21).

The time is short. People need the Lord. Invest your life wholeheartedly in the proclamation of the gospel to those around you. Faithfully fulfill your calling as a minister of reconciliation, a peacemaker.

And know that the grace of God is the most powerful force for change on earth. Once you have truly embraced it yourself, you are qualified and equipped to spread it to others. And just watch what happens when you do.

Here's a story of that amazing grace:

> When I was young, I was sexually abused by my father. This wasn't a frequent event by any means. I only remember it happening once. I don't recall details, but I remember enough to know that things happened that shouldn't have happened between a father and daughter.

When I was saved in 1988, I was 35 years old. I felt a release from anger almost immediately. There was an internal peace I had never known.

However, seven years later I found myself still struggling around my father's birthday and Father's Day—those occasions that required a card or call. I never was able to pick a card that said "I love you" or any other intimate sentiment. It was troubling to me, and so finally one day during my devotions I brought this up to the Lord. I asked, "Lord, why do I go through these struggles around these times?" The answer came quickly and clearly. It was simply, "You don't respect him." I started to object, laying all the groundwork for the argument that "one needs to earn respect," and so on.

I realized after a few minutes how useless my arguments were. All I heard was silence. I asked the Lord, "Is this a sin against You?" Again, the response was quick and clear. "Yes." I felt devastated, but at the same time free. I confessed the sin, and then the Holy Spirit graciously flooded me with memories of the times my father *had* done things that deserved my respect, but I had deliberately withheld it.

Within a few weeks of this experience, I was talking to my dad on the phone. TALKING! We had never had a conversation before. This conversation lasted almost 15 minutes! That was the longest I had ever talked to my dad. At the end of the conversation we both said that we loved each other. It wasn't just words, but something we both felt sincerely.

My dad passed away this past February, which was about four years after that devotional time. When I was visiting him in his last few weeks, I asked him for forgiveness for the times I was unkind and disrespectful. I also told him that I forgave him. I didn't go into detail of what it was I was forgiving him for; it was sufficient that we both knew. The very next day I asked him if he would pray to Jesus and ask for forgiveness of his sins. He did! I praise

God for this, as he had always been extremely resistant to the gospel. I praise God for the words He gave to me at the end of my dad's earthly life. I have peace knowing that my dad is with God now and that I will see him again in eternity.

Dear heavenly Father, thank You for Your life in me, for making all things new again. Thank You for restoring to me the life, dignity, joy, intimacy with You, acceptance, security, and significance that had been lost through sin. Open the eyes of my heart, Lord, so that I can begin to grasp the full extent of Your care and provision for me, so that I will never again look for life and love in the wrong places. I now ask that You would liberate and empower me to freely express to others this wonderful grace of Jesus. In His name I pray, amen.

The Need to Forgive

*Anger is brief madness and, unchecked, becomes
protracted madness, bringing shame and even death.*
                                                —PETRARCH

≈

T his was the most important night of my life," the young
man said after a message I had just given at a conference in New York. While I was speaking on our need to
forgive others who have hurt us, I had noticed that he was
crying. Friends had gathered around his wheelchair to console him right after I was through speaking. He had wheeled
over to me a few minutes later as I was gathering my materials
to leave.

After we had talked briefly, I set up an appointment to
meet with him and a close friend the following morning. I was
curious to know what God was doing in his life.

"Jeffrey, can you tell me why last evening was the most
important night in your life?" I asked, leaning forward and
fixing my eyes on his.

"I was born prematurely, and while I was being transferred
from one medical facility to another, I was denied the oxygen
I needed," he began.

Jeffrey was unable to walk or use his arms. His hands were
locked in a clawlike position. If his weight happened to shift

forward or sideways too much, he would have to get help to be set straight again. He was, in one sense, trapped in a body that would not and could not do what his extremely sharp mind told it to. But he had spent 19 years in bondage of another sort as well, as he went on to explain.

"I have been so angry with God and those people who did that to me. I have prayed so many times that I could be healed, but nothing. My sister was in an industrial accident and a heavy piece of machinery fell on her foot and crushed it. After several months, she went to a healing service in a church and God miraculously healed her.

"Of course I was happy for her. But I couldn't help crying out to God, 'Why her, Lord, and not me? She was crippled for a few months; I've been this way for 19 years!'"

Knowing that Jeffrey had experienced more pain and suffering in 19 years than I likely will in a lifetime, I had enough sense to stay quiet and just listen.

"Last night, I was finally able to forgive those men who had done that to me when I was a newborn."

I just sat there in silence for a while, drinking in the holiness of that moment. After a while, Jeffrey made the decision to let go of the anger that he had harbored against God for allowing all this to happen. In some ways this was even harder for him.

As part of the healing process, Jeffrey then went on to thank God for the parts of his body that didn't work. Then he prayed and asked God to glorify Himself through his legs, arms, and hands, one by one. As we concluded our time together, I told Jeffrey, "You know, there are millions of Christians walking around with strong, able bodies, but who are in deep emotional and spiritual bondage. Because of your decision to forgive and release your anger, Jeffrey, even though you are confined to this wheelchair, you are more free than any of them!"[1]

Living with Wounds

Jeffrey had what the Bible calls "infirmities" (KJV) or "weaknesses." *Strong's Concordance* defines them as "feebleness (of body or mind); by [implication] *malady*; [moreover] *frailty*: disease, infirmity, sickness, weakness."[2] *Vine's Expository Dictionary* uses these words of "infirmity": "want of strength,...weakness, indicating inability to produce results."[3]

Infirmities or weaknesses are wounds—visible or hidden—that inhibit our ability to perform at a higher level. They cause us to be feeble, frail, helpless, inefficient; deficient in strength, dignity, or power. They can be physical conditions, but they also can be mental, emotional, or spiritual.

Jeffrey is not alone in his weaknesses. We all have them. We have holes or wounds or both in our souls that are there because of someone else's abuse, neglect, ignorance, irresponsibility, maliciousness, or foolishness. Some infirmities are simply the by-product of living in a fallen world. We have all been victims of people or circumstances to one degree or another.

There are no promises that we will not be victimized again, but as believers in Christ we need no longer *live* as victims. That is the beauty and power of the presence of Christ in our lives. Though we cannot turn the clock back and change our past, we *can* be free from its negative control over us. When we make the decision to forgive others from the heart, we set ourselves free from the past to be victorious overcomers and more than conquerors through Him who loved us (Romans 8:37).

After a recent phone conversation with a friend, I was struck by grief. After years of suffering through the discovery that his wife had been sexually abused by a relative, my friend and his wife more recently had to endure the agony of finding out that their oldest daughter had been the man's prey as well. Now it appears that their youngest daughter was also victimized, most likely as an infant and toddler.

Though the perpetrator is behind bars, serving what amounts to a life sentence, the pain is still there. My friend said honestly, "If he got out of prison, I'd kill him."

I know this man, and I don't believe he would really do that, because he loves Jesus too much to take that kind of revenge. But the pain is real and the wound is raw. The whole family is reeling from an infirmity that will take the grace of God to heal.

Jesus Was Wounded Too

Jesus doesn't view our infirmities coldly and dispassionately from His throne in the sky,

> for we do not have a High Priest who cannot sympathize with our weaknesses [infirmities], but was in all points tempted as we are, yet without sin. Let us therefore come boldly to the throne of grace, that we may obtain mercy and find grace to help in time of need (Hebrews 4:15-16 NKJV).

The Lord Jesus Himself went through the most heinous rejection, torture, and abuse ever perpetrated on a man, by dying on the cross for our sins. We cannot even begin to comprehend the unspeakable horror of the Holy One becoming sin for us (2 Corinthians 5:21). And yet throughout all the hell He went through, Jesus never sinned.

Our Response to Wounds

Suffering is not a license to sin. Infirmity is not an excuse for iniquity. Experiencing hurt is not resolved by getting bitter. Being wounded ourselves does not give us permission to wound others.

In our woundedness we cry out that it isn't fair—and it seems only just that we pay others back for the pain we've been given. But listen to Peter's description of how Jesus handled the excruciating pain that sinful men inflicted on Him, and note the ramifications for those of us who are His followers:

This finds favor, if for the sake of conscience toward God a man bears up under sorrows when suffering unjustly. For what credit is there if, when you sin and are harshly treated, you endure it with patience? But if when you do what is right and suffer for it you patiently endure it, this finds favor with God. For you have been called for this purpose, since Christ also suffered for you, leaving you an example for you to follow in His steps, who committed no sin, nor was any deceit found in His mouth; and while being reviled, He did not revile in return; while suffering, He uttered no threats, but kept entrusting Himself to Him who judges righteously (1 Peter 2:19-23).

Unfortunately, we cannot claim that same clean slate of sinless treatment of our fellow man. Though God has extended to us total forgiveness in Christ, we have not always extended that same grace and mercy toward those who have hurt us. We have often harbored anger, resentment and bitterness toward others.

Forgiveness—The Only Way Out

When Peter asked Jesus how many times it was necessary to forgive, the disciple volunteered what must have seemed to him a generous number, seven. Jesus, of course, told him that wasn't sufficient. Seventy times seven was more like it. In other words, don't keep track, but as many times as someone sins against you, forgive (Matthew 18:21-22).

To drive home His point even more strongly, Jesus followed with a story (18:23-35). The gist of it was that a certain king decided to declare a "National Debt Payoff Day." The clock had run out on everyone who still owed him money. It was "pay up or else."

One man came before the king owing the equivalent of millions of dollars. The debt was way beyond what he could earn in a lifetime. He pulled out the loose change in his pocket, looked in his wallet, visited the ATM, called his stock-broker, checked the status of his portfolio on the Internet (a loose translation), and still found himself several million short.

The king decided to cut his losses by selling the man, his wife, and his children as slaves. His home and all his posses-sions were going to go on the auction block as well. The king had a right to do all this because he was, after all, the king!

Realizing that he was about to lose everything he owned and everyone he loved, the man fell down before the king and pleaded for mercy. Amazingly, the king heard his plea and can-celled the entire debt.

Incredible! The man was free, and everything that he was about to lose was restored to him. On his way home he hap-pened to meet a guy who owed him a few thousand dollars—about six month's wages. No small change, but chicken feed compared to what the first man had owed the king.

Unbelievably, the first man was unwilling to cancel the debt of the second, and had him thrown in prison. Word got out and traveled back to the king, who was not pleased at all. Let's go directly to Jesus' words to catch the ending:

> Then summoning him, his lord said to him, "You wicked slave, I forgave you all that debt because you pleaded with me. Should you not also have had mercy on your fellow slave, in the same way that I had mercy on you?" And his lord, moved with anger, handed him over to the torturers until he should repay all that was owed him (verses 32-34).

That is a sobering enough conclusion to the story as is, but Jesus didn't stop there. He added an epilogue for the dis-ciples then and for you and me today (verse 35): "My heavenly Father will also do the same to you, if each of you does not for-give his brother from your heart."

The Turmoil of Unforgiveness

What was Jesus referring to when He spoke of being, "handed...over to the torturers"? Jesus doesn't explain what they are in this passage of Scripture, but the root word means "to experience pain, toil, or torment, and to toss or vex."[4] Clearly then, the phrase "the torturers" is referring to those natural or supernatural forces that cause intense pain and turmoil of the body and soul.

Frederick Buechner said it about as pointedly as one can:

> Of the seven deadly sins, anger is possibly the most fun. To lick your wounds, to smack your lips over grievances long past, to savor to the last toothsome morsel both the pain you are given and the pain you are giving back. In many ways it is a feast fit for a king. The chief drawback is that what you are wolfing down is yourself. The skeleton at the feast is you.[5]

There is only one way out of the bondage of bitterness, and that is by forgiving from the heart, as described in this woman's story:

> There was a time in my life when I was angry with everyone! My mom left when I was 18 and my father kicked me out, my husband cheated on me and my oldest child wasn't perfect! There came a point in time five years ago when my child was taken from me and I was accused of all sorts of things. I became very angry and vengeful. Nothing seemed to work! One night I was alone in the house and I picked up Neil's book *The Bondage Breaker* and read through it. I began going through the "Steps to Freedom in Christ" and when I got to the section on forgiveness the list was so long I had to take the phone off the hook. As I began to pray, the picture came to mind of me struggling through life pulling a huge bag of "stuff" behind me. Then the picture changed to that of Christ carrying that bag with the cross up to Calvary. Freedom came—to love people as they are and to forgive and live!

The "temper" I thought was hereditary left and I was free to forgive as Christ forgave me.

Is Unforgiveness an Option?

Are some things so terrible that they should never be forgiven? The editors of *Parade Magazine* seem to think so.

> While we may admire those who can find forgiveness in their hearts, forgiveness may not always be the answer. Andrew Vachss, a writer and attorney who represents abused children, has noted: "A particularly pernicious myth for victims of abuse is that 'healing requires forgiveness' of the abuser." This only leads to further victimization, he added….And there are some things that cannot be—and should not ever be—forgiven. As Elie Wiesel, the Nobel Laureate and Holocaust survivor, said in a prayer at the 50th Anniversary of the liberation of Auschwitz: "God of forgiveness, do not forgive those murderers of Jewish children here."[6]

If you have suffered greatly in your life, there may be a part of your heart that resonates with Elie Wiesel's words. Perhaps angrily so. You might be saying, "How can you tell me to forgive? You don't know how much this person has hurt me!" You're right, we don't. But we do know that the person is still hurting you, because the pain is still obviously there and you are still bound to the past. You don't heal in order to forgive. You forgive in order to heal. Although we wish we had the opportunity to sit down with you and hear your story, that is just not possible. Fortunately, Jesus knows, and He is willing and able to hear your story, heal your wounds, and set you free from your past through forgiveness—first His forgiveness of *your* sins, and then your forgiveness of *others*.

The Way of Healing

In rebuttal to Mr. Vachss's comments, forgiveness is indeed necessary for healing. But forgiveness does not mean tolerating sin and placing oneself back under the power of an abuser. God never tolerates sin, and neither should we. We must take appropriate steps to protect ourselves from continuing abuse. In some cases that may mean separation from an abusive family member, or it may even mean calling the police. In milder cases it may mean simply learning to say "no" to people who try to take advantage of you, setting wise boundaries to protect yourself from being used by people.

If you or someone you love is in an abusive situation, get help. As Christians we are not called to passively accept the injustices of life. God has ordained the higher authority of government to protect us from criminal behavior. And the church ought to step in to give counsel, aid, and sanctuary to the hurting people God sends her way (Luke 10:29-37).

To Mr. Wiesel, we would say that God's forgiveness of any sin, including the sins of Holocaust villains, is contingent on one thing and one thing alone—sinners' repentance and trust in Jesus Christ as the Savior who made atonement for their sin. Whether they receive God's forgiveness is between those people and God Himself. But the necessity for us as God's people to forgive the offender is commanded in Scripture (Colossians 3:5-8,12-13):

> Consider the members of your earthly body as dead to immorality, impurity, passion, evil desire, and greed, which amounts to idolatry. For it is because of these things that the wrath of God will come upon the sons of disobedience, and in them you also once walked, when you were living in them. But now you also, put them all aside: anger, wrath, malice, slander, and abusive speech from your mouth....So, as those who have been chosen of God, holy and beloved, put on a heart of compassion, kindness, humility, gentleness and patience; bearing with one another, and forgiving each other, whoever has a complaint against anyone; just as the Lord forgave you, so also should you.

We don't forgive another person for his or her sake. We do it for our *own* sake. To forgive is to set a captive free—and then realize that *we* were the captive. What is to be gained by forgiving is freedom from our past. If we fail to forgive, we can experience serious mental torment, being haunted by our painful memories and trauma.

The Need to Forgive

After the 1997 shooting deaths of three girls at Heath High School in West Paducah, Kentucky, some of the grieving families filed wrongful death suits against the school district. That is not particularly surprising, but what is unsettling is that lawsuits were also filed against the police, the parents of killer Michael Carneal, and even against seven students who allegedly had advance notice of the crime. Unbelievably, even the young man who led the school prayer circle and talked Carneal into giving up his weapon has been named as a defendant.[7]

The story of the shooting at Columbine High School is similar. At one point at least 19 families had filed suit or intent-to-sue notices in the wake of the spring 1999 slayings. Among them, to the chagrin of local residents, were Tom and Susan Klebold, who claimed that authorities should have warned them to keep their son, Dylan (one of the murderers), away from Eric Harris, who is believed to have been the instigator behind the horror.[8]

And that was not the end of the angry controversy that welled up in the aftermath of the Columbine massacre:

> The anger over the killings continues to boil over into everyday life. A controversy erupted, for instance, over whether the Columbine library, where many of the students were shot, should be renovated and left where it is or moved to a new location in the school. Another battle brewed when the school invited all students' families to paint tiles to be affixed to the wall above the hall

lockers. One stipulation was that the tiles not have a religious theme, lest they provoke lawsuits protesting an affront to the separation of church and state. When some families ignored the rule, they were either denied the chance to put up tiles or had their artwork chiseled off the walls—a policy that, predictably, triggered a lawsuit. Then, in September, several parents of shooting victims cut down two linden trees, symbolizing Klebold and Harris, among 15 that had been planted at a local church to memorialize all who died at Columbine.[9]

Is their anger justified? Is their subsequent behavior justified? Some of these people have suffered tremendous losses. Is it realistic to expect them not to be angry and to act out their anger? Is it right that God calls these people who have been so deeply traumatized to forgive?

Freedom from the Past

The following story demonstrates that forgiveness in the face of a horrible atrocity is not only possible but necessary if one is ever to be free from the past. Tom Bowers' sister, Margie, was brutally murdered by Thomas Vanda, and Tom vowed never to forgive him. The son of foreign missionaries, Tom recounts how he felt at Vanda's trial:

> One year after the murder I sat in a courtroom. As the trial unfolded I felt a burning anger. The prosecutor presented the horrific details of that April night. Vanda expressed no remorse. None! As I sat directly behind the smirking killer, it crossed my mind more than once that I could reach across the railing and strangle him.[10]

After years of struggling with how to be free from the anger and torment inside, God's words filled Tom's mind one day while he was driving through the Blue Ridge Mountains. *It's time. Just forgive.*[11] Tom's testimony is one of overcoming an anger that had festered for too long:

Margie would not have wanted my torment to continue. God did not want it. In obedience to God as well as for my own sake, I had to forgive. At last I said the words aloud and with conviction: "Thomas Vanda, I forgive you." I said them again and again. "Thomas Vanda, I forgive you." As I declared my forgiveness, a crushing burden lifted from me and I was filled with a transcendent peace. I finally understood Esther's words: "I have been given wings." [Esther was Margie's roommate and Thomas Vanda's ex-girlfriend. She had needed to forgive herself for not being there when Margie was killed, for Esther was the one Vanda was really after. When she did forgive herself, the freedom she experienced was like being given wings to fly.][12]

We can read these stories with detached interest, maybe even secretly wondering why it is taking some of them so long to "get over it" and "get on with life." Most of us have not suffered such nightmarish horror, but we all have been hurt by someone else. Nursing small grudges can keep us in bondage and disrupt our fellowship with God as much as bitterness can in the wake of severe trauma. Maybe we avoid others in church because of an unkind or thoughtless word spoken years ago. We dread family reunions because "that person" will be there. We spend extra hours at the office because we don't want to face the conflicts at home. Unresolved anger, resentment, and bitterness can cause many to be defiled (Hebrews 12:15).

We Can Forgive As Christ Forgave

The good news is that Jesus Christ knows what it means to suffer much more than we will ever suffer. And He knows what it means to forgive, for He did so on the cross. Though fully God, Jesus was also fully man. He suffered as a man. He died as a man. He also forgave as a man. He did not secretly turn off His humanity on the cross and thus somehow become dulled to the intense suffering of crucifixion. When the nails were hammered through His wrists, He felt real pain. When

He gasped for air, He felt real agony. When He bled, He felt real weakness. When He died, His brain and heart really stopped working.

And when He said, "Father, forgive them; for they do not know what they are doing" (Luke 23:34), He gave real hope. For the same Jesus lives in all true children of God, and He is always there to give us the grace to forgive.

We Can Forgive Ourselves As Christ Forgave Us

For some people, the hardest person to forgive is the one they see in the mirror. Looking back on a life ravaged by their own wrong choices, sinful behavior, and ruined relationships, their hearts are wracked with guilt, shame, and regret. This personal experience illustrates that serious problem:

> I am still learning how to be free from my anger. I have come a long way, but still have a long way to go. I grew up in a violent home and was subjected to sexual abuse by a family member. There was also divorce and all it destroys in the family. My family was middle-class and very concerned about looking "good" to others and hiding. I was therefore given to angry outbursts toward just about everyone and everything. I was also consumed with unforgiveness, which led me to destructive behavior (drugs, sex, and so on). When I met Jesus, many things were healed and I experienced great freedom. My anger was not so easily released, however. I have spent the last several years learning who I am in Christ, how to forgive others, and how to forgive myself. The last one has been the hardest, and my anger is sometimes directed toward myself or my failures.

Though we may be convinced of the power of the shed blood of Jesus to cleanse *others* from all sin, sometimes we view *ourselves* as the exception. Seeing firsthand how we have messed up our lives and the lives of others, we listen to the accuser of the brethren as he relentlessly assaults us with his litany of lies. Because we instinctively know that sin should be punished, we allow his brutal barrage to continue, feeling it is justified. We have come to believe that we *should* feel bad for what we've done.

If this is your life in a nutshell, it is time to stop giving in to the "bully of your soul." It is time to stop listening to and believing his lies, lies such as "My life is ruined and beyond repair"; "God has put me on the shelf"; "I'll never amount to anything"; "I'm only getting what I deserve."

Our Forgiveness Is "in Christ"

We hope that you read chapters six and seven (on God's grace) with an open heart. You may need to read them again and again, looking up and meditating upon the Scriptures we have considered. In time, the truth of your total forgiveness and cleansing in Christ will become real to you in your emotions. These things are already completely true of you in Christ; right now they just may not *feel* real.

Child of God, will you open your heart to receive the heavenly greeting and blessing, "Grace to you and peace from God our Father and the Lord Jesus Christ" (Philippians 1:2)? As you grow to receive those words, the steps to forgiveness at the end of the next chapter will become powerfully liberating for you. We encourage you to go through that process prayerfully and thoroughly.

Releasing Our Anger Toward God

There is one more area of forgiveness that we need to touch on before closing this chapter. And that concerns our dealing with anger toward God. Entire books have been written concerning the problem of evil and suffering, seeking to explain why those things exist and why God allows them at times to overwhelm us.[13] The best book on the subject is in the Bible itself. It is called the book of Job. Though the subject is vast and far beyond the scope of our book, we do want to address this sensitive subject briefly.

The following personal story is from a man who has spent his entire life feeling left out, rejected, and abandoned. The context of the pain and anger toward God that is expressed in his words below was his being passed over for several promotions. Any one of those new jobs would have taken him out of work that was sheer drudgery. In addition, he would have been placed in a situation where he could have better provided for his family as well as being able to serve God full-time.

> God had saved me when I was 19. All I'd ever wanted was to serve Him; all He seemed interested in was humiliating me. I wouldn't renounce Him. Like Job (13:15), I'd continue to depend on Him for my eternal destiny. But He'd gone out of His way repeatedly to show me that He had no need of my services and that He couldn't be trusted to oversee my earthly existence. Day and night alike were black to me. If my kids grew up without a father, God obviously didn't care! I maintained my church and devotional routines, but an immense wall stood between my Lord and me—one through which no light or love would pass.

Maybe that's where you find yourself or a loved one today. "Why?" questions angrily launched heavenward are about the only semblance of "prayer" you feel capable of uttering. To you it's like making a desperate phone call to heaven—and all you get on the other end of the line is silence. Or a recorded message that sounds hollow and trite (unfortunately, all too often recited by well-meaning but unhelpful Christians).

Be Real with God

We want to give you permission right now to be real with God. In fact, the truth is that you simply cannot be right with God until you are real with Him. And that principle applies whether your anger is directed toward God, other people, or even yourself. God already knows your pain and anger, and so you will neither hurt nor surprise Him by being honest. He can take it. But you can't take *not* being honest. Suppressing your emotions or holding on to your anger will damage and may possibly destroy you.

The prophet Jeremiah was in despair as he helplessly watched the systematic destruction of his beloved homeland. He was clearly depressed, but he was also very angry with God, and he wrote about it in the book of Lamentations:

> I am the man who has seen affliction because of the rod of His wrath. He has driven me and made me walk in darkness and not in light. Surely against me He has turned His hand repeatedly all the day....He has besieged and encompassed me with bitterness and hardship....He has walled me in so that I cannot go out;...even when I cry out and call for help, He shuts out my prayer....He is to me like a bear lying in wait, like a lion in secret places. He has turned aside my ways and torn me to pieces....I have become a laughingstock to all my people, their mocking song all the day. He has filled me with bitterness....My soul has been rejected from peace; I have forgotten happiness. So I say, "My strength has perished, and so has my hope from the LORD" (Lamentations 3:1-3, 5,7-8,10-11,14-15,17-18).

Were Jeremiah's words true? In one sense they were—they were a true representation of how he felt. But were they true in their depiction of God? Is God really like a bear or lion to His people? No, not at all. But Jeremiah could not have reached back into his heart and recovered the truth about who God really is without first telling the truth about how he really felt. Listen to the change in the prophet's perception of God once he was able to be emotionally honest:

> Remember my affliction and my wandering, the wormwood and bitterness. Surely my soul remembers and is bowed down within me. This I recall to my mind,

therefore I have hope. The LORD's lovingkindnesses indeed never cease, for His compassions never fail. They are new every morning; great is Your faithfulness. "The LORD is my portion," says my soul, "therefore I have hope in Him." The LORD is good to those who wait for Him, to the person who seeks Him (Lamentations 3:19-25).

Freedom and Healing from Anger Toward God

Perhaps you are angry with God today because He did not stop the awful abuse that was perpetrated on you as a child or as an adult. You cried out to Him, and it seems as though He turned a deaf ear to your cries. You felt crushed, and perhaps concluded as a result that you were on your own in this world. Maybe you refuse to take the risk any more of leaning on anyone else because you are convinced that no one, not even God, can be trusted.

Perhaps you have watched the terrible suffering of loved ones and God has seemed so distant and uncaring. And so you are angry. And bitter.

Whatever your situation, there is freedom for you if you are willing to face some difficult issues. There are some fundamental steps to be taken to bring about recovery and healing, but they require your cooperation as you step out in faith.

First, as we have already stated, be completely real with God concerning how you feel. Don't hold back your emotions or feel the need to cloak your anger in pious-sounding religious language. Be honest.

Next, admit to yourself and to God that you don't have all the answers. You need to come to the place where you admit that you do not possess all wisdom and understanding. This will be a humbling moment for you, but that was the point that Job (despite all his horrible pain and suffering) had to come to (see Job 38–42). And so do you.

Third, by faith tell God that you believe that His ways and thoughts are higher than yours (Isaiah 55:8-9). You have known that His ways and thoughts are *different* than yours. Now it is time to admit that they are *higher*.

The next step will be tough, but it is essential. Release the right to have all your questions answered this side of heaven. We believe there are many things we are incapable of understanding until we come into God's presence. And so, as you let go of your questions, by faith, thank Him that He is all-wise and that He knows what He is doing.

Next, make the choice to release your anger toward God. Many times we wrongfully blame God for the mistakes we have made and their consequences in our lives. Proverbs 19:3 (NIV) says, "A man's own folly ruins his life, yet his heart rages against the LORD." Though He has never done anything wrong, you may find it helpful to verbalize your prayer as "Lord, I forgive You for..." The steps at the end of chapter 9 will aid you in this prayer. The Lord will also gently lead you in this time to confess that you have been wrong in holding on to your anger toward Him.

Finally, prayerfully ask the Lord to reveal Himself to you in your painful memories—not angrily demanding that He do this, but humbly asking Him to touch you and heal your hurt. He longs to do that if you will let Him.

Your Father Cares About You

We conclude this chapter with a letter from your caring Father to you,[14] followed by a closing prayer. We sincerely hope that you will hear His voice of love as you read and pray.

> *My Child, you may not know Me, but I know everything about you. I know when you sit down and when you rise up. I am familiar with all your ways. In Me you live and move and have your being. I knew you even before you were conceived. I chose you when I planned creation. You were not a mistake, for all your days were written in My book. I determined the*

exact time of your birth and where you would live. You are fearfully and wonderfully made. I knit you together in your mother's womb and brought you forth on the day you were born.

I have been misrepresented by those who don't know Me. I am not distant and angry, but am the complete expression of love. It is My desire to lavish my love on you, simply because you are My child and I am your Father. I offer you more than your earthly father could, for I am the perfect Father. My plan for your future has always been filled with hope because I love you with an everlasting love. My thoughts toward you are as countless as the sand on the seashore, and I rejoice over you with singing. I will never stop doing good to you, for you are My treasured possession. I am able to do more for you than you could possibly imagine.

I am also the Father who comforts you in all your troubles. When you are brokenhearted, I am close to you. As a shepherd carries a lamb, I have carried you close to My heart. One day I will wipe away every tear from your eyes, and I will take away the pain you have suffered on this earth.

I am your Father and I love you even as I love My son, Jesus. For in Jesus My love for you is revealed. He came to demonstrate that I am for you, not against you. Come home and I will throw the biggest party heaven has ever seen. I am waiting for you.

Love,
Your Abba Father

Dear heavenly Father, this matter of dealing with the anger I have held inside is a life-and-death issue, isn't it? Many people have died because of their own or someone else's unwillingness to forgive. Now I know that I cannot truly live until I forgive those who have hurt me. That includes forgiving myself. Sometimes that is the hardest one of all. And I must release my anger toward You if I am ever going to get past this terrible *wilderness in my soul. I am sobered to know the terrible power of bitterness, but I am given hope because Your grace is greater than all my sin. I surrender to Your will and ask that You would teach me how to forgive from my heart. In Jesus' name I pray, amen.*

9

Forgiving
from the Heart

*Resentment is like taking poison and waiting for
the other person to die.*
                    —MALACHY MCCOURT

$\sim$

When I (Rich) was an adolescent, I hated my brother, Tom. This was not just sibling rivalry, this was all-out hate. He is three years older than I am, and I was constantly trying and failing to keep up with him. I resented him. I was jealous of him. He represented everything that I was not—good-looking, popular, friendly, athletic. I didn't like being around him. Just seeing him was a painful reminder of how much a failure in life I was.

Tom's attitude toward me was typically older-brother-to-younger-brother stuff. There were times, however, when he was verbally and physically abusive, and those times just poured gasoline on my anger.

One time I was so angry with him that I hit him in the back of the head with a well-thrown "smart bomb." We were outside at the time, and he turned and chased me back toward our house, snarling and breathing threats all the way. Frantically trying to figure out the safest place in the house to hide, I ran for my life toward the bathroom.

I made it just in time and slammed the bathroom door shut. As I was trying to lock it, my brother pushed it open and stuck his hand through to grab me. Suddenly "the hunted" became "the hunter" as I squeezed his trapped hand between the door and the doorjamb. I enjoyed the feeling of power and control, because depending upon how hard I would push on the door, I could get all different levels of screams out of my brother!

I wanted him to be hurt as he had hurt me. Reluctantly I released my prey once my hysterical mother appeared on the scene. One other time I intentionally shot Tom in the face with a BB gun, dangerously close to his eye. I would spend endless hours in my room trying to devise terrible traps that would unleash their fury on my brother when he would open my door (kind of like that old Mouse Trap game). It's obvious I had a terrible problem with anger, resentment, and bitterness toward my brother.

Part of my problem in dealing with my brother was that he was always bigger than me—until I reached my late teens. I had grown to six-foot-two, 175 pounds, and Tom was about five-eleven, 145 pounds. I was so excited! My time of vengeance had come. The thing I had dreamed of all my life could now be reality. I could finally pulverize my brother. What a sick goal!

But at the age of 18 I became a Christian, and the Lord told me I needed to forgive my brother from the heart. It was unbelievably hard to do. I remember saying, "Just once, Lord! It's not fair!" I'm sure I even would have been willing to pound him in "Christian love," if God would have let me.

You know the answer, of course. Forgiving others or not forgiving others is not up for negotiations with God, no matter how extenuating the circumstances might be. And so I forgave. In retrospect, I am so glad I did.

What Is Forgiveness?

Having established in our last chapter the biblical mandate to forgive, we need to make sure we understand what forgiveness is and what it isn't. Mark 11:25 says, "Whenever you stand praying, forgive, if you have anything against anyone, so that your Father who is in heaven will also forgive you your transgressions."

Biblically then, someone owes a "debt" when another person is holding something against him or her. To forgive means that the one offended cancels the debt and releases the offender from any obligation to pay back or make restitution. It is always good (and makes forgiveness that much easier!) when the offender asks forgiveness and makes any and all restitution possible, but when we forgive we cease to demand that either be done.

Charles Stanley offers this definition:

> Forgiveness is "the act of setting someone free from an obligation to you that is a result of a wrong done against you." For example, a debt is forgiven when you free your debtor of his obligation to pay back what he owes you. Forgiveness, then, involves three elements: injury, a debt resulting from the injury, and a cancellation of the debt. All three elements are essential if forgiveness is to take place.[1]

When someone sins against you, it is like throwing a heavy chain around your neck or casting a strong fishing line toward you and snagging you with the hook. You feel the crushing burden and pain of what was done to you. The longer you hang on to your anger, the heavier the burden becomes—the more deeply the hook sets in.

The Results of Not Forgiving

The pain that you initially felt from the offense is only made worse by your choice not to forgive. Your efforts to get back at your offender by remaining angry are in actuality bringing torment to your own soul. You suffered from acts of the abuse or neglect, and now you are suffering from bitterness. For some sick reason we think that staying bitter is part of getting back at one who has hurt us, but it is only hurting ourselves. That is why we are warned not to take revenge in Romans 12:17-21:

> Never pay back evil for evil to anyone....Never take your own revenge, beloved, but leave room for the wrath of God, for it is written, "Vengeance is mine, I will repay," says the Lord. "But if your enemy is hungry, feed him, and if he is thirsty, give him a drink; for in so doing you will heap burning coals on his head." Do not be overcome by evil, but overcome evil with good.

The Process of Forgiveness

There is only one way to be free from the past, and that is to forgive. When you do so, you throw the chain off your neck and pull the hook out of your flesh. You are free, though you may still be wounded emotionally. Healing will still need to take place, but the good news is that now it can, because the wounding agent has been removed through forgiveness.

How deeply you were crushed and wounded by the offense and how long you harbored unforgiveness will affect how long it takes for your emotions to heal. But God does promise to nurse us back to health, for Jesus has come to "bind up the brokenhearted" and proclaim "liberty to captives, and freedom to prisoners" (Isaiah 61:1). Scripture teaches that "the LORD is near to the brokenhearted and saves those who are crushed in spirit" (Psalm 34:18).

The Only Way to Stop the Pain

You may ask, "What about the offender? Why should I let him off my hook?" That is precisely why you should forgive, so that you will no longer be hooked to him or her. The people we forgive are off *our* hook, but they are not off *God's* hook until they come to Christ for their own salvation, forgiveness, and cleansing. Tragically, some will never come to Christ. In that case, the perpetrators of evil against us will discover that

Jesus Christ the gracious Savior will become to them Jesus Christ the righteous Judge. And they will learn that "it is a terrifying thing to fall into the hands of the living God" (Hebrews 10:31).

Forgiveness is a painful process, but it is the only way to stop the pain. Left unchecked, our flesh will often seek revenge. If that is not possible, in the flesh we will rationalize our attitudes and actions, and seek other options. To counter the arguments of the flesh, Dr. Stanley writes that forgiveness is not—

- justifying, understanding, or explaining why the person acted toward you as he or she did.

- just forgetting about the offense and trusting time to take care of it.

- asking God to forgive the person who hurt you.

- asking God to forgive you for being angry or resentful against the person who offended you.

- denying that you were really hurt; after all, there are others who have suffered more.[2]

There is nothing wrong with having compassion for the person who offended you. Knowing, for example, that the one who abused you may have been abused as a child may genuinely help you to forgive. But having such understanding is not a substitute for forgiveness. What was done to you was wrong, no matter what reason or excuse the person might have for doing it. You still need to make the choice to forgive. Time (under the grace of God) may help heal all wounds, but it will not remove the crushing chain or piercing hook of the offense. These are only removed when we forgive.

No Shortcuts

It is biblical to ask for God's mercy on the offender. Jesus said, "Love your enemies and pray for those who persecute you" (Matthew 5:44). It is also biblical to confess your sin of bitterness and unforgiveness, for He taught us to pray, "Forgive us our debts" (Matthew 6:12). But Jesus continued by saying, "...as we also have forgiven our debtors." He went on to drive home His point on the necessity of forgiveness by teaching, "If you forgive men for their transgressions, your heavenly Father will also forgive you. But if you do not forgive others, then your Father will not forgive your transgressions" (Matthew 6:14-15).

There are no bypasses or shortcuts around the responsibility we have to forgive from the heart. We don't believe that Jesus is teaching in Matthew 6 that a true born-again believer in Christ will go to hell if he or she doesn't forgive another person. If you are a true born again-believer, your destiny is not at stake, but your daily victory *is*. Though you remain His child, you will not experience the blessings and benefits of that relationship on earth. In fact, you can experience torment. The restoration of the blessing of daily victory comes only as you choose to forgive.

Forgiveness Is Not Forgetting

Forgiveness does not mean that we forget the sin. Forgetting may be a long-term *by-product* of forgiving, but it is never a *means* of forgiving. When Scripture teaches that "their sins and their lawless deeds I will remember no more" (Hebrews 10:17), it does not meant that God forgets. God couldn't forget even if He wanted to, since He is omniscient (all-knowing). It means that He will not bring up our past sins and use them against us. He has removed them as far from us as the east is from the west (Psalm 103:12). So when we keep bringing up other people's past offenses, we are actually saying, "I haven't forgiven you."

By the grace of God, over time our memories of sins committed against us will fade. We should not feel guilty if we still remember them, but we shouldn't relish them or dwell on them, or our emotions will be stirred up again. When we forgive, we will find that the sting is gone, even if the memories are not. Our memories will not be filled with the pain and torment that we once experienced before exercising the grace and mercy of forgiveness.

For eternity, Jesus the Lamb will bear the marks on His body of His suffering and death on the cross. He, and we, will never forget that heinous act done to Him for our sake. But, praise God, He will not hold that sin against us!

Forgiveness Is Always Possible

Some believe the lie that forgiveness is impossible. But whatever God has commanded us to do, we can do by His grace. To sin is human, but to forgive is divine, and God "is able to do far more abundantly beyond all that we ask or think, according to the power that works within us" (Ephesians 3:20). God cannot do our forgiving for us, but He will empower us to do that which He has commanded.

For some of God's people who have not been hurt very severely and who struggle only mildly with anger, the thought of forgiving others is no big deal. It's like walking up a small hill. But for others who have been terribly hurt and abused and who have been harboring festering anger for years, the thought of exercising forgiveness may be like thinking about climbing Mt. Everest. It seems an insurmountable peak. But whether it's a small hill or a mighty mountain, Jesus Christ Himself will make the climb with you, every step of the way. And the freedom and exhilaration at the top are well worth the climb!

Jenny was 16 years old, but she looked three or four times her age. Her face had been hardened and toughened by years of anger boiling just below the surface. Her dad had left when she was two years old, and though she did not know the man, she despised him. Sitting in a counseling session with her girlfriend and a youth worker, I saw the hatred glaring from her eyes. When I brought up the subject of her needing to forgive her father, Jenny would not speak. She just stared at me, daring me to come any closer, defying me to make her budge from her carefully constructed fortress of anger.

There was nothing that I could do. No amount of praying, urging, or warning was able to break through. I was disappointed, and Jenny remained in bondage to her bitterness. But God wasn't through with Jenny. I was invited back to speak at the same conference a year later, and guess who was there? Jenny. I never thought I'd see her again, and I certainly never figured she'd come back to such an intense spiritual setting. But there she was.

And I took one look at her and I knew she was free. With a beaming smile on my face I reintroduced myself to her. Her smile was warm and genuine, so I asked her, "Jenny, you finally admitted you hated your dad, didn't you?"

"Yes," she said, nodding.

"And you were able to forgive him, weren't you?" I already knew the answer.

Smiling again, she said "Yes." And it was clear she was enjoying the view from the top of the mountain.

Forgiving from the Heart

In Matthew 18:35, Jesus said we need to forgive others "from the heart." If we just say the words "I forgive you" but don't really mean them, they are meaningless. Forgiveness must come from the heart, which is the core of our being. Only in the heart do the mind, emotions, and will come together. Forgiveness has to come from here, the core of our being. The only successful way that we know how to do this is to say, "Lord, I forgive this person for..." and then specify all the sins of commission and omission. If you are not willing to face the hurt and the hate, your attempt will not be successful. Trust God to bring to your mind all those you need to forgive, and then trust Him to bring to your mind every offense. We have also found it helpful to say in regard to each offense, "because it made me feel this way..." and then describe specifically what effect the offense has had on you. The more specific we are in describing our emotions, the more complete and meaningful the forgiveness will be.

Emotional Vulnerability

It is fairly easy and safe to say something like "It made me angry" or "It hurt me," but those words are quite general and they may not express what you are truly feeling. Below is a list of some words and phrases that may help you pinpoint your feelings more clearly. Feel free to add more of your own.

confused	frustrated	disappointed	exasperated
furious	betrayed	dirty	rejected
worthless	unlovable	unloved	disrespected
helpless	unimportant	fearful	condemned
stupid	crazy	disillusioned	vulnerable
heartbroken	alone	abandoned	foolish
incompetent	manipulated	used	not good enough
ripped apart	thrown away	ganged up on	humiliated
controlled	trapped	insecure	full of dread
anxious	ashamed	embarrassed	cut down
devastated	demoralized	evil	unwanted

We are not trying to make forgiving harder, we are trying to make it complete so that you won't have to revisit it ever again. It's true that we are vulnerable when we get honest with God and ourselves about how the offense made us feel. We may be afraid that our emotions will get out of control. That fear often causes us to suppress them. But that is the worst thing we can do, because in so doing we short-circuit the healing process. In essence we end up keeping Jesus at a comfortable distance so that He cannot complete the healing process. We remain stuck in the same emotional rut and don't experience the healing and freedom He wants us to have.

We have to be emotionally vulnerable to be emotionally free. A trusted friend can help you through the process, as can a reliable Christ-centered pastor or counselor. We have found it to be more effective if you work through the entire "Steps to Freedom in Christ" with someone else. And even if you can't be this honest with others, you *can* be with Christ. He already knows what you are thinking and what you are feeling.

Being specific about what was done to you and how it made you feel will bring a much more complete freedom. Vagueness in forgiveness results in vagueness in freedom. Notice the difference between these two statements:

> *I forgive my brother for calling me names because it made me mad.*

> *I forgive my brother, Sam, for always calling me a "jerk" and laughing at me in front of my friends. It made me feel totally humiliated, and I would get so furious with him that I wanted to punch his lights out. I'm feeling anger toward him now, Lord, but I release that anger to You and relinquish my right to seek revenge by choosing not to hold this sin against him any more.*

The second person is fulfilling Jesus' instruction to forgive his brother from the heart. The first person is evading the real issues, trying to get through the process without being real or vulnerable. He will likely complain at a later time, "I forgave my brother, but I can't seem to stop being angry with him." In reality, he hasn't forgiven him at all, because he hasn't dealt with the core issues of forgiveness.

Canceling the Debt

Another aspect of forgiving from the heart involves canceling the debt owed to you because of the damage done to your sense of worth. It is one thing to acknowledge that you were angry; it is another thing to admit that your view of yourself was damaged by the offense against you. Because of the sins committed against you, you may have come to view yourself as something far less than you are in Christ. The devil, called "the accuser of the brethren," tries to heap words of condemnation on you, even though Romans 8:1 tells us that "there is now no condemnation for those who are in Christ Jesus."

In some cases, your forgiveness of the offender will need to include a statement about how your view of yourself suffered due to that person's sin. Here is an example:

> *Lord, I choose to forgive my mother for always criticizing my work. Her perfectionism made it impossible to please her, though I tried and tried and tried. I became increasingly angry with her and with myself, and came to see myself as totally incompetent and unable to do anything right. I feel like any sense of value I had, just withered under her fierce scrutiny and disapproval. It has even affected my ability to undertake things You have told me to do, because I have feared that I was just not good enough. But I choose to forgive my mother, and I reject all the lies about who I am. I choose to accept my new identity as a child of God.*

Living with the Consequences of Others' Sin

We are to forgive as Christ has forgiven us. He did that by taking our sins upon Himself. By forgiving others, we are agreeing to live, as Jesus did, with the temporary consequences of their sin. You may protest, "But that's not fair." Of course it isn't fair, but it is *reality* in a fallen world. We are all living with the consequences of other people's sin. We are all living with the consequences of *Adam's* sin. The *only real choice* we have is whether we live with the consequences of others' sin in the bondage of bitterness—or in the freedom of forgiveness.

The sinless Lamb of God paved the way for our forgiveness and has granted us the grace to forgive as we have been forgiven. Isaiah 53:4-6 explains this.

> Surely our griefs He Himself bore, and our sorrows He carried; yet we esteemed Him stricken, smitten of God, and afflicted. But He was pierced through for our transgressions, He was crushed for our iniquities; the chastening for our well-being fell upon Him, and by His scourging we are healed. All of us like sheep have gone astray, each of us has turned to his own way; but the LORD has caused the iniquity of us all to fall on Him.

Every murder, every sexual molestation, every racial slur or hate crime, every word of rejection, every lie, every abortion, every act of greed, every act of worship of a false god, every vile act of witchcraft, and every other callous, unkind, or evil attitude, word, or action ever committed by any human being was heaped on the Holy One. Jesus willingly took on our sin and bore the eternal consequences of that sin in His body. He suffered an agonizing death that we might live. "We do see Him who was made for a little while lower than the angels, namely, Jesus, because of the suffering of death crowned with glory and honor, that by the grace of God He might taste death for everyone" (Hebrews 2:9).

Jesus suffered the eternal consequences for all our sins. Now He asks that we take upon ourselves the temporal consequences of the sins of a few. We can lose a promotion, pay raise, a job, custody of children, or even our spouse. We may suffer serious damage to our reputation and lose the respect of others, and even lose their friendship. We might be damaged physically or suffer the loss of material possessions and comfort.

We may even undergo the agony of the death of loved ones, as when someone close to use is killed by a drunk driver.

The damage may also be internal, to our soul—to our sense of worth. Whatever the situation, God makes no guarantees that we will not have to suffer from the temporal consequences from another person's sins. In heaven, however, "He will wipe away every tear from their eyes; and there will no longer be any death; there will no longer be any mourning, or crying, or pain" (Revelation 21:4). In the midst of our infirmities, His grace is sufficient, as the apostle Paul discovered and wrote about in 2 Corinthians 12:7-10:

> There was given me a thorn in the flesh, a messenger of Satan to torment me—to keep me from exalting myself! Concerning this I implored the Lord three times that it might leave me. And He has said to me, "My grace is sufficient for you, for power is perfected in weakness [infirmity]." Most gladly, therefore, I will rather boast about my weaknesses [infirmities], so that the power of Christ may dwell in me. Therefore I am well content with weaknesses [infirmities], with insults, with distresses, with persecutions, with difficulties, for Christ's sake; for when I am weak, then I am strong.

The Deep Channels of God's Power and Grace

The deepest wounds that we have experienced at the hands of others can become the deepest channels of God's power and grace flowing into and through our lives—if we make the choice to forgive and endure the temporary consequences of sin. Consider the following stories* that reveal the grace of God in the most grievous situations:

> A 29-year-old police officer whose wife is pregnant with their first child is shot on the streets of New York City. For days his life hangs in the balance, his struggle to live transfixing New Yorkers. At last it appears he will

---

*Reprinted with permission from *Parade*, © 2000.

pull through—but he will be a quadraplegic. A young woman in Texas is raped, beaten with a hammer, stabbed and left for dead. She manages to survive, but the crime leaves her devastated. "I felt unlovable, untouchable, a throwaway person," she said. In Cleveland, a 7-year-old boy's mother is murdered. His father is arrested for the crime. In a sensational trial, his father is convicted and sent to prison. Ten years later, after a retrial, his father goes free. But by then the boy's childhood is gone. The family has been shattered.

Today, Steven McDonald, the former police officer, occupies a wheelchair and is attached to a ventilator. He travels the country telling his story, speaking about the forgiveness he has found for his assailant. Ellen Halbert, who said the attack she experienced was so degrading that she was never going to talk about it, now devotes her life to aiding crime victims—and those convicted of crimes. And Sam Reese Sheppard, whose father, Dr. Sam Sheppard, was convicted and then acquitted of murder in two sensational trials, publicly prays for those who have wronged him and his family.[3]

Christ's Work Paid *Everything*

Nothing good can come from holding on to our anger and bitterness. A church marquee declared, "A grudge is the only thing that doesn't get better when you nurse it." Ephesians 4:26-27 tells us not to let the sun go down on our anger, else the devil will have a place (ground) to operate. Paul urges the church at Corinth to forgive "so that no advantage would be taken of us by Satan, for we are not ignorant of his schemes" (2 Corinthians 2:11). The devil can take advantage of an entire church when the members are unwilling to forgive.

Paul also exhorted us to "get rid of all bitterness, rage and anger, brawling and slander, along with every form of malice" (Ephesians 4:31 NIV). Unforgiveness is cancer to the soul and to the life of a church. We must be "kind and compassionate to one another, forgiving each other, just as in Christ God forgave you" (Ephesians 4:32 NIV). Forgiveness is the only surgery that will work on such a malignancy.

When we are hurt, it is as if we take out our video camera and capture the event on tape. And when we do not forgive, instead of erasing the images, it is as if we pull out the videotape and pop it in to the VCR in our brain, then push play… and rewind…and play…and rewind…and play….Over and over again we punish people for their sins, even though Jesus Christ Himself proclaimed on the cross "It is finished!" (literally, "Paid in full!").

Jesus Christ declared that His shed blood and sacrificial death were the full and total payment for the sins of mankind—including the sins committed against you! We simply cannot add to that which Christ has declared complete.

In fact, to choose not to forgive is to repudiate the finished work of Christ on the cross. It is making the decision to play prosecutor, judge, jury, and executioner against the offender, something that we cannot do fairly and, in reality, should never dare to do at all. It is a violation of love, which "does not take into account a wrong suffered" (1 Corinthians 13:5). We are commanded to forgive others, but it is really for our sake that we do it, as this poem so powerfully illustrates:

> Once I held in my tightly clenched fist, ashes.
>
> Ashes from a burn inflicted upon my ten-year-old body.
>
> Ashes I didn't ask for. The scars were forced on me.
>
> And for seventeen years the fire smoldered.
>
> I kept my fist closed in secret, hating those ashes yet unwilling to release them.
>
> Not sure if I should. Not convinced it was worth it.
>
> Marring the things I touched and leaving black marks everywhere, or so it seemed.

I tried to undo it all. But the ashes were always there to remind me that I couldn't. I really couldn't. But God could.

His sweet Holy Spirit spoke to my heart one night in tearful desperation.

He whispered, "I want to give you beauty for your ashes. The oil of joy for mourning. And a garment of praise for your spirit of heaviness."

I had never heard of such a trade as this! Beauty for ashes?

My sadly-stained memory for the healing in His Word?

My soot-like dreams for His songs in the night?

My helpless and hurting emotions for His ever-constant peace?

How could I be so stubborn as to refuse an offer such as this?

So willingly, yet in slow motion, and yes while sobbing, I opened my bent fingers and let the ashes drop to the ground.

I heard the wind blow them away, away from me forever.

I am now able to place my open hands gently around the fist of another hurting soul and say with confidence,

"Let them go. There really is beauty beyond your comprehension. Go ahead, trust Him. His beauty for your ashes."[4]

We urge you with all we have in Christ to take time right now to forgive those who have offended you, no matter who they were, when it was, or what it was. Even if it was years ago, we urge you to let the perpetrators off your hook so Christ can be free to bring His healing power to your wounded soul.

Steps to Forgiveness

We encourage you to go through the following steps to forgiveness (and if your wounds are deep, again we strongly recommend you have a trusted friend or respected pastor or counselor with you).

1. Ask God to show you the people you need to forgive, and jot their names down on a piece of paper as He brings them to mind. Be sensitive to your need to forgive yourself if you have been angry with yourself for things you did or didn't do in the past. Forgiving yourself is accepting God's forgiveness of you in Christ.

2. Don't worry about writing down *all* the things that the people on your list did to hurt you, unless you feel it would aid you in forgiving them.

3. Pray for God's gracious presence to guide you through this process. Ask Him to bring to your mind specifically all the offenses against you and how they made (or make) you feel.

4. Begin by confessing to God your sin of harboring anger and bitterness. Then make the choice to forgive. Don't say, "Lord, help me to forgive." He is already helping you. And don't say, "Lord, I want to forgive." Say, "Lord, I forgive…"

5. We encourage you to model your prayer on something like the following:

   Lord, I choose right now to forgive (name) for (specifically say what this person did to hurt you), which made me feel (express to God honestly the emotions you have felt).

6. Stay with each name on your list until you cannot think of any more painful memories concerning that person.

7. Conclude your forgiveness of each individual by praying something like this:

   Dear Lord, I choose not to hold anything against those who have hurt me. Thank You that I am forgiven for my anger and bitterness. I now ask You to bless those who have cursed me. I give up my right to seek revenge, and I ask that You would heal my broken heart. In Jesus' name I pray, amen.

8. Once you have finished this process, give thanks to the Lord. Spend some time praising and worshiping Him for His grace in setting you free!

In conclusion, we invite you to pray together with us.

Dear heavenly Father, what can I say that You don't already know? And yet I feel that I need to confess my thoughts and feelings. I have been hurt in my life, and I have felt it was my right to pay back those who hurt me. It felt good and gave me some temporary relief. But Lord, I've been deceived. I didn't fully realize what I was doing to my own soul, and I certainly didn't realize what I was doing to You. Now I see the sin, my sin. I was wrong in thinking that two wrongs would make a right. Thank You, once again, for Your grace in forgiving me. I receive it. Now I ask for an even greater grace to forgive those who have hurt me. I know that is what You want me to do. It is what I need to do, because it's right. Thank You that Your grace is sufficient, even for this. In Jesus' name I pray, amen.

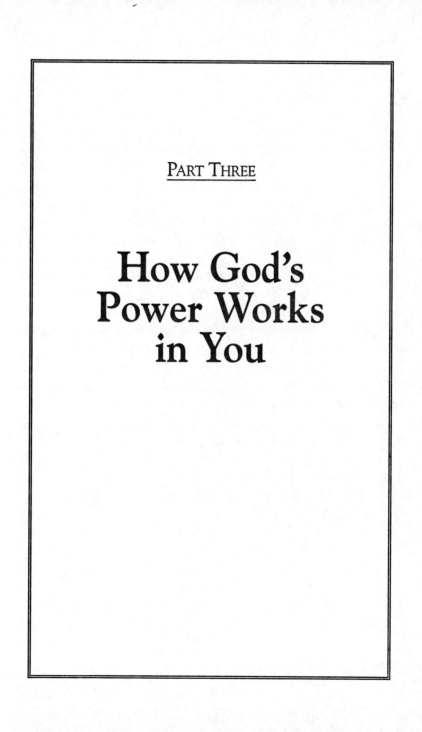

PART THREE

How God's Power Works in You

It's a Mad, Mad World

No man who is in a hurry is quite civilized.

—WILL DURANT

~

Sometimes the best way to see something is to be away from it for a while. I (Rich) was driving down Smoky Park Highway near our new home outside of Asheville, North Carolina, and I noticed something peculiar. The other cars were traveling at or even under the speed limit! I couldn't believe it. I was actually passing more cars than were passing me!

I shook my head as I recalled numerous death-defying trips on the interstates around my former home in Atlanta, Georgia. Countless times I had been cut off, tailgated, and honked at. Other drivers had used gestures and uttered words I have not been able to find in my Bible. All too frequently, I had retaliated by imagining my dashboard controls were actually able to launch heat-seeking missiles into the tailpipes of offending vehicles.

Then I pulled into the parking lot at Asheville Regional Airport and noticed something else. No crowd, no frenzy, no stress, no angry people. How strange! I breathed a sigh of relief and walked into the main concourse. There was a small restaurant where a calm, kindly man dished me up a plate of eggs, bacon, and grits. I sat down, relaxed, and enjoyed my meal. A few other people trickled in and read the newspaper or engaged in quiet conversation. *Amazing*, I thought. *Do people still live this way?*

Wandering down to my gate, I saw people waiting peacefully for the boarding call. Then she arrived! Wearing a power business suit neatly pressed, she frantically brushed her colored blond hair from her eyes and yanked out her cell phone from her purse. She then desperately tried to reach someone who could check to see whether she had locked her car doors. A major crisis?

She was a "stress carrier." Activated by a perpetual self-perceived state of emergency, stress carriers can change the climate of a room or a highway almost instantly. This women would have fit in perfectly at Atlanta's Hartsfield International (where we were headed), but she seemed grossly out of place at Asheville Regional.

Settling into my seat on the plane, I relaxed even more as I gazed out my window at the Appalachian Mountains. The morning mist was still in the valleys, and the leaves were starting to change color. It was peaceful, even serene. I didn't even mind the little bag of "Granola Berry Crunch" thrust my way (instead of the pretzels I was hoping for).

I'm Not Keeping Up!

Absentmindedly I pulled out my copy of *ASA Connections* (the airline's in-flight magazine). On the front of the inside cover Jack Welch was grinning at me aggressively from a photo of the cover of the book *Jack Welch and the GE Way*. The ad yelled at me, "PROBLEM. So many great business books. So little time. 1,200 important books like this one come out every year. Of course, you know that, as an executive in today's business environment, you must keep current with the expanding base of knowledge. Can you possibly keep up with all that reading? Yes, you can. If you subscribe to..."[1]

Another stress carrier. Feeling my anger and anxiety levels rise, I flipped ahead and read an article about duck hunting in Georgia. Interestingly, I found this:

> Bill Bowles, manager of Albany's Wynfield Plantation...[a duck-hunting lodge], agreed, "I sat on the front porch with a visitor who told me that as soon as he hit [rural] Georgia, his stress level went down 50 percent. As soon as he came through our gate, his stress level went to zero. I see executives come in with pagers and flip-tops—and by the time they come into the lodge for dinner, the pagers and phones are gone," Bowles continued. "They can stay in touch with their offices if they want to." He grinned and added, "Most don't."[2]

People are having difficulty keeping up with the rapid rate of change. The rat race is producing more and more stress, which elevates levels of anger and anxiety. The average person simply can't handle any more pressure. Can you relate? We are convinced that if the god of this world can't entice us to evil, he will try to drive us to be so busy that we are simply unable to cope.

The good news is that we are not helpless victims, because it is possible to take decisive action to reduce the unnecessary stress in our lives and thus decrease the pressures that provoke anger. It is not only possible, it is essential. And it doesn't require moving to the mountains either.[3] It just requires the Lord (Psalm 121:1).

The World's Invisible System of Beliefs

Though "the earth is the Lord's" (Psalm 24:1), and though God loves the people of the world (John 3:16), all is not well on planet Earth. Scripture describes unbelievers as living "according to the course of this world, according to the prince of the power of the air, of the spirit that is now working in the sons of disobedience" (Ephesians 2:2).

In 1 John 2:15-17 we are admonished not to be governed by the world system:

> Do not love the world nor the things in the world. If anyone loves the world, the love of the Father is not in him. For all that is in the world, the lust of the flesh and the lust of the eyes and the boastful pride of life, is not from the Father, but is from the world. The world is passing away, and also its lusts, but the one who does the will of God lives forever.

John concludes that "the whole world lies in the power of the evil one" (5:19). Clearly then, no matter how beautiful this earth can be, there is an invisible system of beliefs that drives a very ugly side of life on the blue planet. This system, composed of the fleshly lusts and pride of men, is choreographed by the devil himself and is categorically anti-God. John warns that it is simply impossible to love this world system and the Father at the same time.

Philosophies Opposed to God

Mark Bubeck offers a helpful definition of "the world" as John uses the term:

> The main Greek word used to describe our enemy, the world, is the word *kosmos*. The main usage of this word describes the order or system that runs this inhabited earth. It is a spiritual system of things that is opposed to God and the Lord Jesus Christ....[It is] the whole world system over which Satan rules (John 12:31; 1 John 5:19). As our enemy, the world is the whole organized system, made up of varying and changing social, economic, materialistic, and religious philosophies which have their expression through the organizations and personalities of human beings. The world system in its function is a composite expression of the depravity of man and the intrigues of Satan's rule, combining in opposition to the sovereign rule of God.[4]

The physical planet Earth is not our enemy, nor is it evil. It is the *philosophies* of this world that work in opposition to the rule of God that are evil. The Christian communities of this world have added a positive influence to our cultures, but they are constantly competing with many godless influences. For example, the practice of giving gifts to others at Christmas can be a true act of love. But it can also be corrupted by the world system as it infects the innocence of gift-giving with a desire to show off one's status in life through the expensiveness of a gift. John calls that attitude "the boastful pride of life." A preoccupation with material gifts to the exclusion of devotion to Christ is nothing more than greed and idolatry. John calls that "the lust of the eyes."

The Modern Way of Life and Thinking

There is nothing inherently wrong with cell phones, pagers, laptops, and the whole lineup of technological gadgets that are commonplace today and that will flood the market tomorrow. Properly used, some of these new inventions can serve us by improving the quality of our life. But they can also become an obsession or distraction from the true values of life, as one author notes:

> In a restaurant one night, I heard a man whining to his companions about never having a moment's peace. Both his beeper and cell phone went off during dinner. After quickly responding to his electronic umbilicals, he continued his complaints. I hoped someone might suggest he *turn off* his equipment but no one did. This man may have been technologically sophisticated, but interpersonally he was clueless! Whether he suffered from self-importance or insecurity, who knows? But it was clear he had made himself a willing victim of technology.[5]

With keen insight into the American psyche, author and speaker C. Leslie Charles suggests that the following is the belief system of our angry, self-centered society. She calls it "The Cranky Code."

- I am entitled to what I want when I want it.

- My time is important and I should not have to be inconvenienced by others.

- I have a right to be impatient or rude when other people are behaving stupidly.

- I am entitled to special privileges because I am who I am.

- I'm a taxpayer; I own part of this road and I have the right to drive as fast as I want.

- I not only have the right to pursue happiness, I *deserve* to be happy and I'll do whatever it takes to achieve it.

- I'm entitled to cheat a little bit in order to get ahead. If I don't take advantage someone else will, and then they'll be a step ahead of me.

- I work extra hard but don't get paid for it so I'm justified in helping myself to a few "souvenirs" from my office to offset what I am rightfully owed.

- I'm too busy to mince around with false politeness and should be able to tell people exactly what I think without having to worry about their feelings.

- I must be more *in the know* than everyone else so I can stay "one up" on them; otherwise they may take advantage of me.

- I deserve the newest, the biggest, the best, and the most. It's my right.

- I'm going to die one day so I may as well get as much as I can right now.

- So what if I'm being rude—I never have to see this person again, so what difference does it make?

- My opinions and views are more valid than anyone else's.

- My emergencies take precedence over anyone else's emergency.

- The world is unfair and opportunities are limited, so I may as well get all I can while I can, regardless of who or what stands in my way.[6]

Though clearly non-Christian in origin, these belief statements can honestly reflect the flesh patterns of believers as well—though we may be very reluctant to admit it!

False Philosophy #1—Materialism

One of the world's philosophies that gives birth to many of the false beliefs listed above is *materialism*. The dictionary defines materialism as "the tendency to be more concerned with material than with spiritual goals or values." It is the "love of money," which Paul warned was the "root of all sorts of evil" (1 Timothy 6:10). A materialist falsely believes that the possession of things can bring love, joy, and peace. But they can't—those are fruits of the *Spirit*. There is nothing wrong with having material possessions unless they take the place of God, as A.W. Tozer explains:

> Before the Lord God made man upon the earth He first prepared for him a world of useful and pleasant things for his sustenance and delight. In the Genesis account of the creation these are simply called "things." They were made for man's use, but they were meant always to be external to the man and subservient to him.

In the deep heart of the man was a shrine where none but God was worthy to come. Within him was God; without, a thousand gifts which God had showered upon him. But sin has introduced complications and has made those very gifts of God a potential source of ruin to the soul. Our woes began when God was forced out of His central shrine and things were allowed to enter. Within the human heart things have taken over. Men have now by nature no peace within their hearts, for God is crowned there no longer, but there in the moral dusk stubborn and aggressive usurpers fight among themselves for first place on the throne.[7]

Materialism in Our Culture

Fueled by life in a wealthy nation, many people want their piece of the materialistic pie, giving rise to a sense of "entitlement." Entitlement lives by the philosophy of "I deserve _____ simply because I am me." Because there is so much stuff available, many people believe that therefore it should be available to *them,* and it should be available *now.* The result of such thinking is billions of dollars in credit card debt in our nation and daily tension and anger in families because of financial stress.

Though we may deny we are materialistic, it is next to impossible to live in a culture such as ours and not be affected or even infected to some extent. Stress has a way of revealing which values we hold dearest and the survival mechanisms we trust most. The American dream is to have the best home we can afford in the best community. To select that home and make that purchase can be very stressful, according to a Christian friend of ours.

> After selling real estate for two decades, I have become increasingly dismayed at the lack of character and basic decency demonstrated by people I have worked with over the past few years....On the whole I have witnessed a

growing fixation on material things and a declining interest in the welfare of others. In short, it seems to me that ours is a culture where people worship things and use people to get those things, as opposed to a society where people love others and use things to serve them....

Each year it seems that the public demands bigger and bigger houses with more and more gadgets in them. No one seems to be satisfied with anything; nothing seems to be large enough or good enough. I've been amazed at how high the temperature can rise during the typical house hunt, negotiations for the sale, and the subsequent renegotiation over the inspection amendment. All along the way, I marvel at the amount of energy spent agonizing and threatening the other parties in "the deal" over every imaginable issue.

Do We Worship Dead Gods?

The American dream can become for some the American nightmare. The ancient words of Psalm 135:15-18 describe the root of the problem:

> The idols of the nations are but silver and gold, the work of man's hands. They have mouths, but they do not speak; they have eyes, but they do not see; they have ears, but they do not hear; nor is there any breath at all in their mouths. Those who make them will be like them, yes, everyone who trusts in them.

Scripture warns that you become like the god you worship. If we worship the true and living God, we will be alive and set free by the truth. But if our god is cold, hard cash and the lifeless things it can buy, what kind of people do you expect we will become? And if you think that materialism is a problem limited to unbelievers, then you need to hear the rest of the story from the world of real estate, as told candidly by our agent friend:

> As sad as the deterioration of society as a whole has been,...I must say that the most disheartening thing I have

observed has been the virtual lack of distinction between the general public and those who claim to be sincere, born-again, evangelical, Bible-believing Christians. It appears to me that the greatest hindrance to the spread of the gospel is affluence....

More often than I can bear to recount, I've encountered the princes and princesses of affluent Christianity, who make it clear that somehow they are due what they want when they want it. After all, they are children of Almighty God, and He does, after all, give us the desires of our heart, doesn't He? When the goal of gross acquisition and the opportunity to proudly display the spoils of real-estate war are blocked, these overgrown children often throw temper tantrums that absolutely defy the imagination....When we forget that we're just passing through on this earth, our priorities and values really do get mixed up. It seems that far too often, we value things over people—and will eventually do just about anything to those people to get those things.

The Bible's Words on Money and Things

Standing in stark contrast to a society gone mad with a sense of entitlement is the Lord Jesus Christ. Listen to His response to a scribe who expressed a desire to follow Him: "The foxes have holes and the birds of the air have nests, but the Son of Man has nowhere to lay His head" (Matthew 8:20).

It is crucial to realize that Jesus wasn't whining or complaining here. He was not engaging in a little messianic self-pity. He was simply telling it like it was. No palatial estates guaranteed. Not even the best lawn in the subdivision. Jesus had slept his first night on earth in a stable, and things hadn't changed much over some 30 years. He warned us, "Beware, and be on your guard against every form of greed; for not even when one has an abundance does his life consist of his possessions" (Luke 12:15).

King Solomon, who was both wealthy and wise, declared, "Whoever loves money never has money enough; whoever loves wealth is never satisfied with his income. This too is meaningless" (Ecclesiastes 5:10 NIV). Jesus presented the wonderful opposite: "Blessed are those who hunger and thirst for righteousness, for they shall be satisfied" (Matthew 5:6). The truth is that "no one can serve two masters; for either he will hate the one and love the other, or he will be devoted to one and despise the other. You cannot serve God and wealth" (Matthew 6:24).

False Philosophy #2—Hedonism

In addition to warning us about the danger of loving money, the apostle Paul also warned us of another dangerous philosophy of life. He called it being "lovers of pleasure" and warned that it stands in direct conflict with being "lovers of God" (2 Timothy 3:4). It is the worldly philosophy of *hedonism*, the pursuit of pleasure *apart from* God, rather than the pursuit of pleasure *in* God.

A number of years ago, Helmut Thielicke, the famous German theologian and pastor, took an extended trip around our nation. At the end of his tour, he was asked what the greatest problem among American Christians was. He responded, "They have an inadequate view of suffering."[8]

In the introduction to his book *Where Is God When It Hurts?* Philip Yancey contrasts older Christian authors' handling of the problem of pain to that of modern Christian authors. His observation is that the older ones were tougher and more able to trust God than their more recent counterparts. His conclusions show how our soft, self-centered culture foments human anger:

> When you read the two categories of books side by side, the change in tone is quite striking. It's as if we in modern times think we have a corner on the suffering market. Do we forget that Luther and Calvin lived in a world without ether and penicillin, when life expectancy averaged thirty years, and that Bunyan and Donne wrote

their greatest works, respectively, in a jail and a plague quarantine room? Ironically, the modern authors—who live in princely comfort, toil in climate-controlled offices, and hoard elixirs in their medicine cabinets—are the ones smoldering with rage.[9]

In a more whimsical moment, I had a picture of Moses called to a modern-day ministry. In this work, he was leading not a million Hebrews but rather a million Americans around in the wilderness for 40 years. No fast-food restaurants. No soft drinks. No TV. Nothing but manna and water! The grumbling of the Jews over the lack of Egyptian garlic, onions, and leeks would pale in comparison to the outrage over no burgers, fries, and Cokes!

When the feel-good god is not appeased, we become irritated, annoyed, and even desperate. In our striving to eliminate suffering in our society, we have only become angrier and more anxious when that inevitable suffering arrives. Jesus "learned obedience from the things which He suffered" (Hebrews 5:8). If the Son of God went through such training in life, what makes us think that we can learn to walk with the Father by an "easier" way?

False Philosophy #3—Selfish Ambition

Another worldly philosophy that fuels societal anger is *selfish ambition*, manifested in a drivenness to compete, get ahead, and "win." A driven person believes, "I must do _____ to keep up, succeed, or win." It is the same belief that pushes mothers to read Shakespeare to their unborn children while pressuring executives to work overtime, neglecting those same children after they're born. Whereas materialism is the lust of the eyes in action, and hedonism the lust of the flesh, selfish ambition is the "boastful pride of life." It is not so much the obsessive desire for things as it is the proud yearning to be top dog—first and best. It's not "Hey, look what I've got!" but rather "Hey, look at me!" And it is born out of men being "lovers of self" (2 Timothy 3:2).

Selfish ambition can show up in Christian ministry. The lure of fame gained through radio, TV, books, videos, big conferences, and so on can be very strong. Commercials for churches advertising "anointed preaching" and "dynamic worship" vie for the attention of unattached worshippers. But how many angry, neglected spouses and children are turned off to God and the church while ambitious preachers advance their careers? Are we called to build the kingdom of God or driven to build our own kingdoms? The Lord Jesus promised to build *His* church, not ours. After all, there are no biblical guarantees that the gates of hell won't prevail against our self-made kingdoms.

A few years ago I was traveling and speaking too much. The opportunities were abundant, the new places exciting, the fruit intoxicating. It can be a real "rush" to be known and admired, and to be the in-demand speaker. Then it became increasingly apparent to me that my young son, Brian, was suffering. He would wake up in the middle of the night screaming and crying.

One early morning as I was shaving, I asked the Lord to show me whether Brian's fear and anger were because of my traveling too much. I sensed the Lord responding, "You know." Gently but firmly He made it clear: "Don't ask questions I've already answered." At the time I was wrestling with whether the Lord wanted me to take a ministry trip to Singapore, the Philippines, and India. I really wanted to go...until that moment. I woke Shirley up and told her I was not going. I determined that I would not sacrifice my son on the altar of my ministry. I was horrified to think that my children might grow up viewing Jesus as the One that takes Daddy away. Now (five years later) the Lord seems to be granting me new permission to travel and minister, but the investment of those years of primarily being home with my wife and children is producing wonderful rewards, both present and eternal.

The "Unholy Trinity" Is Driving Us to Distraction

Materialism, hedonism, and selfish ambition constitute the "unholy trinity" of the world system. Unless we turn to the one God, these false gods will grow bigger, stronger, and louder, demanding more and more of our attention and energy. The stakes are being raised all the time, and the costs to our human souls are staggering. Too many of us are climbing the corporate ladder and realizing too late that it is leaning against the wrong wall. Consider this observation:

> Spend a moment reflecting on the structure of your typical day and whether you're surrounded by nonstop mental commotion. If your chores, concerns and queues of incoming data are stacked like incoming flights landing at O'Hare International over the Thanksgiving holiday, you're precariously poised for a bad case of crankiness! An occasionally busy, demanding day filled with mental distraction is one thing, but an unrelenting succession of them takes its toll. Crankiness is a sign that you're suffering from too much pressure, too often. Your judgment can suffer as you bound from one activity to the other without relief, and so can your mood.
>
> Somewhere, somehow, there has to be a limit. You can't always completely control your schedule or magically trim down your workload, but you always have options in your personal life. How do you spend your personal time? The media would have you think that you can't survive without the latest headline, newest scandal update, or tonight's lineup of sitcoms and dramas, but sometimes turning your back on these things is exactly what you need.[10]

Our Family's Experiment

When we moved from Atlanta to Asheville, I decided to try an experiment. It began as a financially driven choice, since money was a little scarce and the freed-up $500 per year would come in handy. I decided not to get cable TV. I was also on the warpath a bit because I felt our children were becoming tube addicts. As much as I knew I'd miss The Weather Channel, ESPN, ESPN2 and Nick at Nite (Shirley's favorite), I went ahead with the experiment. But what about the children? How would they react? I felt very strange when taking this step, almost like those "radicals" who ditch their television sets altogether, as Neil had done when his children were young.

The experiment is still going on, but after a year of no cable TV, what is the result? A houseful of angry, deprived kids (and parents) withering from being deprived of "must-see TV"? Hardly! Michelle, our oldest, reads constantly instead of vegging out in front of the TV. Brian takes self-defense classes and loves playing with his friends and siblings. All of them get to watch a video a day if they want to (and Emily, our third, really loves videos!), but never do I hear them complaining about missing such-and-such a show. It seems as though they couldn't care less.

I discovered that trying to keep up with personal and work-related phone calls, e-mails, faxes, and letters, as well as sporting events on TV and fast-breaking news stories, contributed to my stress and anger. I felt like a demanding world was invading my home and taking over my time. Peace was rare. Joy was fleeting. Love was strained.

I had to take decisive action. I started taking weekends off from e-mail. We turned off the ringers on our phones. We chose to let the answering machine take the calls in the evening so we could return the calls after the children had gone to bed (why did the phone *always* ring when I was reading to them?). Now I check the sports scores in the paper for five minutes in the morning instead of watching the games. Maybe it's not as exciting that way, but the time I now have with my wife and children is priceless!

Nothing Left to Give

This mom's story is all too true of many Americans:

> "I'm a stay-at-home mom, and after breakfast, I get the other two kids off to school. I'm loading laundry, running errands, feeding and changing our youngest and cleaning before they come home. I do dinner, homework supervision, baths and bedtime stories," she said. "I drive the kids to all their appointments, sports activities and friends' houses. I hate even scheduling the kids' appointments because of all the time I have to spend on the phone. My husband travels a lot and I hate to be cranky when he comes home from a trip, but I'm going full speed on about four hours' sleep." [11]

As Americans we are indeed "overwhelmed, overworked, overscheduled and overspent." [12] Our lives are often daily efforts to live out the Olympic motto: *citius, altius, fortius* (faster, higher, stronger). Was the prophet Daniel seeing a vision of our twenty-first-century America when he wrote, "Seal the book until the time of the end; many shall run to and fro, and knowledge shall increase" (Daniel 12:4 NKJV)?

Why not take a sober look at your life? Are you finding yourself becoming short with your co-workers and loved ones because you feel like you are perpetually behind? When all our energies are being drained away in an effort to "keep up," we will find we have nothing left to give in our relationships. In fact, we will find that we lose our tempers at the smallest intrusion of needs or demands from the people around us, including our families. With our plates too full, we end up forcing our loved ones to eat the crumbs that fall off the table.

Wednesdays are busy days for me. In addition to my normal workload, I have to take Brian to practice at 4 P.M., grab something for dinner, and head out the door by 6 to a men's study at church. On one particular Wednesday, I also decided to finish staining the railing on our deck, as well as exercise to a 45-minute workout video. And all this between 3 and 5 P.M.!

While sloshing on the stain, I was reeling under the pressure of lack of time when Brian came trotting out holding the portable phone. "Pastor Steve's on the phone, Daddy," he said, handing me the phone.

"I don't have time to talk right now," I snapped. I was angry at Brian for interrupting me and angry at Steve for invading my world. I then called Brian an unkind name and angrily snatched the phone from his hand.

I pushed the "talk" button on the phone and spoke sweetly and kindly into the mouthpiece, "Hello, this is Rich."

Silence. I pushed the "talk" button again, and tried my sweet greeting again. Steve greeted me in return this time.

With a feeling of horror, I realized what had happened. The phone had been turned on the entire time I had been so mean and nasty to Brian, and my pastor had heard it all!

The Lord used that experience to show me that I was trying to accomplish too much and that I would get angry when something or someone blocked my goal. I profusely apologized to my gracious son. When I got to church, I went straight to Steve and apologized for all I had said and done over the phone. Turns out he hadn't heard a thing! But God had and that was what really mattered.

Distracted—from God

As Christian parents, we need to reduce the stress in our homes by managing our own lives better. Our children are faced with the opportunity for activities every day of the week, and generally they don't have the discernment to know when enough is enough. But how can we build wisdom into our children's lives when we are double-booking ourselves? And how can we teach them that their worth comes from who they are in Christ, when we are still seeking to get our needs met through the world?

Where is God in all our busyness? We are not excusing laziness nor denying the need to do our work heartily for the Lord—but why are we so stressed out so often? It is not time we lack, because we have precisely the right amount of time to do God's will. The problem is, we have shoved Christ out of the center of our lives and compromised our Christian values.

If you're tired of being out of breath, out of time, and out of sorts, the next chapter is for you. In it we'll talk about how to get out of the rat race while still living in the real world. Let's join togther in prayer.

> *Dear heavenly Father, I have been caught up in a world that is driven, competitive, and greedy. I confess that I have allowed the values of this world to influence me. I have been angry, short-tempered, irritable, and easily annoyed. My anger has hurt others and has damaged my witness as Your child. I know that I am forgiven and I thank You for it, but I need to confess this to You. "Teach me Your way, O Lord; I will walk in Your truth; unite my heart to fear Your name" (Psalm 86:11). In Jesus' name, amen.*

A Peace of Your Mind

He that can take rest is greater than he that can take cities.

—BENJAMIN FRANKLIN

~

I was angry. Not a loud, reactive, belligerent kind of *thumos* anger, but more like a simmering, deep-down-in-the-soul *orge* anger.* It wasn't the vicious barking of a junkyard dog, but the low growl from a stray on the street. It was as if my emotions were giving off low-level distress signals but I was too busy to pick up on it.

Fortunately for my sanity, I had programmed into my schedule a right-after-work-before-dinner walk, a brisk walk for aerobic exercise and to clear my mind. (This walk serves as a great transition between the office and the family. I'm grateful that I live on a pleasant street near some challenging hills that I can use as my "track.")

Reluctant to drop below my "target heart rate," I protested briefly when I sensed the Lord saying "Stop." But I did. I took a deep breath and smelled the freshly mown grass. I looked through the woods and let the color green refresh me. And I listened to the Lord's gentle counsel.

Unknown to me, I had been angry at myself for being slow to change in a certain area of my life. I was also angry with a church that seemed determined to excel at being lukewarm.

---

*See chapter 2 for a discussion of these Greek words for "anger."

I was frustrated over an untimely case of writer's block. And the list went on. But as quickly as I became aware of my anger, I dealt with it in the presence of the Shepherd. I had to, because I know myself. What starts out as an annoying drone in my soul can erupt with a loud roar, usually at my children.

God's peace and then peace of mind flowed in again as I sensed the Shepherd urging me to lie down in green pastures, or at least to stop and smell the mown grass! Sanity returned, and my soul was restored.

Living Like the Prince of Peace

Not surprisingly, the earthly life of Jesus Christ, the Prince of Peace, provides a wonderful contrast to the hectic American way of life. Notice what He did when the pressures of life started mounting: "The news about Him was spreading even farther, and large crowds were gathering to hear Him and to be healed of their sicknesses. But Jesus Himself would often slip away to the wilderness and pray" (Luke 5:15-16).

This example of Jesus' habit is important for three reasons. First, this was a time in His earthly work when Jesus was well-known and in great demand. He was in real danger of becoming totally overwhelmed by the sheer numbers of people coming to Him.

Second, Jesus knew where His strength and direction came from. Though He possessed a perfect heart of compassion and loved to be with people, that was not where His life came from. Rather, everything flowed to Him from the Father.

Third, Jesus had developed a lifestyle of slipping away to pray. It had been woven into the fabric of His life on earth. It probably required a sacrifice of physical comfort. Mark 1:35 gives us insight into the "when" of Jesus' solitude: "In the early morning, while it was still dark, Jesus got up, left the house, and went away to a secluded place, and was praying there."

Time for Silence

In his book *Spiritual Disciplines for the Christian Life*, Donald S. Whitney makes this comment:

> One of the costs of technological advancement is a greater temptation to avoid quietness. While we have broadened our intake of news and information of all kinds, these advantages may come at the expense of our spiritual depth if we do not practice silence and solitude.[1]

He's right. We are a nation that has grown accustomed to activity and noise, and we find it awkward to be alone and silent. When was the last time you drove in the car alone without the radio or the cassette or CD player on? When was the last time you put your luggage down in your motel room and *didn't* turn on the TV? Our spiritual condition may be assessed by how well we handle solitude. In the following Psalms, David admonishes us to wait in silence before God and put our trust in Him:

> My soul, wait in silence for God only, for my hope is from Him. He only is my rock and my salvation, my stronghold; I shall not be shaken. On God my salvation and my glory rest; the rock of my strength, my refuge is in God. Trust in Him at all times, O people; pour out your heart before Him; God is a refuge for us (Psalm 62:5-8).

> O LORD, my heart is not proud, nor my eyes haughty; nor do I involve myself in great matters, or in things too difficult for me. Surely I have composed and quieted my soul; like a weaned child rests against his mother, my soul is like a weaned child within me. O Israel, hope in the Lord from this time forth and forever (Psalm 131).

> The LORD is my shepherd, I shall not want. He makes me lie down in green pastures; He leads me beside quiet

waters. He restores my soul; He guides me in the paths of righteousness for His name's sake (Psalm 23:1-3).

Time for Prayer

With a busy life and a full plate, I have found it crucial for my own well-being to get up early to meet with God before the rest of the house rises (we have four children age ten and under!). The best time for you to get away may be in the morning, or later in the evening when things quiet down. If you are employed, what about using a portion of your lunch hour to take a quiet walk or find a quiet place? If nothing else, you can go sit in your car to get away!

Jesus talked about praying to the Father in secret, either in a room or closet. He promised that your Father, who sees you there, will indeed reward you (Matthew 6:6). Richard Foster, in his book *Celebration of Discipline*, has some challenging thoughts on this matter:

> We can find or develop a "quiet place" designed for silence and solitude. Homes are being built constantly. Why not insist that a little inner sanctuary be put into the plans, a small place where any family member could go to be alone and silent? What's to stop us? The money? We build elaborate playrooms and family rooms and think it well worth the expense. Those who already own a home could consider enclosing a little section of the garage or patio. Those who live in an apartment could be creative and find other ways to allow for solitude. I know of one family that has a special chair; whenever anyone sits in it he or she is saying, "Please don't bother me, I want to be alone."[2]

Susanna Wesley, mother of 19 children (including her sons Charles and John), used to pull her apron over her head when she needed a reprieve in God's presence. It told her children that she was not to be disturbed. The older ones watched the younger children while their mother was refreshed and renewed.

The Challenge for Single Moms

Single moms clearly have a serious challenge in finding time for quiet prayer and reflection. Not only are they generally working full-time, but they have all the other responsibilities of a home and family to tend to during their "free" time. If that is your situation, it is going to be essential that you create a network with other moms, so you can take turns watching each other's children to give yourselves the breaks you need. Churches that are sensitive to the needs of single moms ought to provide these services at little or no cost. The pressures of working and single-parenting are so high, and the dangers of stressed-out anger erupting into violent abuse are so real, that a proactive approach to seeking silence and solitude must be taken. If you wait until things get really bad before acting, you may end up deeply regretting it.

This mom's experience is a story of hope:

> Just recently God has showed me I have anger that I need to deal with. I never realized it before. But you know God works on us slowly and surely. I had been lashing out and snapping at my children and I didn't know where it came from. Through much prayer God has showed me I have anger from past hurts. I have done a lot of forgiving, but there was still some underlying anger I needed to deal with. I have asked God to prompt me every time it comes up with my girls so that I can ask the Holy Spirit to go before me in speaking to my children in love. God is faithful and I am overcoming this anger. But it means being in the Word every day and also maintaining that one-on-one personal time with the Lord and being in His presence throughout the day. When I put on praise music and praise Him, the enemy is scattered. Alleluia, we have the victory!

Time in God's Presence

Scheduled time alone with the Lord sets the stage for walking with Him during the rest of the day. Why not take periodic "Jesus" breaks (just like coffee breaks!), when you can relax and just focus on Him. Whether in the shower, in the car, walking the dog, or going out to pick up the mail, moments of talking and even venting in God's presence can be lifesavers. Brief periods of time in silent reflection or worship can calm your spirit and defuse your anger.

Any time you can get away from the place that is the center of your stress, it will be well worth it, especially if you can slip off to a place of natural beauty. Even sitting by a fountain in the office lobby can provide refreshment. It's amazing that God has wired us so that certain sounds, smells, colors, and tastes can provide rest in the midst of stress. Sometimes that's all it takes to keep from exploding (or imploding) during a tense and hectic day.

For 30 years the staff who work at the Christian Training Center International in Franklin, North Carolina, have served the body of Christ in the midst of some of the most beautiful scenery in the western part of that state. It is an ideal place for getting away and sitting at the feet of Jesus. Over the past years, small groups of believers have gathered there to do just that. Every three or four months, from Thursday evening to Saturday noon, they conduct a "Sitting at the Feet of Jesus" retreat. With no agenda except to be quiet, worship, and listen to the Lord, these retreats have brought renewal and refreshment to many of His people.

"At first we felt like we were going through withdrawal," said Susan Pons, wife of CTCI director Larry Pons. "But the times have been transforming for us. I can't begin to tell you all that God has shown us, but the predominant theme is His love. He is showing us more and more deeply how great His love for us is."

In addition to their quarterly gatherings open to the public, the staff, led by Larry, gathers for a similar though shorter time of seeking God's face every Monday morning. (What would the average church become if the staff set aside a similar "tithe" of their workweek to sit at Jesus' feet and receive encouragement, correction, and guidance from Him?)

Let us encourage you to seek the Lord and ask Him how you might incorporate a regular habit of sitting at the feet of Jesus into your own life and the life of your family. Maybe you are not able to take half a day per week, but what about half an hour a day? That is about 2 percent of your time. Maybe it's not possible to set aside a day-and-a-half every quarter, but what about half a day once a month?

Armed with your Bible (you might want to prayerfully read through one of the four Gospels) and a notebook to journal your thoughts and impressions, you will find it a safe haven from the stress and resultant anger of this world. If you enjoy praise and worship music, you might want to take a cassette-tape or CD player along.

Cleansing from Busyness

Paul exhorted us, "Do not be conformed to this world, but be transformed by the renewing of your mind" (Romans 12:2). If we are not actively allowing our minds to be renewed, we *will* by default be slowly but surely squeezed into this world's mold, a world that lives as if busyness were next to godliness.

Between His prayer that the Father would keep His disciples "from the evil one" (John 17:15) and His request that the Father would "sanctify them in the truth" of the Word (verse 17), Jesus declares, "They are not of the world, even as I am not of the world" (verse 16). Though we are *in* this world, we are not *of* it. Neither is Jesus. The *devil* is the god of this world, and he will rule over our lives to the degree that we love this world. God's Word, however, will sanctify us—set us apart—from its angry, corrupting influences.

No matter how much the world has already infected you, Jesus can cleanse you. He said, "These things I have spoken to you, so that in Me you may have peace. In the world you have tribulation, but take courage; I have overcome the world" (John 16:33). Through our faith, we have the victory that has overcome the world as well (1 John 5:4). How is that possible? Because through the cross "the world has been crucified to me, and I to the world" (Galatians 6:14). In Christ, we don't dance to the beat of the world's drum anymore. We march to the tune of the gospel and find our rest in Christ.

Sitting at Jesus' Feet

Scripture tells the stories of some privileged people who sat at the feet of Jesus. Doing this was a life-changing moment for them, and it can be for you, too.

We are told in Luke 8:26-39 how a man terribly tormented by demons encountered the Lord of hosts. This man, possessed with supernatural strength, had lived in the tombs, breaking every chain that was put upon him to restrain him. Luke describes the transformation in him once Jesus set him free:

> The people went out to see what had happened; and they came to Jesus, and found the man from whom the demons had gone out, sitting down at the feet of Jesus, clothed and in his right mind; and they became frightened (Luke 8:35).

From shame to dignity. From torment to liberty. From uncontrollable rage to absolute peace. For this man, his place at the feet of Jesus became the place of *serenity*.

Luke also tells us about an immoral woman who found her way into the house party of a Pharisee named Simon (7:36-50). Much to this man's chagrin,

> she brought an alabaster vial of perfume, and standing behind Him [Jesus] at His feet, weeping, she began to wet His feet with her tears, and kept wiping them with

the hair of her head, and kissing His feet and anointing them with the perfume (verses 37-38).

After rebuking Simon for his lack of love, Jesus delivered the punch line, saying to the woman, "Your sins have been forgiven....Your faith has saved you; go in peace" (verses 48-50).

This woman, at first standing, soon found herself seated at the feet of Jesus. Whether it was the compassion in His eyes or the mere fact He would allow her to touch Him, we don't know. But for this sinful woman, her place at the feet of Jesus was a place of *repentance and healing.*

One day Jesus entered the house of His dear friends Mary, Martha, and Lazarus in Bethany (Luke 10:38-42). Martha was busily preparing the meal, but Mary "was seated at the Lord's feet, listening to His Word" (verse 39).

Martha became very upset that Mary had left her to do all the serving, and she complained to Jesus about it. She instructed the Lord to set her sister straight. Jesus' reply ought to be indelibly imprinted on all our hearts:

> Martha, Martha, you are worried and bothered about so many things; but only one thing is necessary, for Mary has chosen the good part, which shall not be taken away from her (Luke 10:41-42).

Martha represents all the type A personalities. Notice that Jesus pointed out that she was "worried and bothered about so many *things*" (10:41, emphasis added). Jesus wanted to have the same fellowship with Martha that He was having with Mary, but Martha was bothered about *things!* Leonard Raven-hill said it well: "This was not a matter of *disposition* but *decision*. Mary had 'chosen' the good part, which would not be taken from her."[3] For Mary, her place at the feet of Jesus became a place of *loving instruction and wisdom.*

Finally, as we're told in John 12, Mary again came into Jesus' presence. This time she brought "a pound of very costly perfume of pure nard, and anointed the feet of Jesus and wiped His feet with her hair; and the house was filled with the fragrance of the perfume" (verse 3). Though Jesus said she had done it to prepare Him for burial (verse 7), she probably did not understand that. For Mary, sitting at the feet of Jesus and pouring out her expensive offering was simply an act of *pure and uninhibited adoration*.

For those who care to take the time, their place of sitting at the feet of Jesus will be a sanctuary, a refuge, and a safe haven from the stress and pressures of an angry world. It will be a place of brokenness, introspection, quiet instruction, restoration, healing, serenity—and finally, a place of peace.

The Peace of His Mind

Don't be surprised if others do not understand your desire to sit at Jesus' feet. In each of the four passages above (you can read the complete stories yourself), there was opposition to Jesus or the one at His feet. The way of freedom will always be opposed by those who don't understand or by those who don't want to give up what the world has to offer them. But you can't let that stop you, "for whatever is born of God overcomes the world; and this is the victory that has overcome the world—our faith. Who is the one who overcomes the world, but he who believes that Jesus is the Son of God?" (1 John 5:4-5).

Here are a few suggestions that we believe will help you experience a peace of His mind.

- Schedule daily times to spend with the Lord as intentionally as you would any other appointment. The Lord will be eagerly awaiting that time!

- Keep your times with God simple and uncomplicated. Don't feel pressured to read huge sections of the Bible or pray through long lists of requests.

- Keep your times with God fresh. Try different things. Worship God along with a CD or tape. Read a short psalm, and journal what your heart is saying to God. Take a prayer walk. Write a poem. Be creative!

- If your health would not be endangered, consider fasting (drink plenty of water!) for a meal or a day. Use the time normally spent eating to pray or serve others in some way. Doing God's will is a richly satisfying "meal" (see John 4:31-34). Extended fasts can be a tremendous spiritual retreat and can even bring healing to the body, but ought to be undertaken only with God's prompting while under a physician's care.

- Consider taking a rest from things that intrude into your world, rob you of privacy, and steal your peace and joy (and that can turn up the hostility thermostat). Turn off the ringer on the phone and turn on the answering machine for an evening. Turn off the beeper and cell phone for a while (unless the safety or health of others would be jeopardized). Resist the urge to check those e-mails one last time. Leave the laptop home when you go on vacation. And by all means, dethrone the one-eyed monster. Turn the tube off early once in a while. The sense of power will make you feel really good!

- Remember that Jesus is always on His throne, and the world will hold together without you. Don't take yourself or your work *too* seriously. Shut down the computer and go for a good walk. Better yet, if you've got kids, go out and play with them!

This poem, based on Psalm 23, provides a fitting conclusion for us:

The Lord is my pacesetter, I shall not rush;

He makes me stop and rest for quiet intervals.

He provides me with images of stillness which restore my serenity.

He leads me in ways of efficiency through calmness of mind.

And His guidance is peace.

Even though I have a great many things to accomplish each day,

I will not fret; for His presence is here.

His timelessness, His all importance will keep me in balance.

He prepares refreshment and renewal in the midst of my activity.

By anointing my mind with His oil of tranquility my cup of joyous energy overflows.

Surely harmony and effectiveness shall be the fruits of my hours

For I shall walk in the pace of my Lord and dwell in His house forever.

—Attributed to Toki Miyashina

Dear heavenly Father, I need to return to the stillness of serenity and peace in You. I choose to be still and know that You are God. With a sigh of relief, I return to my rest in You. I choose to take time to sit at Your feet and learn from You. And even when I am busy, show me how to live my life in Your presence rather than succumbing to the world's pressure. Restore to me the joy of my salvation and the childlike delight in life. And teach me how to have fun again. In Jesus' name I pray, amen.

Connecting to the Power

I believe that it is impossible for any Christian to be effective either in his life or in his service unless he is filled with the Holy Spirit who is God's only provision of power.

—DR. HENRIETTA MEARS

~

It was a great fall day for a trip to the mountains. The kids had the day off from school, and with a full weekend of speaking coming up, I decided to take the day off as well. Shirley and I had settled on leaving at 10 A.M., and I was really looking forward to getting out, seeing the fall colors, and hiking in Amicalola Falls State Park in northern Georgia.

A heavy volume of e-mails to answer kept me busy until 10:15 that morning. Shirley, noticing I had not come out of the office, poked her head in, asking when I'd be ready.

"Let's shoot for 10:30," I said, hurrying to finish up my correspondence.

Shutting down the computer, I raced downstairs, jumped in the shower, shaved, brushed my teeth, and dressed. I emerged triumphantly at 10:29, ready to go. But what I saw did not make me a happy hiker.

Of our four kids, only two were ready. The TV was on, and one of the others was relaxing in the presence of Barney.

He had obviously not heard the "call of the wild." I groaned and rolled my eyeballs. A couch potato at the age of four!

"Shirley! We said we were going to leave at 10:30! I'm ready, why aren't the kids?"

For some reason, however, she did not immediately take my point of view and shot back, "Maybe if you had helped a little bit and hadn't spent all morning in your office, we'd be on time!"

"Righteously indignant," I stormed around the house, roughly putting clothes on kids and chasing them out to the van to get buckled in. I was intent on proving that it is not that hard to get four kids ready for a day trip. Smugly satisfied, I stood back to admire my work. Then I realized that all four still needed to use the bathroom one final time before leaving. By this time I was in the midst of a full-blown "flesh attack."

Angrily unbuckling them and shooing them back into the house to use the toilet, I stalked around the back yard, muttering under my breath. Once everyone, including Shirley, had finally gotten into the van, the digital clock on the dash glared at me in defiance: 11:00.

"Daddy, can we listen to the kids' praise tape?" Emily, our four-year-old, asked sweetly.

Actually, I was tempted to stomp the life out of the kids' praise tape. "Before we leave, I've got something to say to this family." You could sense impending doom in the air as I opened my mouth wide and firmly inserted both feet.

"This is without a doubt the slowest, least organized family in the world! And I'm sick of it!" I declared, scowling at all four kids and my wife. I purposefully allowed my angry gaze to linger a little longer on Shirley.

"But if you had helped—" she protested.

I quickly cut her off. "Don't give me any of that! Look at the clock. We are half-an-hour late!"

With that final pronouncement, I punched in the kids' tape and slammed the van into reverse. Everyone else seemed to recover quickly from my angry outburst as the happy praise music played on. But, the longer it played, the more annoyed I got.

The Lord Intervenes

I was such a mess that I found myself coming under conviction when "Kum Ba Ya" was playing. I don't even know what "Kum ba ya" means! I had not heard that song in a decade and, to be perfectly honest, I would not be upset if another ten years went by before I heard it again.

That was bad enough, but it got worse. The kids on the tape sang, "If you're happy and you know it, clap your hands…" Our kids clapped their hands. I gripped the steering wheel harder and gritted my teeth. I wasn't happy—and I knew it.

Graciously, the Lord got my attention, and after several minutes of battling my pride, I pulled off the road and ate a huge piece of humble pie. I asked each of the kids and Shirley to forgive me for my anger, impatience, and unkind words. Fortunately, they were far more eager to forgive than I was to ask for forgiveness.

As I pulled back on to the road, I was relieved and refreshed. I was even able to clap my hands, stomp my feet, and say "amen" when that song came on again.

The Power to Experience a Holy Moment

After lunch in the state park, Michelle and Brian (our two oldest kids) and I went on a hike. Shirley stayed with the younger two on the playground. After climbing to the top of a particularly steep ridge, Brian called out.

"Daddy! Daddy! Can we build an altar to the Lord?" he panted, trying to catch his breath.

I had told them earlier about how their mom and I had once built an altar of 12 stones on the top of a mountain. It was there that we had reaffirmed our commitment to follow the Lord together, no matter what He told us to do.

Not knowing all that God had planned, I sent Brian and Michelle scurrying off to find 12 stones. They placed them carefully on top of each other, then we gathered around our newly built altar.

"Brian, in the Bible, people built altars like this when they were surrendering to God in a new way. Are you willing to give your whole life to Him like that?"

"Yes, Daddy, I am. But I want to think a minute about what I am going to say."

I didn't dare speak, for I knew we were on holy ground.

"Dear Lord," he began, "I give my whole life to You, for You to do what You want with me. In Jesus' name, amen."

Through my deep joy, my mind flashed back to my earlier anger. I knew that, had I slammed the door in the face of the grace of God and refused to repent, that holy moment on the mountain would most certainly have been lost.

What had been my problem? Clearly, I had elevated the desire to leave at 10:30 to a driving goal. When my family blocked that goal by being late (in part because of my negligence), I became furious. How silly to wound my family members and almost ruin a wonderful day over 30 minutes of delay! In my foolishness, I had chosen to walk according to the flesh and not according to the Spirit. Although I had the Spirit's presence in my life, I had not been experiencing His power.

The Struggle

It's encouraging to know that even the apostle Paul had a struggle similar to the one I described above. In fact, every child of God who has ever lived can echo at some point in life Paul's words in Romans 7:

> What I am doing, I do not understand; for I am not practicing what I would like to do, but I am doing the very thing I hate....So now, no longer am I the one

doing it, but sin which dwells in me. For I know that nothing good dwells in me, that is, in my flesh; for the willing is present in me, but the doing of the good is not. For the good that I want, I do not do, but I practice the very evil that I do not want (verses 15,17-19).

Confused. Frustrated. Paralyzed. Controlled. Despairing. These are words that describe Paul in the verses above. It is the description of a man in bondage. A man who knows the truth but just does not seem able to make it happen in his life.

Maybe that is where you find yourself as you read these words. If so, don't give up. The Helper, the Holy Spirit, is here! But before we dive into the solution in Romans 8, we need to look further into the problem, in Romans 7. The cure will be much more powerful once we understand the disease.

Our Hearts Are Righteous

Notice that Paul's heart was righteous. He *wanted* to do what is right. The "willing" to do good was present in him. Paul didn't need convincing that God's Word was right and true and to be obeyed. He understood and agreed with it.

God says that under the new covenant of grace, "I will put My laws upon their heart, and on their mind I will write them" (Hebrews 10:16). This is in fulfillment of Ezekiel 36:25-27, where the prophet writes,

> I will sprinkle clean water on you, and you will be clean; I will cleanse you from all your filthiness and from all your idols. Moreover, I will give you a new heart and put a new spirit within you; and I will remove the heart of stone from your flesh and give you a heart of flesh. I will put My Spirit within you and cause you to walk in My statutes, and you will be careful to observe My ordinances.

God, through Ezekiel, had promised to put in our bodies (our flesh) a new, clean heart. This heart would not be of stone (hard, stubborn, and unyielding), but one of flesh (soft, teachable, humble). And the very Spirit of God would come to dwell within us, uniting Himself with our new, alive spirit to empower us to do good.

According to Jeremiah 17:9, "The heart is more deceitful than all else and is desperately sick; who can understand it?" That statement is totally true of an unsaved person, but was never meant to be applied to true believers in Christ. We've been given a new heart! We are new creations in Christ to the very core of our being.

Our Identity Is the Key

Many of God's people have been taught that their hearts are wicked, deceitful, and sick. They have assumed that Paul's Romans 7 experience is the normal Christian life! Consequently they have felt doomed to battle their anger and rage all their lives, hoping for, at best, brief moments of victory.

Child of God, nothing could be further from the truth! Paul said that "nothing good dwells in me, that is, in my flesh" (Romans 7:18). He didn't say *he* was no good. Neither did he say that nothing good dwelled in him *at all*. What he did say was that nothing good dwelled in his *flesh*. In fact, he went on to identify the culprit—it was *sin* dwelling in his flesh that was operating counter to God.

We have a new identity, a new heart, and a new nature in Christ. The very presence of God dwells within us! However, there still remains *a residual part of us* that is bent toward self-reliant, self-centered living. And in that place that the Bible calls *flesh*, the power of sin resides, exercising its influence through our physical bodies. Sin is not *us*, but it dwells *in us*.

If you happened to have pancreatic cancer, you would not say, "I am cancer." You would say, "I have cancer." By the same token, as believers in Christ we should never say "I am evil," but rather "I have evil (sin) in me." That's exactly what Paul said in Romans 7:21-23:

I find then the principle that evil is present in me, the one who wants to do good. For I joyfully concur with the law of God in the inner man, but I see a different law in the members of my body, waging war against the law of my mind and making me a prisoner of the law of sin which is in my members.

How Does Evil Do Its Work?

Have you felt like there was a civil war inside of you? Have you sensed the inner struggle between the desire to do what is right versus an evil presence that pulls you the other direction? The Spirit of truth, working through your mind, is being opposed by sin, which seeks to operate through your flesh. Author Bill Gillham gives a good picture of how sin fights against the truth in our minds:

> When the power of sin speaks to your mind, it does not use the pronoun "you," but the pronoun "I." Instead of experiencing the communication "Why don't *you* go ahead and give her a piece of your mind!" it will be served up to your mind as, "Well, *I* have a good mind to tell her off! By George, *I'm* going to do it!" And you often wind up "doing the very thing you hate." You grab the idea and convert it into action. You sin! Yes, *you* did the evil thing, but the *genesis* of it, the *origin* was the power of sin, *not* your mind.[1]

In the story at the beginning of this chapter, do you think I really *wanted* to disrupt my fellowship with God, hurt my family, and ruin the day for all of us? Not at all! In my inner man, I wanted to do what is right. I love God and my family and desire nothing more than to be in right fellowship with both.

But sin spoke to my mind, and I swallowed its lies hook, line, and sinker. Sin said, "I can't believe they're doing this to me! Their slowness is wasting my time and ruining my day. I need to set them straight." So my flesh took control away from the Spirit of God in my life, and sin worked through my body (predominantly my big mouth, but also my cold eyes and angry hands and feet). The deed of my flesh was obvious—an outburst of anger. James sums up what happened very well:

> Let no one say when he is tempted, "I am being tempted by God"; for God cannot be tempted by evil, and He Himself does not tempt anyone. But each one is tempted when he is carried away and enticed by his own lust. Then when lust has conceived, it gives birth to sin; and when sin is accomplished, it brings forth death. Do not be deceived, my beloved brethren (1:13-15).

James makes it clear that we are fully capable of generating sin by ourselves, through our own fleshly lusts. In addition, however, the world system governed by Satan makes its appeal to our minds through those lusts (1 John 2:15-17). Finally, the devil's enticing voice coming from *without* can sound identical to the tempting voice of sin coming from *within*. In essence, we are being triple-teamed by the world, the flesh, and the devil!

Sin is deceptive (Hebrews 3:13). It promises pleasure, fulfillment, and satisfaction, but it lies. It delivers only "passing pleasures" (Hebrews 11:25). And then comes the ugly payoff. The consequences are always greater than the "benefits." Always.

The old black preachers used to say, "Sin will take you places you don't want to go. Sin will cost you more than you want to pay. And sin will keep you longer than you want to stay." And they are exactly right.

The Results of Walking According to the Flesh

If you choose to walk according to the flesh and not by the Spirit, you will find yourself crying out along with the apostle Paul, "Wretched man that I am! Who will set me free from the body of this death?" (Romans 7:24).

Notice Paul did not say, "*Wicked* man that I am!" He said, "*Wretched* man that I am!" "Wretched" means "miserable," and bondage to sin will inevitably lead to misery, as this man's story illustrates:

> I have been a police officer for almost 20 years. I am divorced and remarried with two children. I have been angry for so long, mostly about past hurts, rejection, my divorce. I was also angry with God, my church, my life. I was angry for so long, I did not know who or what I was angry at or why. To put it bluntly, I was miserable. I left my church because I was angry at the people. I was so angry that when I walked in the front door of the church I would just be in a rage. I could also be very verbally nasty to people when I was angry. Needless to say, when I dragged my family away from our small church I hurt some feelings and caused turmoil in my family. There is so much to tell.
>
> My misery was so great. I hated being angry. I don't know if this is possible to understand, but I would get so angry and I would lash out—and then feel so guilty and hope I didn't hurt anyone too badly. I had a silent rage within me as well and I was actually beginning to be afraid of it.

The Missing Element

Despite how overwhelming the misery of walking in the flesh is, no believer in Christ need remain in that condition any longer! The apostle Paul didn't. Listen to his words of victory in Romans 8:1-4:

> There is now no condemnation for those who are in Christ Jesus. For the law of the Spirit of life in Christ Jesus has set you free from the law of sin and of death. For what the Law could not do, weak as it was through the flesh, God did: sending His own Son in the likeness of sinful flesh and as an offering for sin, He condemned sin in the flesh, so that the requirement of the Law might

be fulfilled in us, who do not walk according to the flesh
but according to the Spirit.

Child of God, despite all that you have done contrary to
the will and Word of God, you are not condemned! God is
for you (Romans 8:31). He's on your side and you're on His!
What *has* been condemned is your sin! Sin was sentenced to
death and executed! That happened at the cross, so that now
you are set free from sin's hold over you and the spiritual death
that was yours apart from Christ!

Paul explained in Romans 6:7-8 that our old sin-loving
self died with Christ and "he who has died is freed from sin."
The fact that you have been letting sin reign in your body and
have been obeying its lusts (Romans 6:12) does not negate
the fact that you are free from sin's control in Christ. You are
like a man pardoned by the judge and released from prison
after years of hard labor—but who keeps on sneaking back
into his jail cell!

Making Freedom Real in Our Experience

Notice how we make this freedom real in our experience.
Romans 8:4 says that the fulfillment of the requirements of
the Law (obedience to God's commands) occurs in those who
"do not walk according to the flesh but *according to the Spirit*
(emphasis added)."

That was the key that was missing in Paul's Romans 7
experience. (Did you notice that not once is the Holy Spirit
mentioned in Paul's description of his struggle?) The knowledge and even the desire to do what was right had been there,
but the power was not!

Tragically, most Christians are living in that same spiritual impotence. They are like the man who took his family to
the car dealership to buy his first car, a brand-new minivan.
After the man had signed the papers and made the down payment, the salesman handed him the keys, pointed him to the
car, and shook his hand to wish him well.

The father, thrilled at his new acquisition, piled his wife and kids into the van—and proceeded to the rear so he could push it home! After miles of this exhausting effort, a friend pulled up alongside him, driving his own car.

"Need some help, Joe?" he asked. "Are you out of gas?"

"Nah, gas tank's full. The salesman said so."

"So why are you pushing it? It's brand-new, right?"

"Yeah, it's new, and I was really excited about it at first, but this is hard work, and I'm getting more and more frustrated with the whole thing. I'm beginning to think that this car-driving business doesn't work for me. It seems to work for you, though."

The friend, realizing that Joe was clueless, asked, "Didn't the salesman give you a key to start it?"

"Yep. Got it right here in my pocket!"

Joe's friend then mercifully explained to him that there was power under the hood that would propel that vehicle effortlessly down the road. All Joe had to do was turn on the ignition, sit behind the wheel, and give it some gas. So Joe joyfully drove off into the sunset.

This parable would never happen in real life of course, at least not with cars. But it is happening every day in the spiritual realm as God's people desperately try (and fail!) to live the Christian life by their own strength rather than by the power of the Holy Spirit.

The Holy Spirit—the Power of the Presence of Christ

Talking about the Holy Spirit makes some people nervous, but Jesus said a lot about the coming of the Spirit, just prior to His death. Here's a sampling of the words of Jesus Himself from the Gospel of John:

> I will ask the Father, and he will give you another Counselor [Helper, NKJV] to be with you forever—the Spirit of truth. The world cannot accept him, because it

neither sees him nor knows him. But you know him, for he lives with you and will be in you (John 14:16-17 NIV).

The Counselor, the Holy Spirit, whom the Father will send in my name, will teach you all things and will remind you of everything I have said to you (John 14:26 NIV).

I tell you the truth: It is for your good that I am going away. Unless I go away, the Counselor will not come to you; but if I go, I will send him to you....When he, the Spirit of truth, comes, he will guide you into all truth. He will not speak on his own; he will speak only what he hears, and he will tell you what is yet to come. He will bring glory to me by taking from what is mine and making it known to you (John 16:7,12-14 NIV).

We think of how wonderful it must have been for the disciples to walk with Jesus: to see Him do His marvelous miracles, to hear His powerful teaching, to experience His love and mercy. But Jesus Himself said it was better for us that He go away. Why? So that the Holy Spirit would come!

While Jesus lived on earth, He limited Himself to time (about 33 years) and space (inside a human body). The best that people could experience in those days was to have God *with* them in the person of Jesus. Now there are no such limitations, and God through the Holy Spirit actually lives *in* all His children!

That reality ought to make us pause to think. The God of the universe, the One with all power and wisdom and love, lives inside every man, woman, and child who belongs to Christ! In fact, our bodies are called "a temple of the Holy Spirit" (1 Corinthians 6:19).

No Power Shortage with God

Have you felt frustrated and powerless against the anger or rage in your life? If you are a Christian, that sense of despair and defeat is based in ignorance, unbelief, or a lie! The power of God, greater by far than any sin, is available within you! Listen again to Paul: "Now to Him who is able to do far more abundantly beyond all that we ask or think, according to the power that works within us, to Him be the glory in the church and in Christ Jesus to all generations forever and ever. Amen" (Ephesians 3:20-21).

What have you been praying for? Have you been asking God to control your temper? Have you been pleading with Him to quell the burning rage in your life? Can God do those things? Yes! The Scripture says that

- God can do *all* you ask Him

- God can do *all* you ask Him *or* even think or imagine

- God can do *beyond* all that you ask or think

- God can do *abundantly beyond* all that you ask or think

- God can do *far more abundantly beyond* all that you ask or think!

There is no power shortage with God! He is eager, willing, and able to do all that is in accordance with His will. Perhaps the most amazing truth of all is that the power source, the generator of such might, lives within you. He, the Spirit, is the very life of Christ! How strong is the power of Christ's life? Paul prays that we would see that reality, in Ephesians 1:18-23·

> I pray that the eyes of your heart may be enlightened, so that you will know what is the hope of His calling, what are the riches of the glory of His inheritance in the saints, and what is the surpassing greatness of His power toward us who believe. These are in accordance with the working of the strength of His might which He brought about in Christ, when He raised Him from the dead and seated Him at His right hand in the heavenly places, far above all rule and authority and power and dominion,

and every name that is named, not only in this age but also in the one to come. And He put all things in subjection under His feet, and gave Him as head over all things to the church, which is His body, the fullness of Him who fills all in all.

Tony Evans once said, "If that doesn't get your bell ringing, your clapper's busted!" The same awesome power that raised Jesus Christ from death to life and brought Him to God's right hand, far above all other authority, is the same strength working in you and me!

Think about that for a moment. Go back to the dawn of that first Easter Sunday. There was a violent earthquake. An angel, like lightning, came and rolled the stone away from the tomb. The mighty Roman guards shook in terror and fell faint like dead men. Jesus Christ rose from the dead! The mightiest human power on earth, the Roman government, could not stop Him. The most awful forces of evil—sin, death, and Satan—could not hold Him.

Jesus rose from the grave and then ascended far above every earthly and heavenly power to sit at God's right hand. And brother or sister in Christ, that very same power that raised Him up is at work in you through the Holy Spirit!

Being Filled with the Spirit of Christ

When a believer in Christ is experiencing the Holy Spirit's powerful presence guiding and directing his life, he is "filled with the Spirit." Paul, by inspiration of God, made it clear that this state of spiritual being is not a luxury but a necessity. It is a command of God.

> Do not get drunk with wine, for that is dissipation, but be filled with the Spirit, speaking to one another in psalms and hymns and spiritual songs, singing and making melody with your heart to the Lord; always giving thanks for all things in the name of our Lord Jesus Christ to God, even the Father; and be subject to one another in the fear of Christ (Ephesians 5:18-21).

Just as the alcohol in wine radically alters the personality of the drinker, so the filling of the Holy Spirit transforms the believer. Instead of angry, hurtful words, there is a flow of praise and worship from the heart through the lips. Instead of grumbling and complaining, there is thanksgiving. Instead of hostility and rebellion, there is humility and submission to the will of God. This kind of living is not just for the spiritually elite. It is the intended, normal Christian life for all believers. As A.W. Tozer explains,

> The Spirit-filled life is not a special, deluxe edition of Christianity. It is part and parcel of the total plan of God for His people. You must be satisfied that it is not abnormal. I admit that it is unusual, because there are so few people who walk in the light of it or enjoy it, but it is not abnormal. In a world where everybody was sick, health would be unusual, but it wouldn't be abnormal. This is unusual only because our spiritual lives are so wretchedly sick and so far down from where they should be.[2]

Desire for the Spirit's Filling

There are three primary prerequisites for the filling of the Holy Spirit. The first prerequisite is *desire*. Jesus said, "Blessed are those who hunger and thirst for righteousness, for they shall be satisfied ['filled' NIV]" (Matthew 5:6). This is not a drowsy, half-hearted, "guess I could use some help" kind of desire. It is the same intense yearning and longing in the spiritual realm that a starving and thirsting man experiences in the physical realm. Jesus tells us about this in John 7:37-39:

> On the last day, the great day of the feast, Jesus stood and cried out, saying, "If anyone is thirsty, let him come to Me and drink. He who believes in Me, as the Scripture said, 'From his innermost being will flow rivers of living water.'" But this He spoke of the Spirit, whom

those who believed in Him were to receive; for the Spirit was not yet given, because Jesus was not yet glorified.

Humility Is Needed for the Spirit's Filling

In order to bring us to the point of such hunger and thirst for Him, God often has to break our stubborn will. That breaking produces the second prerequisite, *humility*. "God is opposed to the proud, but gives grace to the humble," James 4:6 says.

We have to come to the point where, when we reach into our fleshly bag of tricks, we find it empty, and realize that we have been living our lives independently of God. We have to come to the point where we humble ourselves under the mighty hand of God (1 Peter 5:6), confess our sins, and repent of living by our own strength and resources.

God Brings Us to the End of Ourselves

It may take a lot to bring some believers to the end of their resources so that they can discover God's resources. If necessary, God will orchestrate our own breaking through discipline. Hebrews 12:5-7 encourages us that God disciplines us in love because we are His sons. He disciplines us for our good, that we might share His holiness (Hebrews 12:10). He knows that living according to the flesh is futile, and so He allows us to come to our own painful conclusion about the futility of our own self-centered ways. Hopefully, we will be wise enough to surrender to His will.

Hebrews 12:11-13 provides a word of encouragement as well as a warning about God's discipline and breaking of our wills:

> All discipline for the moment seems not to be joyful, but sorrowful; yet to those who have been trained by it, afterwards it yields the peaceful fruit of righteousness. Therefore, strengthen the hands that are weak and the knees that are feeble, and make straight paths for your

feet, so that the limb which is lame may not be put out
of joint, but rather be healed.

God orchestrates the circumstances of our lives to reveal
fleshly living, breaks us of that self-centered lifestyle, and
paves the way for a fresh filling of the Spirit. Like most
believers, I had to learn the hard way. I first became aware of
the Spirit-filled life during my junior year in college. After my
salvation two years prior, I had battled God over who was
going to really be the Lord of my life. Through the misery of
life lived for self, God finally got my attention, and I opened
myself wide to the Holy Spirit's powerful, guiding presence.

Suddenly, the Christian life was not a drag or a duty but a
delight. I joyously witnessed for Christ and found my love for
the Word of God insatiable. The fruit of the Spirit began to
develop in my character, and my sarcastic, cynical tongue
began to preach God's truth.

God Is Faithful to Continue Disciplining Us

No matter how long one has walked with God in the
power of the Holy Spirit, there are always new areas on which
the Lord puts His finger. For the Miller family, the latest one
has been dealing with our adopted son, Luke. Let me begin
by saying that Shirley and I have absolutely no doubts that
God brought him into our family. He is a precious gift from
the Lord and overall a very happy, even delightful, child. He
is energetic, affectionate, and funny.

But I can honestly say that no human being has ever
pushed my buttons the way that little five-year-old boy has!
Earlier in this book I wrote about his temper tantrums. There
was something about the defiance, out-of-control rage, shrill
screaming, angry yelling, and destructive behavior that cried
out for a fleshly response. He was (and still is at times) an
explosive child—and unfortunately, when we first got him I
exploded right back.

As someone who has known how to be filled with the Spirit for more then 25 years, I am ashamed at how carnally I responded to Luke. When he would yell, I would yell louder. When he glared at me, I would glare back. I was determined to win the power struggle, but my methods were purely of the flesh.

One day after I was particularly harsh with him verbally, I closed his door, fell to my knees, and wept. I knew that my behavior was grieving God and hurting Luke, and I wanted out. At that moment, God broke me of my self-reliance and fleshly retaliation. With a new surrender to God's Spirit, I sensed peace, joy, and gentleness return to me. By God's grace, I have not gone back. Some of Luke's behavior still angers me, but now it is on the level of annoyance and irritation instead of hostility and rage.

Once we exhaust all our human efforts at overcoming our anger and fury (and other sins), and we finally give up trying to fix our problems by ourselves, then we are prime candidates for the Spirit's filling.

Putting Off and Putting On

Stephen Kellough, chaplain at Wheaton College in Illinois, made these observations after the 1995 movement of God's Spirit on that campus, which was characterized by heart-wrenching confession, repentance, and brokenness:

> With the confession of sin, sincere repentance, and a commitment to purge our lives from every known sin, we are "putting off" ungodly and self-destructive behavior. The biblical challenge is to follow the putting *off* with a putting *on*. The scriptural imperative is to follow an emptying with a filling....[In Ephesians 3:14-21] the apostle is praying for power—spiritual power. The apostle is calling down power from heaven—power for "the inner being," power for living, because it is in the "inner being" where life is really lived. Now maybe all of this talk about "spiritual power" and "the inner

being" sounds theoretical, impractical, or even mystical. But in reality, nothing could be more practical. Paul is seeking strength for the soul, where all decision-making and choices for life are made.[3]

Aren't you tired of reacting in fleshly anger? I sure was. Wouldn't you like to find yourself responding according to the fruit of the Spirit rather than according to the deeds of the flesh? Believe me, the difference is like night and day. It is a choice you can make today.

Faith for the Spirit's Filling

Once we come to the point of deeply desiring God's Spirit to fill (direct and empower) us, and we are truly humbled and broken of self-reliance, we must respond to God in *faith*. Faith is the third prerequisite to being filled with the Holy Spirit. Hebrews 11:6 teaches, "Without faith it is impossible to please Him, for he who comes to God must believe that He is and that He is a rewarder of those who seek Him." Do you believe that God will reward you when you seek Him to fill you with the Spirit? If you do, that is faith.

Jesus showed us God's eagerness to fill us with the Holy Spirit, when He asked,

> Now suppose one of you fathers is asked by his son for a fish; he will not give him a snake instead of a fish, will he? Or if he is asked for an egg, he will not give him a scorpion, will he? If you then, being evil, know how to give good gifts to your children, how much more will your heavenly Father give the Holy Spirit to those who ask Him? (Luke 11:11-13).

God wants you to be filled with the Holy Spirit! It is His desire, His command (Ephesians 5:18). He would not declare something to be His will and then turn around and be reluctant to bestow it, would He?

Life in the Spirit

As believers in Christ, we don't need to ask for the Holy Spirit to come in; He's already there. Paul makes this clear in Romans 8:9, where he declares that "if anyone does not have the Spirit of Christ, he does not belong to Him." The human spirit of every true born-again child of God is in union with the Holy Spirit (Romans 8:16). What we need is for the life of Christ to be fully manifested in our spirit, soul, and body. That is what it means to glorify God in our bodies, that is, to manifest the presence of God. Some believe that there are also movements of God's Holy Spirit from outside us, which Andrew Murray clarifies:

> Dear believer, please do not waste your time deciding which of these is the right one. God blesses men in both camps. When the flood came all the fountains of the abyss were broken up and the gates of heaven were opened. It came simultaneously from beneath and from above. God is prepared to bless men in both camps. He desires to teach us to know and honor the Spirit who is already within us. He also desires to bring us to wait upon Himself in a spirit of utter dependence, and to beseech Him that He as our Father would give us our daily bread, the new, the fuller influx of His Spirit. Do not allow yourself to be held back by this question. *God understands your petition.* He knows what you desire. Believe that God is prepared to fill you with His Spirit; let that faith look up to Him with unceasing prayer and confidence. He will give the blessing.[4]

The Spirit-filled life is essentially the same as abiding in Christ, who is our life. The Lord Jesus spoke explicitly about this intimate connection in John 15:

> Abide in Me, and I in you. As the branch cannot bear fruit of itself unless it abides in the vine, so neither can you unless you abide in Me. I am the vine, you are the branches; he who abides in Me and I in him, he bears

much fruit; for apart from Me you can do nothing (verses 4-5).

The branch of a grapevine does not, by itself, generate the fruit that hangs from it. The life, energy, and nourishment that create the fruit flow up through the vine and into the branch. Apart from the vine, the branch will be useless and fruitless. But a branch properly connected to the vine will bear fruit.

So it is with our relationship with Jesus. If we try to live the Christian life in our own strength, we cannot bear fruit because the fruit of the Christian can only be "the fruit of the Spirit" (Galatians 5:22-23). The only power source capable of producing such fruit is the Holy Spirit who dwells within us.

An outburst of anger is a deed of the flesh (Galatians 5:20). The goal is not simply to stop the deeds of the flesh. The goal is to be filled with the Spirit. Love must replace hate. Joy overcomes grumbling. Peace replaces anxiety. Patience replaces anger. Kindness overcomes hostility. Goodness replaces malice. Faithfulness overcomes a lack of trust. Gentleness replaces rudeness. Finally we have self-control, where before we lost control.

The Choice of Faith

We have a choice as to whether we are going to live by the Spirit or live according to the flesh. These two are in direct opposition to each other, according to Paul in Galatians 5:16-17:

I say, walk by the Spirit, and you will not carry out the desire of the flesh. For the flesh sets its desire against the Spirit, and the Spirit against the flesh; for these are in opposition to one another, so that you may not do the things that you please.

As Mark tells us, Jesus sent the disciples out across the Sea of Galilee after feeding the 5000 (Mark 6:45). The Master, however, stayed behind to pray on the mountain. Late that night, Jesus and the disciples had an encounter, one that can change our lives just as it did theirs:

> Seeing them straining at the oars, for the wind was against them, at about the fourth watch of the night He came to them, walking on the sea; and He intended to pass by them. But when they saw Him walking on the sea, they supposed that it was a ghost, and cried out; for they all saw Him and were terrified. But immediately He spoke with them and said to them, "Take courage; it is I, do not be afraid" (Mark 6:48-50).

Many of us are like the disciples. We are struggling and straining, trying to live the Christian life on our own power, and we are getting nowhere. If you want to row against the storms of life, go ahead. God will let you do so until you collapse in exhaustion, for Jesus always intends to pass by the self-sufficient person. As long as we think we can do it ourselves, He will let us. But those who call upon the name of the Lord will be saved. When the disciples acknowledged their need for help by crying out in fear, Jesus came to them. He responded immediately once they admitted their weakness.

Isn't it time to break the cycle of defeat in your life? If that is your desire, won't you join us in a prayer of faith, asking God to bring the filling of His Spirit?

> *Dear heavenly Father, I have lived too long in the bondage and defeat of the Romans chapter 7 struggle. I want to enter into the life of victory of Romans chapter 8. You have shown me so clearly that I cannot overcome anger in my own strength and by my own resources. In pride I have been rowing against the storms of life. I have come to the end of my resources. I now ask You, by Your grace, to fill me with the Holy Spirit. I surrender to Your will and wisdom, and I receive Your love and power. Be my strength to overcome the deeds of my flesh and to bear the fruit of the*

Spirit in my life. I choose to abide in Christ and bear much fruit. I choose by faith to believe that You will enable me to live above the power of sin. Should I fall to temptation and resort to living by the flesh, I pray that You will convict me, that I may again be filled by Your Holy Spirit. Give me sensitive spiritual ears to be led by the Spirit of truth. In Jesus' name I pray, amen.

Breaking Strongholds of Anger,
Part One

To rule one's anger is well; to prevent it is still better.

—T*RYON* E*DWARDS*

~

G ary's strong, athletic shoulders were hunched over and his head was bent down as I walked into his coach's office. His discouragement was understandable. The last ten days had been pretty humbling for the 23-year-old college senior.

He had been arrested for drunk and disorderly conduct and had spent a night in jail. He had been suspended from the baseball team for a week. Because of this he had been going to AA meetings for seven days straight. Now he was faced with the prospect of airing his dirty laundry in front of this complete stranger called in as a counselor, with two coaches present.

I found Gary to be friendly, respectful, likeable, intelligent, and articulate. There was nothing immediately apparent to suggest he had a problem with anger and violence. Yet by his own admission Gary had a history of fighting since his early teens. His intense rage was the result of suffering verbal and physical abuse from his stepfather. It boiled over in angry battles with peers, with Gary usually coming out on top. The victories made him feel better, he said, at least for a few minutes. His peers certainly respected him, and feared him as well.

"I've never backed down from a fight in my life. I can't," he admitted during our first session together. "When my stepfather would slap me and throw me around the room, I would fight him. I did that 'cause I hoped he'd kill me. I really did. I wanted to kill myself."

In high school, he took out his aggression on the football field, as a defensive end. Gary liked football. His anger fueled his play, and he was not afraid to fail. In football, he told me, there is so much action during any given play that rarely does one mistake stand out. But baseball was different. It posed more of a threat, since it's harder to hide on a baseball field, and there's nowhere to let out your aggression.

Gary told me that other people thought he was cool because he was a good athlete, but he knew deep down that his life was controlled by a terrible fear of failure and rejection. All anybody else ever saw was the competitive fire and the anger. That is all Gary would *let* them see.

Without football to act as a release valve for his steaming-hot rage, he turned to alcohol to numb his pain. But it only added fuel to the angry fire inside him, and the result was his arrest, hearing, and possible sentencing to community service or a fine. Plus he had to make an appointment with me.

Gary had a stronghold of anger, but he had an even deeper stronghold of rejection. The rejection, his sense of worthlessness, and his self-loathing had spawned the anger and the violent temper.

Gary is a believer in Christ, but like most Christians, he has yet to learn to trust Jesus not only as Savior but also as Lord and Life. Gary needs to know who he is in Christ and needs to learn to walk by faith in the power of the Holy Spirit.

A Journey to Freedom

To break the strongholds of anger, we encourage you to first work through the "Steps to Freedom in Christ" located in the back of this book. Those steps will enable you to do a thorough, broad-based spiritual "housecleaning" in your life. Then come back and work through the steps outlined in this chapter and the next. These will act like a spiritual laser beam, focusing intensely and precisely on the issue of anger.

The following process is really a journey to freedom. It is the same journey that the Lord is taking Gary on. These steps represent a summary of the biblical realities that need to be at work in an individual's life in order for him or her to break free from the control of fleshly anger and rage. But this is a guide, not a god. Making these spiritual strides is only possible through the enabling grace of God, and doing so does not in any way make us more acceptable to Him than we already are in Christ.

You will see that each step requires either a liberating act of grasping the truth or a critical decision of repentance and faith, or both. Though we have placed the steps in a particular order, the Holy Spirit has the right to take each of us on our own very personal journey of freedom, moving us through these steps in whichever order He sees fit. In reality, He will likely have us working on several of them simultaneously.

We will spend the next two chapters exploring the principles contained in each step. We will conclude with some suggestions for maintaining our freedom in Christ.

STEPS TOWARD
BREAKING STRONGHOLDS OF ANGER

1. I know that I am now a child of God and that my old, angry self was crucified with Christ.

Every born-again believer is a new creation in Christ (2 Corinthians 5:17). We are not forgiven sinners, we are redeemed saints. Like an ugly caterpillar inside its cocoon changes into a beautiful butterfly, so we died, were buried, and were raised into newness of life in Christ (see Romans 6:1-4). Romans 6:5-7 proclaims,

> If we have become united with Him in the likeness of His death, certainly we shall also be in the likeness of His resurrection, knowing this, that our old self was crucified with Him, in order that our body of sin might be done away with, so that we would no longer be slaves to sin; for he who has died is freed from sin.

We have been transferred out of the kingdom of darkness into the kingdom of God's beloved Son (Colossians 1:13). We are no longer "in Adam," we are now alive and free "in Christ." Being dead to sin means that we are no longer slaves to sin. Sin is no longer our master (Romans 6:14), because the power of sin has been broken. By the enabling grace of God we can say "no" to sin. We can live "self-controlled, upright and godly lives" (Titus 2:11-12 NIV). We can choose to walk by the Spirit and not fulfill the lusts of the flesh (Galatians 5:16-17).

This truth has tremendous ramifications for believers controlled by fleshly anger and rage. All excuses are gone—but so is our helplessness. We cannot say, "I just can't help it. That's the way I am." That is not true if we have Christ in our lives. We now can say, "In Christ I *can* live a righteous life. I can walk by the Spirit and not carry out the desires of the flesh. Sin is no longer my master, since I am now a bondservant of Christ."

Now We Can Live in Hope

Knowing all this to be true brings hope. Since I am no longer a child of the devil, but a liberated child of God (Ephesians 5:8; 1 John 3:1-3), all my heavenly Father's resources are now available to deal with my problems of anger. I am not alone, abandoned, helpless, or hopeless.*

---

* If you are struggling with grasping your new identity as a child of God, we recommend Neil's books *Victory Over the Darkness* and *God's Power at Work in You*. They were written to help you experience the truth of who you already are in Christ and show how you can conform to the image of Christ.

Maybe you've worn the label "rage-aholic." Maybe you've even served time for crimes committed in anger. Maybe you have clutched onto your anger as a "deserved" badge of honor, thereby broadcasting to the world that you are an abuse survivor. Maybe you have wielded the sword of anger in order to ensure self-protection and to make sure you get your own way. Maybe you fear you will never overcome the angry, edgy defensiveness that lies barely restrained beneath the surface of your soul.

Know today, child of God, that all fleshly anger and rage lost its power over you the moment you trusted Christ as Savior. Shed the labels that try to declare you bound to the darkness, and receive the pure truth that you are sealed in Christ as a child of the Father through the Holy Spirit! The key to lastingly liberate us from the chains of anger must be forged from the truth of our new Father–child relationship with the living God. (Reliance upon a vague "Higher Power" or self-created "God as we have come to know Him" simply will not be sufficient.)

Kent was undergoing counseling, and part of his therapy was to attend a men's Bible study I was leading on "breaking the chains" in our souls. He would reluctantly show up, listening but not participating. The look on his face ranged from amusement to anger to indifference.

Kent just did not seem to be able to get the Christian life to work for him, and he was angry, especially with God and himself. Here is what he said about his life:

> The truth contained in Ephesians 2:8-10 freed me from my own little brand of legalism [for salvation]. But I still tend to impose on myself a set of rules that are impossible to attain. The current rule that I struggle with is faith. I can't trust God. I try and I want to, but I fail miserably. I want to trust God with my doubts about myself and His involvement in my life. But I have a voice inside that tells me I am no good and worthless and that I can't trust God. Sure,

> some days I feel pretty good about myself, then it returns—the doubt and self-hate. The more others put expectations on me, the more I struggle.
>
> Hardly a day goes by that I don't experience tremendous emotional pain from this feeling of failure. I have come to realize that I am a spiritual failure and accept myself as one. Unable to trust God with my worries and concerns, I just hope I can make it through this time in my life without seriously hurting my wife and family.

Later, when Kent shared his testimony of freedom in a small group at a men's retreat, I was amazed. Gone were the anger, depression, and sense of failure that had trapped him. What had triggered the downward spiral into the trap? Feeling very inadequate when asked to serve in a position of church leadership. What had set him free? Knowing that he was a totally accepted child of God, adequate in Christ to serve in any way He saw fit, and free from the slavery of sin.

2. I confess that I still have a problem with fleshly anger, which is sin, and that by myself I am incapable of overcoming its control over me.

The truth of our new identity in Christ does not negate the reality that all of us battle flesh patterns to one degree or another. It is a denial of reality when we refuse to face the facts that clearly indicate we have a problem with fleshly anger. Healing can only come when we courageously face the truth that we have a problem beyond our ability to solve. Pride will try to deceive us into thinking we can overcome our anger in our own strength, but Jesus said, "Apart from Me you can do *nothing*" (John 15:5, emphasis added).

Do you anger easily? Do people say you have a temper? Is anger an emotion you readily display, or never dare to show? Do you believe you have a right to be angry? Do you require medication to relieve stress or stress-related maladies? Are you uptight? Do you find yourself easily irritated or impatient? Do you resent other drivers and vehicles on the road? Are you a sore loser? Do you tend to get upset by matters over which you have little or no ability to control? In the wisdom literature we read,

> A fool always loses his temper, but a wise man holds it back (Proverbs 29:11).

> A fool shows his annoyance at once, but a prudent man overlooks an insult (Proverbs 12:16 NIV).

> He who is slow to anger has great understanding, but he who is quick-tempered exalts folly (Proverbs 14:29).

> Do not associate with a man given to anger, or go with a hot-tempered man, or you will learn his ways and find a snare for yourself (Proverbs 22:24-25).

> A man of great anger will bear the penalty, for if you rescue him, you will only have to do it again (Proverbs 19:19).

> He who is slow to anger is better than the mighty, and he who rules his spirit, than he who captures a city (Proverbs 16:32).

> A man's discretion makes him slow to anger, and it is his glory to overlook a transgression (Proverbs 19:11).

In the kingdom of God we don't try to control or manipulate others through anger. God calls people who do this *fools*, and He is not the least bit impressed by their ability to angrily manipulate people and circumstances. In fact, Scripture warns that such people will fall into trouble, as will those who hang around them.

From Denial to Honesty

The second step to freedom from controlling anger involves getting out of denial and coming face-to-face with your anger problem. As my counseling times with Gary have continued, I have been refreshed by his honesty. Recently he declared, "I know why I've had such problems with anger. I have tried to do everything myself, and what I've been doing hasn't worked."

David once kept silent about his sin, and he shared the consequences of his cover-up in Psalm 32:3-4: "When I kept silent about my sin, my body wasted away through my groaning all day long. For day and night Your hand was heavy upon me; my vitality was drained away as with the fever heat of summer." His psychosomatic illness was due to unconfessed sin, which finally led him to walk into the light. "I acknowledged my sin to You, and my iniquity I did not hide; I said, 'I will confess my transgressions to the LORD,' and You forgave the guilt of my sin" (Psalm 32:5).

The Lord won't let one of His children live in denial, because He loves them too much. Jeremiah wrote, "In spite of all these things, yet you said, 'I am innocent; surely His anger is turned away from me.' Behold, I [God] will enter into judgment with you because you say, 'I have not sinned.'" (Jeremiah 2:34-35).

Do not make the mistake of ignoring or denying your anger problem. God's grace for healing awaits, but it is only to the humble man that He gives it (James 4:6). Do not resist God's humbling process as He breaks down your fleshly defenses and brings you to the end of your own resources. "A broken and a contrite heart, O God, You will not despise" (Psalm 51:17). You may find it very painful to see your coping mechanisms crumbling. You may not like what you see in yourself at all. But know that the Lord will never despise you as you come face-to-face with your weakness and the failure of the flesh.

3. I choose to believe that the presence and power of Christ within me is my only hope for breaking free from anger's control.

This book has no power to set you free from the power of sin, nor does any personal counselor or counseling procedure. No set of video- or audiocassettes can free you from the chains of controlling anger. The power to deliver you and me from any sin lies solely in the Lord Jesus Christ and in the truth of His Word. He can and does work through a book, seminar, sermon, pastor, or counselor as His instruments, but it is the Son who sets us "free indeed" (John 8:36). If you are putting your trust in any person (including yourself) or any human method, your faith will prove misguided and futile. But "he who believes in Him will not be disappointed" (Romans 9:33). Jeremiah 17:5-8 tells us why:

> Thus says the LORD, "Cursed is the man who trusts in mankind and makes flesh his strength, and whose heart turns away from the LORD. For he will be like a bush in the desert and will not see when prosperity comes, but will live in stony wastes in the wilderness, a land of salt without inhabitant.
>
> "Blessed is the man who trusts in the LORD and whose trust is the LORD. For he will be like a tree planted by the water, that extends its roots by a stream and will not fear when the heat comes; but its leaves will be green, and it will not be anxious in a year of drought nor cease to yield fruit."

When we use the Steps to Freedom in Christ to help people resolve their personal and spiritual conflicts, we encourage those we counsel to seek as much prayer support as possible. In addition, we strongly urge people who come to us to bring along a trusted friend to bathe the entire session in prayer. Each one of the Steps begins with a prayer requesting that God bring to mind the issues that He wants each individual to deal with. Frequently we will pause during the session to ask the Lord for wisdom, strength, freedom from confusion, or protection. We pray in faith because we know that Jesus has come to bring good news to the afflicted, to bind up broken hearts, to proclaim liberty to captives and freedom to prisoners (Isaiah 61:1). As we pray, God gives us the strength to not be discouraged but to persevere until the person we're counseling breaks through to resolution and freedom.

Discouragement is one of Satan's most effective weapons. He wants us to give up on God and to disbelieve that Christ is willing and able to set us free. We are often like the man Mark tells about whose son was terribly demonized. He pleaded with Jesus, "If You can do anything, take pity on us and help us!" (Mark 9:22).

"Jesus said to him, '"If You can?" All things are possible to him who believes.' Immediately the boy's father cried out and said, 'I do believe; help my unbelief.'" (verses 23-24).

Jesus quickly set the boy free, and later explained to the disciples the reason for the failure of their earlier attempt to help the boy: "This kind cannot come out by anything but prayer" (verse 29). Prayer demonstrates our dependence upon God.

Be honest with God. If you are struggling with unbelief, tell God that your faith is weak. Ask Him to help your unbelief. As we see in Mark 9, Jesus accepted the honesty of the man who came to Him, and He will accept yours as well.

And take a proactive approach to pulling together an army of prayer warriors who will call upon the Lord Jesus Christ and claim the fact that the power of sin and Satan in your life has been broken. Make prayer your number-one priority. James 5:13 says, "Is anyone among you suffering? Then he must *pray*" (emphasis added). We only give lip service to our dependence upon God if we neglect to pray. But "the effective prayer of a righteous man can accomplish much" (James 5:16).

Consider these powerful prayer promises:

> Truly I say to you, if you have faith and do not doubt, you will not only do what was done to the fig tree, but even if you say to this mountain, "Be taken up and cast into the sea," it will happen. And all things you ask in prayer, believing, you will receive (Matthew 21:21-22).

> If you abide in Me, and My words abide in you, ask whatever you wish, and it shall be done for you (John 15:7).

> Truly, truly, I say to you, he who believes in Me, the works that I do, he will do also; and greater works than these he will do; because I go to the Father. Whatever you ask in My name, that will I do, so that the Father may be glorified in the Son. If you ask Me anything in My name, I will do it (John 14:12-14).

Self-control Is God's Will for You

Do not believe the devil's lie that God will help others but will not help you. If you are a believer in Christ, "it is God who is at work in you, both to will and to work for His good pleasure" (Philippians 2:13). Is it God's will for you to be free from anger's control? Of course it is! Then know and choose to believe that you can do all things through Christ who strengthens you (Philippians 4:13). Self-control is a fruit of the Spirit (Galatians 5:23). To keep a deed of the flesh from manifesting itself, stop and pray. Ask the Lord to fill you with His Spirit, and then believe that He has. Here are some suggestions that might help you draw upon the Spirit's power rather than reacting in the flesh:

1. *Be especially prayerful when you are about to go into a situation that or be with a person who pushes your anger buttons,* though of course we must always be spiritually alert. Jesus said, "Keep watching and praying that you

may not enter into temptation; the spirit is willing, but the flesh is weak" (Matthew 26:41).

2. *Recognize the buttons that stimulate your old flesh patterns.* These are things like irritating noise, someone yelling at you, guilt-manipulation, attacks on your competence, and so on. Be aware of your body's "cues" that you are starting to get angry (for example, tenseness, restlessness, lack of concentration, clenched fists, and so on).[1] Deep-breathing exercises and muscle-relaxation techniques can be quite helpful, but steer clear of anything that would require you to passively empty your mind.

3. *Try to get some space between yourself and the stimulant to anger.* Don't put yourself in situations of great temptation. Paul said, "Flee from youthful lusts" (2 Timothy 2:22). Politely excuse yourself from a conversation if you need to, and come back when you have cooled down. Proverbs 17:14 says, "The beginning of strife is like letting out water, so abandon the quarrel before it breaks out."

4. *Make good use of "anger blasters,"* constructive diversions that can get your mind off the anger stimulant for a while.[2] You can jog, ride a bike, take a walk in the woods, pump iron, or go for a drive in the country. A lot of the tension you feel when you are angry is your body's inborn mechanism preparing you to fight. By engaging in a physical activity, you diffuse that angry energy. The more pleasing the surroundings to which you retreat, the more soothing they will be to your soul.

5. *Slow down and focus your mind on truth.* Some people find it helpful to count to 10, or to count to 100 backwards if they are really angry. We encourage you to

recite Scripture in your mind when your flesh patterns are stimulated by someone or something.

6. *Ask yourself these questions: "Is this really worth my attention? Is my anger justified? Do I have a right or ability to do anything about it? Is this a goal or a desire?"* There is "a time for war and a time for peace" (Ecclesiastes 3:8), but we have to make sure our anger is justified before we "go to war." Make sure you choose wisely, for the person who fights over everything wins nothing. And when you need to stand your ground, speak the truth in love (Ephesians 4:15)

∾∾∾

In closing, listen to how God is helping this woman learn to break a stronghold of anger in her life:

Anger, issues of control, and selfishness have been consuming too much of my life for too long. They affect me in all areas of life. Finally, God has placed me with a husband who has struggled with his own controlling and selfish nature. I am slowly learning the power of biting my tongue and going to prayer instead of to war. Usually the triggering issues are trivial, which is all the more reason to let them go. I hear over and over "let go and let God." For me, it's not always that simple, but I am learning to give Him more of me each day. It is overwhelming how unworthy I feel, and how small, when I continually let anger win, and yet God has continued to bless me and open doors I didn't think would open in my life. I confess I still fail with my anger, but I believe as I honestly and humbly open my heart each day that He is continuing to wash me and speak to me and most amazingly...wait PATIENTLY.

Please join together with us in prayer.

Dear heavenly Father, You are worthy of all honor, glory, and praise. You are gracious and merciful, slow to anger, and abounding in lovingkindness. I thank You for the liberating power of Your Spirit and Your Word. I present myself to You, knowing that You have so much more work to do in me to make me a loving, patient, peaceful, kind, gentle person. Thank You for the freedom You have already brought me into in Christ. I welcome the continuing process of breaking strongholds of anger in my life. Don't stop, Lord, no matter how much I complain or how often I run. I need You desperately. I thank You that You will never leave me nor forsake me. In Jesus' name I pray, amen.

14

Breaking
Strongholds of Anger,
Part Two

Anger begins with folly, and ends with repentance.
—H.G. BOHN

~

E ugene Peterson's contemporary rendering of 2 Corinthians 10:3-6 gives a fresh view of the warfare involved in tearing down strongholds. He writes,

> The world is unprincipled. It's dog-eat-dog out there!
> The world doesn't fight fair. But we don't live or fight
> our battles that way—never have and never will. The
> tools of our trade aren't for marketing or manipulation,
> but they are for demolishing that entire massively cor-
> rupt culture. We use our powerful God-tools for smashing
> warped philosophies, tearing down barriers erected
> against the truth of God, fitting every loose thought and
> emotion and impulse into the structure of life shaped by
> Christ. Our tools are ready at hand for clearing the
> ground of every obstruction and building lives of obedi-
> ence into maturity (THE MESSAGE).

When we look at how much we have struggled with anger
in our lives, it is easy to just focus on our weakness. We may
seriously consider just giving up and giving in to the rule of
anger. After all, it *is* easier to drive in a rut than to try to move
the car out of it.

But God wants us to be reminded of the divinely powerful weapons we have at our disposal. There is no sin that is stronger than Jesus, and there is no sin for which it is worth sacrificing a clear conscience, an intimate walk with God, and a peaceful night's sleep.

A Quick Review

Before moving on to the fourth principle of breaking strongholds of anger, let's review the ground we've already covered. Once again, the following statements constitute the biblical realities that need to be at work in an individual's life in order for him or her to break free from controlling anger.

1. *I know that I am now a child of God and that my old, angry self was crucified with Christ.*

2. *I confess that I still have a problem with fleshly anger, which is sin, and that by myself I am incapable of overcoming its control over me.*

3. *I choose to believe that the presence and power of Christ within me is my only hope for breaking free from anger's control.*

When it comes to facing the sin in our lives, it is easy to excuse ourselves or rationalize our sin. Therefore, if we are serious about getting well, we need to make an appointment with the Great Physician, the only "heart doctor," before whose eyes all things are open and laid bare (Hebrews 4:13).

4. I place myself on the Holy Spirit's examination table so that He can reveal my sinful, angry behavior, as well as the lies I have believed that keep me enslaved to fleshly anger.

David prayed, "Search me, O God, and know my heart; try me and know my anxious thoughts; and see if there be any hurtful way in me, and lead me in the everlasting way"

(Psalm 139:23-24). At first glance, asking God for such a revelation of our inner condition may seem frightening. But there is no need to fear the truth, especially when that truth is revealed by our loving God.

In placing ourselves upon the Holy Spirit's examination table we are, in essence, giving Him the keys to every "room" in the house of our lives. We are granting Him permission to go everywhere in our past and present, even if it means discovering the skeletons in our closets. We are admitting that we don't have all the answers to our anger problem, but that He does. He alone can make the perfect diagnosis and prescribe the perfect remedy.

Again, one excellent way to do this is by taking unhurried time in the presence of God to walk through the "Steps to Freedom in Christ." Many people have done this on their own, but it is even better to have a trusted friend guide you and pray with you through them.

Researchers in different parts of the country are in the process of conducting studies to determine the long-term effects of going through the Steps on the spiritual and emotional states of believers. They have developed survey questions that enable them to quantify individual and group levels of anger, and preliminary reports are quite encouraging.

For example, a group from Oklahoma was surveyed right before and four months after going through the Steps to Freedom. The study showed that during that period of time, anger had decreased by more than one-third among those surveyed.

Results from a Texas study showed that anger had decreased by more than one-half *three months* after the surveyed group had gone through the Steps. Those results are particularly encouraging since the group had indicated that same decrease in anger just a *week* after processing the Steps to Freedom. This means that some lasting, long-term transformation had clearly taken place.

Hidden Causes Revealed

It is amazing how the Spirit of God often reveals, through tools like the Steps to Freedom in Christ, the hidden root causes of our problems—root causes we had totally forgotten or not considered important before.

Jeff asked for a personal appointment because he was confused about how to handle a situation on the job. A co-worker was on his case continually, and Jeff didn't know what to do. I suggested that we pray and ask the Lord to show him whether his problems were primarily circumstantial or internal.

Five days later, Jeff came into my office with some real answers to that prayer. In the time since I had first seen him, he had become very defensive with his co-worker when she had (unjustly) accused him of doing no work. And he had vehemently denied his wife's contention that he came home grumpy, even though he did!

Ordinarily, Jeff would have chalked those incidents up as normal behavior on his part. But the Spirit of God opened his eyes and revealed that Jeff feared the disapproval of others. He was bound and determined to present an image of himself that was so likeable and efficient that he could never be criticized. But all phobias are rooted in lies. Jeff believed that he needed the approval of others in order to accept himself. He came to realize that his anger was a defense mechanism designed to protect this false image whenever it was threatened by others' words.

In prayer, Jeff renounced the lie and chose to believe the truth that he was already loved and accepted in Christ. It will take time for his mind to be fully renewed and his behavior transformed, but he would not even be on the right track were it not for his eagerness to allow the Spirit of God to reveal his wrong behavior and beliefs.

5. I choose to forgive from my heart each and every person with whom I am angry, including myself and God, and I choose to open my heart to Christ's healing touch.

This step may be the most powerfully liberating for you. Making the choice to forgive ourselves and others from the heart is almost without exception a major stepping-stone toward experiencing freedom from anger's control. That is why we devoted two chapters in this book to forgiveness. Each of those chapters (chapters 8 and 9) has practical steps to take in order to forgive yourself and others, and to release any anger built up against God.

If you have not already prayerfully and thoroughly worked through those chapters, we urge you to do so at this time. Forgiving from your heart is the crucial third step in the Steps to Freedom in Christ.

Once you forgive others from your heart, don't be surprised if hours, days, even weeks afterwards, other people come to mind that you need to forgive. Or the Lord may bring up other incidents involving those you have already forgiven. Don't be discouraged—the Lord is just helping you recover one layer at a time. If this happens, it in no way invalidates the work that you have already accomplished. It simply means that the Lord is continuing to reveal areas of bondage, layer by layer. He knows what and how much we can handle at any certain moment.

If more issues involving forgiveness do come up, you know what to do. Simply make the choice to forgive from the heart in accordance with the guidance offered in Step 3. Don't become anxious about issues that remain unrevealed. You are responsible to deal only with what you know. Wait for the Lord. Be patient with His timing. He desires your freedom even more than you do, and He "is at work in you, both to will and to work for His good pleasure" (Philippians 2:13).

Sometimes, even after faithfully following the suggested guidelines for forgiving from the heart, you may still feel anger toward those who have offended you. You may wonder if you were sincere in your forgiveness. If that occurs, ask God to search your heart again. Sometimes there are things that have not been dealt with at all or have been visited only superficially. Many times we bypass the emotional core because the feelings seem too painful to face. If this is the case, then the Lord will guide you through the forgiveness process again. Having another person pray with you through this Step will also help ensure that you are being thorough and honest. It is also possible that your anger may be justified and God wants you to take action to correct a wrong.

Many times, however, even after we have forgiven an offender, a deeper healing work needs to take place. Your emotions are damaged, and you need the Lord Jesus' healing touch in order for you to be whole. I have seen the Lord do a dramatic work of healing in my life in response to a heart cry for His touch. He will do the same for you as well, once you make the choice to forgive.

6. I specifically and thoroughly confess and repent of all attitudes and practices of fleshly anger, and I renounce the lies that I have believed that have fueled my anger.

Jesus said that it is the truth that sets us free from our slavery to sin (John 8:32). That being true, it is clear that lies keep us in bondage to sin. Whether it is controlling anger, rage, or any other sin of the flesh, there is at least one (and usually more than one) lie that keeps us chained to that sinful behavior.

Below we have listed some of the more common sinful attitudes and behaviors that can be based in rage and anger. We also have listed the more common lies that can result in fleshly anger and rage. After those lists are prayers of confession and renunciation for you to use. Whether you use these prayers or your own, it is imperative that your repentance come from your heart.

Psalm 24:3-5 makes this solemn warning and encouraging promise:

> Who may ascend into the hill of the LORD? And who

may stand in His holy place? He who has clean hands and a pure heart, who has not lifted up his soul to falsehood and has not sworn deceitfully. He shall receive a blessing from the LORD and righteousness from the God of his salvation.

Before we go any further, let's go to the Lord in prayer.

Dear heavenly Father, I ask You to search me and know my heart and thoughts and show me if there is any hurtful way in me. Reveal to me any and all sinful attitudes and actions that are related to my anger or rage. I want to confess these attitudes and actions to You and turn from them so that You might lead me in Your everlasting way. Please expose the lies I have believed so that I may renounce them and walk in the truth. In Jesus' name I pray, amen.

Sinful Attitudes and Behaviors

- ❏ Arguing and quarreling
- ❏ Screaming and yelling
- ❏ Threatening
- ❏ Contentiousness (picking fights)
- ❏ Bitter or jealous heart
- ❏ Critical and judgmental spirit
- ❏ Legalistic and religiously rigid spirit
- ❏ Gossip, slander, and backbiting
- ❏ Refusal to forgive
- ❏ Causing factions and divisions in the church
- ❏ Defensive reactions to criticism

- ❏ Throwing objects
- ❏ Fighting
- ❏ Gang-related violence
- ❏ Criminal behavior (for example, vandalism, theft, rape, murder)
- ❏ Abusing the innocent or weak (people, animals)
- ❏ Substance abuse (food, alcohol, drugs, and so on)
- ❏ Eating disorders
- ❏ Sexual promiscuity
- ❏ Lying and deceiving
- ❏ Controlling and manipulative behavior
- ❏ Overaggressive or rude driving
- ❏ Overcompetitive spirit in work or play
- ❏ Passivity or refusal to accept responsibility
- ❏ Resistance or rebellion toward authority
- ❏ Sulking or silent treatment
- ❏ Stubborn refusal to listen or yield
- ❏ Controlling fears
- ❏ Running away
- ❏ Withdrawal from family, friends, church
- ❏ Withholding sexual intimacy in marriage
- ❏ Vengeful or malicious thoughts, words, or deeds

❑ Self-injury or self-mutilation

❑ Satanism and witchcraft

❑ Suicidal urges or actions

Prayer of Confession and Repentance

> *Dear heavenly Father, I confess that I am angry and that this anger has shown up in my sinful attitudes and actions of (<u>list all that the Holy Spirit reveals to you</u>). I thank You for Your forgiveness and cleansing, and I repent of all these sinful attitudes and actions, in Jesus' name, amen.*

It is one thing to confess a sin. It is another to have the power to walk in obedience to God's Word. Chapter 12, "Connecting to the Power," provides the biblical instruction you need to walk by the Spirit so that you don't have to carry out the desires of the flesh. You may want to go back and reread that chapter once you have finished this process.

Common Lies Resulting in Angry Attitudes and Behavior

❑ No one loves me, not even God.

❑ I can't do anything right.

❑ I am a failure.

❑ I will never amount to anything.

❑ I have no talents, gifts, or anything to offer.

❑ I don't fit in.

❑ I am on my own in this world.

❑ I have to take care of myself.

❑ God will not defend me.

❑ God has forgotten me.

❑ I cannot trust anyone.

❑ I cannot be free.

❑ There's no hope for me.

❑ The Christian life doesn't work for me.

❑ I am dirty (or evil).

❑ I am worthless.

❑ I must be perfect to be accepted.

❑ I must be perfect to accept myself.

❑ I must never show weakness or let others beat me.

❑ I must prove to others that I am competent (a man, and so on).

❑ I must control others to feel safe.

❑ I am alone.

❑ I must perform to a certain level in order to feel good about myself.

Prayer for Renunciation of Lies

> *Dear heavenly Father, I renounce the lie that (name the lie). I refuse to allow it to have any hold over me any more. I cancel out any and all ground gained in my life by the enemy through my believing that lie, and I choose now to walk in the truth of God's Word. In the name of Jesus, the truth, I pray, amen.*

It is essential, once you renounce lies that have controlled you, that you replace those lies with the truth. Rehearsing the truth again and again until it is firmly entrenched in our minds will set us free. We must let the peace of Christ rule in our hearts and we do that by letting the word of Christ richly dwell within us (Colossians 3:15-16). The truths of who we are "in Christ" (see the end of chapter 4, "Mental Strongholds") are well worth memorizing and meditating upon so that your mind will be renewed (Romans 12:2).

7. I renounce using the parts of my body as instruments of angry unrighteousness and I present my entire body and its members to God as instruments of righteousness.

After two months of weekly two-hour discipleship appointments with Gary, I have almost worked myself out of a job. He has learned how to walk by the Spirit, and has become more like the Lord Jesus. The biggest breakthrough came when he chose to surrender fully to Christ's lordship in his life and to begin to draw upon the power of the Spirit to live.

"All my life I have tried to rise up and be someone great," Gary sighed as he sat across the table from me in his college's snack shop. "I would step on the field trying to prove to my parents, trying to prove to myself, that I was good enough—and someone special."

"My view of success has always been getting awards, having people respect me, coming through in the clutch, and respecting myself. God didn't run my life," he continued, broken in spirit, "I did. Everything I believe has been about me. But what is important to God is for me to give everything to Him. I'm kind of afraid to do it, though."

But he did. One by one Gary listed off the parts of his body that had been used in pride, fear, anger, and violence. His brain, his mouth, his eyes, his ears, his hands, his feet, and so on. He confessed that he had misused those members of his body as instruments of unrighteousness.

The most significant to Gary were his hands. They had always symbolized success or failure to him. Whether it was clutching a baseball bat, throwing a ball, or trying to punch the lights out of an enemy, his hands had been his power.

Gary humbly invited the Lord to use his hands and the rest of his body for His good purposes. And then he "climbed up on the altar" and presented his body as a living and holy sacrifice to God (Romans 12:1).

Romans 6:11-13 provides the biblical basis for such a life-changing decision:

> Consider yourselves to be dead to sin, but alive to God in Christ Jesus. Therefore do not let sin reign in your mortal body so that you obey its lusts, and do not go on presenting the members of your body to sin as instruments of unrighteousness; but present yourselves to God as those alive from the dead, and your members as instruments of righteousness to God.

We invite you now to make the same decision of surrender that Gary did. Instead of obeying sin's lustful cries, which lead to slavery, surrender to God's ways—which lead to freedom! When you make it in humble sincerity, this choice will be your gateway to a new life of love, joy, peace, patience, and power.

Prayer of Surrender

> *Dear heavenly Father, I confess that I have used my (name the parts of your body) as instruments of unrighteousness by (say specifically what you did). I am sorry for defiling the temple of the Holy Spirit in that way. I now choose to present myself to You as a living and holy sacrifice and my (name the parts of your body) to You as instruments of righteousness, for Your glory. In Jesus' name I pray, amen.*

8. I actively stand firm against Satan's attacks on my mind and body by putting on the full armor of God, and I confess and renounce all the sins of my ancestors and other earthly influences in my life. I choose to take every thought captive to the obedience of Christ.

Satan takes advantage of our bitterness and magnifies it into out-of-control rage and revenge. The devil is a liar, a deceiver, and an accuser (John 8:44; Revelation 12:9-10). He seeks to manipulate our emotions and behavior by controlling our thinking with distorted ideas about God, ourselves, and others.

But Jesus came to destroy the devil's works (1 John 3:8), and so Satan was disarmed and defeated at the cross (Colossians 2:15). Since Jesus Christ now has all authority in heaven and on earth (Matthew 28:18), when we humbly submit to God's rule in our lives and resist the devil, he will flee from us (James 4:7).

Resistance requires active participation on our part. We have to put on the armor of God, stand firm, and resist. The King James Version renders the beginning of Ephesians 6:12 as "We wrestle not against flesh and blood...." Rather, we wrestle against demonic powers. To "wrestle" implies a struggle requiring energy, focus, and skill.

But this battle is neither waged nor won on a physical or fleshly level, "for the weapons of our warfare are not of the flesh, but divinely powerful for the destruction of fortresses" (2 Corinthians 10:3). God has mercifully given us His armor of truth, righteousness, peace, salvation, faith, and the Word of God so that we can wage a victorious battle in prayer against the enemy's schemes (see Ephesians 6:10-20). But we must make the choice to put on and take up these weapons.

For a complete view of the enemy's tactics and the believer's protection in Christ, we strongly urge you to read my (Neil's) book *The Bondage Breaker*. In short, however, the primary ways in which Satan gains access to a believer's life are through—

- involvement in the occult and other counterfeit religions and practices

- our passively allowing lies and worldly philosophies to dominate our belief system

- abuse, molestation, neglect, and hurt from the past, and our subsequent believing of lies and harboring of anger and bitterness

- rebellion

- pride

- involvement in sins of the flesh, especially sexual sins

- passive acceptance of the sins of our ancestors

Taking Up God's Means of Protection

If you had heard that a serial killer was loose in your neighborhood, you would not take a casual approach to protecting yourself! You would make sure every door and window were completely closed and locked. You would make sure your security system was on full alert. You would probably have your cell phone handy.

Satan is an exploiter. You give him an inch, he'll take a mile. Therefore, we urge you again, if you have not already carefully and prayerfully walked through the Steps to Freedom in Christ, to do so. By submitting to God in confession and repentance, you will be taking back any ground that Satan may claim as his own in your life. You are in essence closing and locking the doors and windows. By resisting the devil in your authority in Christ, you are turning on the lights and grabbing your weapons and driving any spiritual intruders off your property. You can be assured that a heavenly security guard will be dispatched to set a watch over your house.

Once the spiritual strongholds of anger and rage have been broken, it is critical that you learn to take every thought captive in obedience to Christ. A large part of that process is guarding what comes into your heart and mind. The media can have a huge impact on our thought lives through books, magazines, TV shows, movies, video and computer games, and Internet sites. Paul advises us in Philippians 4:8, "Brethren, whatever is true, whatever is honorable, whatever is right, whatever is pure, whatever is lovely, whatever is of good repute, if there is any excellence and if anything worthy of praise, dwell on these things."

After surrendering fully to Jesus as his Lord, Gary was convicted over some of the TV shows and books he had formerly tolerated or even enjoyed. He had to walk out on one show his buddies were watching because it bothered him so much. His anger is now being replaced by a growing peace and joy as he has immersed himself in the Bible, a devotional book, and C.S. Lewis's Chronicles of Narnia.

9. I humble myself by seeking reconciliation with and making restitution to those whom I have wounded in my anger, whenever it is possible and wise to do so.

Choosing the path of humility will go against your fleshly feelings, but it is one of the more significant steps to freedom when orchestrated by the Holy Spirit. God gives grace to the humble. Relationships that we have damaged or destroyed through our sinful anger can often be repaired and restored. Ultimately, this is God's work. Our responsibility, however, is to be obedient to the Lord and to seek reconciliation and healing.

Romans 12:18 says, "If possible, so far as it depends on you, be at peace with all men." Reconciliation is not always dependent upon us. Another person can refuse to be reconciled to you even after you have prayed, humbly admitted your wrongdoing, and reached out in love. The restoration we desire to happen immediately may take time, or it may never happen. When God prompts you to "go and do your part," you must go regardless of the outcome.

Matthew 5:23-24 provides biblical guidelines for seeking reconciliation with another person:

> If you are presenting your offering at the altar, and there remember that your brother has something against you, leave your offering there before the altar and go; first be reconciled to your brother, and then come and present your offering.

Guidelines for Restitution

This is serious business with God. If we have hurt another person with our anger or rage, we need to go to that person and make restitution. If distance is a problem, a phone call is the next best thing. We don't recommend writing a letter or using e-mail because such communication can easily be misread, misunderstood, passed on to the wrong people, and even used against you legally.

If your safety or well-being would be jeopardized by going to the other person alone, then take someone with you (if that would provide sufficient protection), or make a phone call from a safe location. Private angry thoughts you've had toward another person (that haven't resulted in action) should be dealt with privately before the Lord. The other party has no awareness of those thoughts and doesn't need to have it. In fact, bringing them up will cause more problems than it will solve.

The only exception is in the case where you have stolen or damaged merchandise or property and the owner is unaware of what you did. In that case, you need to go to the person, humbly confess your wrongdoing, and ask him or her how to make it right. Be willing to suffer the consequences of your wrongdoing. That may be part of God's breaking and healing of you. First pray and ask God for the right words, right attitude, and right timing. Make sure you have already forgiven the other party, if he or she offended you.

When confessing your misdeeds, label your action as *wrong*. Be specific and admit what you did. Make no defenses or excuses. Don't blame the other person or demand an apology. That is between him or her and God. Ask specifically, "Will you forgive me?" then wait for the answer. Trust God for the outcome, no matter what it is.

One time I (Rich) was in a prayer meeting, and I inappropriately prayed in anger about a former pastor of mine. He happened to walk into the room about that time, and I happened to peek. I knew I had done something wrong. The next morning I was trying to spend time with the Lord, but I wasn't connecting. He turned my attention to Matthew 5:23-24 and I knew immediately why He was displeased. I knew that I needed to call the pastor and each of the men in that group and ask forgiveness for my sin. By the grace of God they were all home and all graciously forgave me. After I'd spent about 20 minutes pulling my foot out of my mouth, the Lord was eager to receive my worship again.

Look Forward in Hope

These nine steps are not laws to be slavishly followed. They merely provide a framework through which the Spirit of liberty can break down strongholds of anger and set you free. Nor are they a shortcut to maturity. It will take us the rest of our lives to be transformed by the renewing of our minds and to be conformed to the image of God. However, freedom is a gate that needs to be walked through in order for growth to occur.

Freedom will be maintained and growth gained as you continue to cultivate an intimate, personal relationship with the living God through consistent worship, prayer, and Bible study.

You also need to intentionally pursue open, honest fellowship with other believers in Christ who will pray for you and your struggles with anger. Give them permission to lovingly hold you accountable for your attitudes and actions. Consider giving them permission to contact your spouse and employer periodically to find out how you are doing in controlling your temper. It's true that, generally, we don't do what people *expect*, but what they *inspect*!

Finally, immerse yourself daily in the liberating truths of your new identity in Christ as an accepted, secure, significant child of God. As part of the bride of Christ, you are a love gift from the Father to the Son (see John 17:2,6,9,24). Jesus has given you the same glory that the Father gave Him (see verse 22). And the Father loves you just as much as He loves the Lord Jesus Christ (see verse 23).

We hope, and we pray, that this final personal story will give *you* hope in your daily battle of overcoming anger.

> I used to be what we term "short-tempered." I would not give anyone the time of day and would angrily burst out at them for asking a simple question. People were eventually afraid to approach me, and I thought I was victorious. I called myself a Christian during this entire ordeal. I would read my Bible and pray and "counsel" others. One of my special prayer requests was to be more like Christ.
>
> Little did I know what I was asking for. Because I would not listen to others, God found a way of dealing with me directly. I joined a Bible study some four years ago and that is when I was brought to my knees. Slowly but surely God worked through my life in all areas. I would discover disturbing things about my life and I would feel that there was no way that I was truly called by God. But every day, and every week in the Bible study, I would discover how much God loved me, no matter what was inside me. That love brought me to the point where I asked Him to change me completely, and I offered myself as a living sacrifice to Him. And even if I squirmed off the altar, I asked that God be patient with me while I got back on again.
>
> Today I am not perfect, but my anger is in check. Hallelujah! Praise His name, I am able to count to 100, and not become angry. Sometimes when I feel I cannot control myself, I excuse myself and go to the restroom and pray,

and ask God to remove the anger from me and fill me with His love and peace that surpasses all human understanding. And it works! I even surprise myself, even though I know I serve a mighty God. His wonders still catch me by surprise. I am sure everyone around me is just waiting for me to blow up like before, as though they are standing on a land mine and the slightest move will make it explode. But little do they know that I serve a truly wonderful Living God!

Overcoming anger is a lifelong process. There will always be new people and circumstances that will test us and push our buttons. Pressures and stresses will come, but Jesus has already overcome the world, the flesh, and the devil. "The Father is with me. I've told you this so that trusting me, you will be unshakable and assured, deeply at peace. In this godless world you will continue to experience difficulties. But take heart! I've conquered the world" (John 16:32-33 THE MESSAGE).

Let's close in prayer together.

> *Dear heavenly Father, the stubbornness of my own flesh, the corruption of this world, and the wiles of the devil are all arrayed against me in this battle to overcome anger. But I praise You, Lord Jesus, that You are the Victor over them all! You say that "those who belong to Christ Jesus have crucified the flesh with its passions and desires" and that through the cross "the world has been crucified to me, and I to the world"! I believe that Jesus has "disarmed the rulers and authorities" and has "made a public display of them, having triumphed over them."[1] Jesus, I choose to abide in You, to cling to You as my lifeline. You are my life and my strength, and Your grace is sufficient for me. May I glorify You in my body, as I seek to be conformed to Your image. I thank You for the day when this perishable body will put on imperishable glory and the victory over sin will be complete. In Your name I pray, amen.*

Steps to Freedom
in Christ

"It was for freedom that Christ set us free; there-
fore keep standing firm and do not be subject again
to a yoke of slavery" (Galatians 5:1). If you have
received Christ as your Savior, He has already set
you free through His victory over sin and death
on the cross. The question is, are you living vic-
toriously in Christ's freedom, or are you living in
bondage, however hidden or subtle?

~

C hrist offers you freedom from personal and spiritual
conflicts...freedom from sin and the negative pro-
gramming of your past...freedom from the damaging
effects of guilt and unforgiveness. Freedom opens the pathway
to knowing, loving, worshipping, and obeying God. It is the
joyful experience of living by faith according to what God says
is true and in the power of the Holy Spirit, and not carrying
out the desires of the flesh. Freedom doesn't mean perfection,
but it does mean a growing and abundant life in Christ, who
alone can meet our deepest needs for life, identity, acceptance,
security, and significance.

Regaining Your Freedom

If you are not experiencing this life of freedom, it may be
because you have not stood firm in the faith or lived according
to who you are in Christ. Somehow you have returned again

to a yoke of slavery (Galatians 5:1). Your eternal destiny is not at stake, but your daily victory is.

No matter how difficult your life might be, there is great news for you. You are not a helpless victim caught between two nearly equal but opposite spiritual superpowers. Satan is a liar and a deceiver, and the only way he can have power over you is if you believe his lies. Only God is omnipotent (all-powerful), omnipresent (always present), and omniscient (all-knowing). Sometimes the reality of sin and the presence of evil may seem more real than the presence of God, but that's part of Satan's deception. Satan is a defeated foe—and we are alive in *Christ*.

The Steps to Freedom in Christ do not set you free.[1] *Who* sets you free is Christ; *what* sets you free is your response to Him in repentance and faith. The Steps provide an opportunity for you to have an encounter with God, the Wonderful Counselor, by submitting to Him and resisting the devil (James 4:7). They are a means of resolving personal and spiritual conflicts that have kept you from experiencing the freedom and victory Christ purchased for you on the cross. Your freedom will be the result of what you choose to believe, confess, forgive, renounce, and forsake. No one else can do that for you.

The Battle for Your Mind

There is a battle going on for your mind, which is the control center of all that we think and do. The opposing thoughts you may experience as you go through these steps can affect you only if you believe them. You may have nagging thoughts like "This isn't going to work" or "God doesn't love me." Don't believe Satan's deceptions; don't pay any attention to accusing or threatening thoughts.

The battle for your mind can only be won as you personally choose truth. As you go through the process, remember that Satan is under no obligation to obey your thoughts. Only

God has complete knowledge of your mind, because He alone is omniscient (all-knowing). Find a private place where you can *verbally* process each Step. You can submit to God inwardly, but you need to resist the devil by reading each prayer aloud and by verbally renouncing, forgiving, confessing, and so on.

These steps address critical issues between you and God. You probably will find it possible to go through them on your own because Jesus is your Wonderful Counselor. However, some people do feel they need additional help. If you experience difficulty, ask your pastor or a counselor or someone familiar with the Steps to help you.

Both gaining and maintaining your freedom will be greatly enhanced if you first read *Victory Over the Darkness* and *The Bondage Breaker*. They will help you further understand the reality of the spiritual world and your relationship to it. While these steps can play a major role in your continuing process of discipleship, there is no such thing as instant maturity. Being renewed in your mind and conformed to the image of God is a lifelong process.

Regardless of the source of any difficulty you may have, you have nothing to lose and everything to gain by praying through the issues. If your problems stem from a source other than those covered in the Steps, you may need to seek professional help. The real focus here is your relationship with God. The lack of resolution of any one of these issues will affect your intimacy with Him and your daily victory in Christ.

Trust God to Lead You

Each Step is explained so you will have no problem knowing what to do. It doesn't make any difference whether or not there are evil spirits present; God is always present. If you experience any resistance, stop and pray. If you experience some mental opposition, just ignore it. It is just a thought, and it can have no power over you unless you believe it. Throughout the process, you will be asking God to lead you. He is the One who grants repentance leading to a knowledge of the truth that sets you free (2 Timothy 2:24-26). Start the Steps with the following prayer and declaration. (It is not necessary to read the words in the parentheses, which are there for clarification or reference.)

May the Lord grace you with His presence as you seek to do His will. Then, having found your freedom in Christ, you can help others experience the joy of their salvation.

Prayer

Dear heavenly Father, I acknowledge Your presence in this room and in my life. You are the only omniscient (all-knowing), omnipotent (all-powerful), and omnipresent (always present) God. I am dependent upon You, for apart from You I can do nothing. I stand in the truth that all authority in heaven and on earth has been given to the resurrected Christ, and because I am in Christ, I share that authority in order to make disciples and set captives free. I ask You to fill me with Your Holy Spirit and lead me into all truth. I pray for Your complete protection and ask for Your guidance. In Jesus' name I pray, amen.

Declaration

In the name and authority of the Lord Jesus Christ, I command Satan and all evil spirits to release me in order that I can be free to know and to choose to do the will of God. As a child of God who is seated with Christ in the heavenlies, I command every evil spirit to leave my presence. I belong to God, and the evil one cannot touch me.

Step 1: Counterfeit vs. Real

The first step toward experiencing your freedom in Christ is to renounce (verbally reject) all past or present involvement with occult practices, cult teachings, and rituals, as well as non-Christian religions.

You must renounce any activity or group that denies Jesus Christ or offers guidance through any source other than the absolute authority of the Bible. Any group that requires dark, secret initiations, ceremonies, promises, or pacts should also be renounced. Begin this step by praying aloud,

> *Dear heavenly Father, I ask You to bring to my mind anything and everything that I have done knowingly or unknowingly that involves occult, cult, or non-Christian teachings or practices. I want to experience Your freedom by renouncing all counterfeit teachings and practices. In Jesus' name I pray, amen.*

Even if you took part in something and thought it was just a game or a joke, you need to renounce it. Satan will try to take advantage of anything he can in our lives, so it is always wise to be as thorough as possible. Even if you were just standing by and watching others do it, you need to renounce your passive involvement. You may not have even realized at the time that what was going on was evil. Still, go ahead and renounce it.

If something comes to your mind and you are not sure what to do about it, trust that the Spirit of God is answering your prayer, and renounce it.

The following "Non-Christian Spiritual Checklist" covers many of the more common occult, cult, and non-Christian religious groups and practices. It is not a complete list, however. Feel free to add others that you were personally involved with.

After the checklist, there are some additional questions designed to help you become aware of other things you may need to renounce. Below those questions is a short prayer of confession and renunciation. Pray it aloud, filling in the blanks with the groups, teachings, or practices that the Holy Spirit has prompted you to renounce during this time of personal evaluation.

Non-Christian Spiritual Checklist

(Check all those that you have participated in)

❑ Out-of-body experience (astral projection)

❑ Ouija board

❑ Bloody Mary

❑ Light as a Feather (or other occult games)

❑ Table-lifting

❑ Magic Eight Ball

❑ Spells or curses

❑ Mental telepathy or mental control of others

❑ Automatic writing

❑ Trances

❑ Spirit guides

❑ Fortune telling or divination (for example, tea leaves)

❑ Tarot cards

❑ Levitation

❑ Magic—The Gathering

❑ Witchcraft or sorcery

❑ Satanism

- ❑ Palm-reading
- ❑ Astrology or horoscopes
- ❑ Hypnosis
- ❑ Seances
- ❑ Black or white magic
- ❑ Fantasy games with occult images
- ❑ Blood pacts or cutting yourself on purpose
- ❑ Objects of worship, crystals, or good-luck charms
- ❑ Sexual spirits
- ❑ Martial arts (mysticism or devotion to sensei)
- ❑ Superstitions
- ❑ Mormonism (Latter-Day Saints)
- ❑ Jehovah's Witness (Watchtower)
- ❑ New Age (books, objects, seminars, medicine)
- ❑ Masons
- ❑ Christian Science
- ❑ Mind Science cults
- ❑ The Way International
- ❑ Unification Church (Moonies)
- ❑ The Forum (est)
- ❑ Church of the Living Word
- ❑ Children of God (Children of Love)

- ☐ Church of Scientology

- ☐ Unitarian Universalism

- ☐ Silva Mind Control

- ☐ Transcendental meditation (TM)

- ☐ Yoga

- ☐ Hare Krishna

- ☐ Bahaism

- ☐ Native American spirit worship

- ☐ Islam

- ☐ Hinduism

- ☐ Buddhism (including Zen)

- ☐ Black Muslim beliefs

- ☐ Rosicrucianism

- ☐ Other non-Christian religions or cults

- ☐ Occult or violent video, computer, and online games

- ☐ Movies, TV shows, music, books, magazines, or comics that the Lord is bringing to your mind (especially those that glorified Satan, caused fear or nightmares, were gruesomely violent, or stimulated the flesh). List them below:

Below are some additional questions designed to help you become aware of other things you may need to renounce.

1. Have you ever seen, heard, or felt a spiritual being in your room?

2. Do you have recurring nightmares? Specifically renounce any accompanying fear.

3. Do you now have, or have you ever had, an imaginary friend, spirit guide, or "angel" offering you guidance or companionship? (If it has a name, renounce it by name.)

4. Have you ever heard voices in your head or had repeating, nagging thoughts such as "I'm dumb," "I'm ugly," "Nobody loves me," "I can't do anything right"— as if there were a conversation going on inside your head? (List any specific nagging thoughts.)

5. Have you ever consulted a medium, spiritist, or channeler?

6. Have you ever seen or been contacted by beings you thought were aliens?

7. Have you ever made a secret vow or pact (or inner vow, for example, "I will never...")?

8. Have you ever been involved in a satanic ritual of any kind or attended a concert in which Satan was the focus?

9. What other spiritual experiences have you had that were evil, confusing, or frightening?

Once you have completed your checklist and the questions, confess and renounce *each* item you were involved in by praying the following prayer aloud:

> *Lord, I confess that I have participated in _____, and I renounce _____. Thank You that in Christ I am forgiven.*

When you have finished confessing and renouncing each item, pray the following prayer:

> *Lord, I confess that I have participated in these wrongful practices. I know they were evil and offensive in Your sight. Thank You for Your forgiveness. I renounce any and all involvement in these wrongful practices, and I choose to believe that Satan no longer has any rightful place in my life because of those involvements. In Jesus' name I pray, amen.*

Evaluate Your Priorities

Our priorities reveal what is important to us. And a priority doesn't necessarily have to be evil in nature in order to usurp God's rightful place in our lives and thus become a false god or idol. Evaluating your priorities can help you recognize where your true allegiance is and, if necessary, restore God's rightful place in your life. (See appendix A, page 309.)

Satanic Rituals or Heavy Occult Activity

There are special renunciations for anyone who either has or suspects that he or she may have had a deeper exposure to Satanism. They provide an opportunity for you to verbally renounce any involvement (voluntary or involuntary) in the "Domain of Darkness" and then affirm your position in the "Kingdom of Light." If you have experienced heavy involvement in the occult, or think you may have been exposed to it, it is important to have an experienced friend, pastor, or counselor guide you through these special renunciations. (See appendix B, page 312.)

Step 2: Deception vs. Truth

God's Word is true, and we need to accept His truth in the innermost part of our being (Psalm 51:6). Whether or not we *feel* it is true, we need to *believe* it is true! Jesus is the truth, the Holy Spirit is the Spirit of truth, and the Word of God is truth; and we are admonished to speak the truth in love (see John 14:6; 16:13; 17:17; Ephesians 4:15).

The believer in Christ has no business deceiving others by lying, telling "white" lies, exaggerating, stretching the truth, or anything relating to falsehoods. Satan is the father of lies, and he seeks to keep people in bondage through deception. It is the truth in Jesus that sets us free (see John 8:32-36,44; 2 Timothy 2:26; Revelation 12:9.) We will find real joy and freedom when we stop living a lie and live openly in the truth. After confessing his sin, King David wrote, "How blessed [happy] is the man...in whose spirit there is no deceit!" (Psalm 32:2).

We have been called to walk in the light (1 John 1:7). When we are sure God loves and accepts us, we can be free to own up to our sins and face reality instead of running and hiding from the truth and painful circumstances.

Start this Step by praying the following prayer aloud. Don't let any threatening, opposing thoughts, such as "This is a waste of time" or "I wish I could believe this but I just can't," keep you from praying and choosing the truth. Even if this is difficult for you, keep working your way through. God will strengthen you as you rely on Him.

> *Dear heavenly Father, I know that You want me to know the truth, believe the truth, speak the truth, and live in accordance with the truth. Thank You that it is the truth that will set me free. In many ways I have been deceived by Satan, the father of lies, and I have deceived myself as well.*
>
> *Father, I pray in the name of the Lord Jesus Christ, by virtue of His shed blood and resurrection, asking You to rebuke all evil spirits that are deceiving me.*
>
> *I have trusted in Jesus alone to save me, and so I am Your forgiven child. Therefore, since You accept me just as I am in Christ, I can be free to face my sin and not try to hide. I ask for the Holy Spirit to guide me into all truth. I ask You to "search me, O God, and know my heart; try me and know my anxious thoughts; and see if there be any hurtful way in me, and lead me in the everlasting way." In the name of Jesus, who is the truth, I pray, amen.*
>
> (See Psalm 139:23-24.)

There are many ways in which Satan, "the god of this world," seeks to deceive us. Just as he did with Eve, the devil tries to convince us to rely on ourselves and to try to get our needs met through the world around us, rather than trusting in the provision of our Father in heaven.

The following exercise will help you discover ways you may have been deceived. Check each area of deception that the Lord brings to your mind and confess it, using the prayer following the list.

Ways You Can Be Deceived by the World

❑ Believing that acquiring money and things will bring lasting happiness (Matthew 13:22; 1 Timothy 6:10)

❑ Believing that excessive food and alcohol can relieve my stress and make me happy (Proverbs 20:1; 23:19-21)

❑ Believing that an attractive body and personality will get me what I want (Proverbs 31:10; 1 Peter 3:3-4)

❑ Believing that gratifying sexual lust will bring lasting satisfaction (Ephesians 4:22; 1 Peter 2:11)

❑ Believing that I can sin and get away with it without any negative consequences (Hebrews 3:12-13)

❑ Believing that I need more than what God has given me in Christ (2 Corinthians 11:2-4,13-15)

❑ Believing that I can do whatever I want and no one can touch me (Proverbs 16:18; Obadiah 3; 1 Peter 5:5)

❑ Believing that unrighteous people who refuse to accept Christ go to heaven anyway (1 Corinthians 6:9-11)

❑ Believing that I can associate with bad company and not become corrupted (1 Corinthians 15:33-34)

❏ Believing that I can read, see, or listen to anything and not be corrupted (Proverbs 4:23-27; 6:27-28; Matthew 5:28)

❏ Believing that there are no consequences on earth for my sin (Galatians 6:7-8)

❏ Believing that I must gain the approval of certain people in order to be happy (Galatians 1:10)

❏ Believing that I must measure up to certain standards in order to feel good about myself (Galatians 3:2-3; 5:1)

Lord, I confess that I have been deceived by _____. I thank You for Your forgiveness, and I commit myself to believing only Your truth. In Jesus' name, amen.

It is important to know that in addition to being deceived by the world, false teachers, and deceiving spirits, we can also deceive ourselves. Now that you are alive in Christ, completely forgiven and totally accepted, you don't need to defend yourself the way you used to. Christ is now your defense. Confess the ways the Lord shows you that you have deceived yourself or defended yourself wrongly by using the following lists and prayers of confession:

Ways to Deceive Yourself

❏ Hearing God's Word but not doing what it says (James 1:22)

❏ Saying I have no sin (1 John 1:8)

❏ Thinking I am something I'm really not (Galatians 6:3)

❏ Thinking I am wise in this worldly age (1 Corinthians 3:18-19)

❑ Thinking I can be truly religious but not bridle my tongue (James 1:26)

> *Lord, I confess that I have deceived myself by* _____. *Thank You for Your forgiveness. I commit myself to believing only Your truth. In Jesus' name, amen.*

Ways to Wrongly Defend Yourself

❑ Denial of reality (conscious or unconscious)

❑ Fantasy (escaping reality by daydreaming, TV, movies, music, computer or video games, drugs, alcohol, and so on)

❑ Emotional insulation (withdrawing from people or keeping people at a distance to avoid rejection)

❑ Regression (reverting to less threatening times)

❑ Displaced anger (taking out frustrations on innocent people)

❑ Projection (blaming others for my problems)

❑ Rationalization (making excuses for my own poor behavior)

❑ Lying (presenting a false image)

> *Lord, I confess that I have defended myself wrongly by* _____. *Thank You for Your forgiveness. I now commit myself to trusting in You to defend and protect me. In Jesus' name, amen.*

Choosing the truth may be hard for you if you have been believing lies for many years. You may need some ongoing counseling to help weed out any defense mechanisms you have relied on to cope with life. Every Christian needs to learn that Christ is the only defense he or she needs. Realizing that you are already forgiven and accepted by God through Christ will help free you up to place all your dependence on Him.

Truth About Your Father God

A major deception of the enemy is to cause us to equate our feelings about our Father God with the way our parents or other authority figures in our lives may have failed or mistreated us. If you harbor negative feelings from your past or present relationships with authority, if you find it difficult to love or feel loved by God, if you have difficulty trusting God, it is important for you to gain freedom from those misconceptions. A true understanding of God is foundational to your freedom. (See appendix C, page 314.)

Are You Anxious or Fearful?

Plaguing fears or anxiety can control our lives and prevent us from walking by faith in the surpassing victory that is ours in Christ. If you feel that fear or anxiety is preventing you from living with boldness and confidence in God's presence and power in your life, you need to renounce it specifically to gain the freedom that is yours in Christ. (See appendixes D and E, pages 316 and 321.)

Faith Must Be Based on the Truth of God's Word

Faith is the biblical response to the truth, and believing what God says is a choice we all can make. If you say, "I wish I could believe God, but I just can't," you are being deceived. Of course you can believe God because what God says is always true. Believing is something you choose to do, not something you feel like doing.

The New Age movement has twisted the concept of faith by saying that we make something true by believing it. No, we can't *create* reality with our minds; only God creates reality. We can only *face* reality with our minds. Faith is choosing to believe and act upon what God says, regardless of feelings or circumstances. Believing something does not make it true. *It's true; therefore, we choose to believe it.*

Just "having faith" is not enough. The key question is whether the object of your faith is trustworthy. If the object of your faith is not reliable, then no amount of believing will change it. That is why our faith must be on the solid rock of God and His Word. That is the only way to live a responsible and fruitful life. On the other hand, if what you believe in is not true, then you will not experience the freedom that only the truth can bring.

For generations, Christians have known the importance of publicly declaring what they believe. Read aloud the following "Statement of Truth," thinking about what you are saying. You may find it very helpful to read it daily for several weeks to renew your mind with the truth and replace any lies you may be believing.

Statement of Truth

1. *I recognize that there is only one true and living God, who exists as the Father, Son, and Holy Spirit. He is worthy of all honor, praise, and glory as the One who made all things and holds all things together.* (See Exodus 20:2-3; Colossians 1:16-17.)

2. *I recognize that Jesus Christ is the Messiah, the Word who became flesh and dwelt among us. I believe that He came to destroy the works of the devil, and that He disarmed the rulers and authorities and made a public display of them, having triumphed over them.* (See John 1:1,14; Colossians 2:15; 1 John 3:8.)

3. *I believe that God demonstrated His own love for me in that while I was still a sinner, Christ died for me. I believe that He has delivered me from the domain of darkness and transferred me to His kingdom, and in Him I have redemption, the forgiveness of sins.* (See Romans 5:8; Colossians 1:13-14.)

4. *I believe that I am now a child of God and that I am seated with Christ in the heavenlies. I believe that I was saved by the grace of God through faith, and that it was a gift and not a result of any works on my part.* (See Ephesians 2:6,8-9; 1 John 3:1-3.)

5. *I choose to be strong in the Lord and in the strength of His might. I put no confidence in the flesh, for the weapons of my warfare are not of the flesh but are divinely powerful for the destruction of my strongholds. I put on the full armor of God. I resolve to stand firm in my faith and resist the evil one.* (See 2 Corinthians 10:4; Ephesians 6:10-20; Philippians 3:3.)

6. *I believe that apart from Christ I can do nothing, so I declare my complete dependence on Him. I choose to abide in Christ in order to bear much fruit and glorify my Father. I announce to Satan that Jesus is my Lord. I reject any and all counterfeit gifts or works of Satan in my life.* (See John 15:5,8; 1 Corinthians 12:3.)

7. *I believe that the truth will set me free and that Jesus is the truth. If He sets me free, I will be free indeed. I recognize that walking in the light is the only path of true fellowship with God and man. Therefore, I stand against all of Satan's deception by taking every thought captive in obedience to Christ. I declare that the Bible is the only authoritative standard for truth and life.* (See John 8:32,36; 14:6; 2 Corinthians 10:5; 2 Timothy 3:15-17; 1 John 1:3-7.)

8. *I choose to present my body to God as a living and holy sacrifice and the members of my body as instruments of righteousness. I choose to renew my mind by the living Word of God in order that I may prove that the will of God is good, acceptable, and perfect. I have put off the old self with its evil practices and have put on the new self. I declare myself to be a new creation in Christ.* (See Romans 6:13; 12:1-2; 2 Corinthians 5:17; Colossians 3:9-10 NIV.)

9. *By faith, I choose to be filled with the Spirit so that I can be guided into all truth. I choose to walk by the Spirit so that I will not carry out the desires of the flesh.* (See John 16:13; Galatians 5:16; Ephesians 5:18.)

10. *I renounce all selfish goals and choose the ultimate goal of love. I choose to obey the two greatest commandments: to love the Lord my God with all my heart, soul, mind, and strength and to love my neighbor as myself.* (See Matthew 22:37-39; 1 Timothy 1:5.)

11. *I believe that the Lord Jesus has all authority in heaven and on earth, and He is the head over all rule and authority. I am complete in Him. I believe that Satan and his demons are subject to me in Christ since I am a member of Christ's body. Therefore, I obey the command to submit to God and resist the devil, and I command Satan in the name of Jesus Christ to leave my presence.* (See Matthew 28:18; Ephesians 1:19-23; Colossians 2:10; James 4:7.)

Step 3: Bitterness vs. Forgiveness

We need to forgive others so Satan cannot take advantage of us (2 Corinthians 2:10-11). We are commanded to get rid of all bitterness in our lives and forgive others as we have been forgiven (Ephesians 4:31-32). Ask God to bring to your mind the people you need to forgive by praying the following prayer aloud:

> *Dear heavenly Father, I thank You for the riches of Your kindness, forbearance, and patience toward me, knowing that Your kindness has led me to repentance. I confess that I have not shown that same kindness and patience toward those who have hurt or offended me. Instead, I have held on to my anger, bitterness, and resentment toward them. Please bring to my mind all the people I need to forgive in order that I may now do so. In Jesus' name, amen.*

(See Romans 2:4.)

On a separate sheet of paper, list the names of people who come to your mind. At this point don't question whether you need to forgive them or not. If a name comes to mind, just write it down.

Often we hold things against ourselves as well, punishing ourselves for wrong choices we've made in the past. Write "myself" at the bottom of your list if you need to forgive yourself. Forgiving yourself is accepting the truth that God has already forgiven you in Christ. If God forgives you, you can forgive yourself!

Also write down "thoughts against God" at the bottom of your list. Obviously, God has never done anything wrong so we don't have to forgive Him. Sometimes, however, we harbor angry thoughts against Him because He did not do what we wanted Him to do. Those feelings of anger or resentment against God can become a wall between us and Him, so we must let them go.

Before you begin working through the process of forgiving those on your list, take a few minutes to review what forgiveness is and what it is not.

- *Forgiveness is not forgetting.* People who want to forget all that was done to them will find they cannot do it. Don't put off forgiving those who have hurt you, hoping the pain will one day go away. Once you choose to forgive someone, *then* Christ can come and begin to heal you of your hurts. But the healing cannot begin until you first forgive.

- *Forgiveness is a choice, a decision of your will.* Since God requires you to forgive, it is something you can do. Sometimes it is very hard to forgive someone because we naturally want revenge for the things we have suffered. Forgiveness seems to go against our sense of what is right and fair. So we hold on to our anger, punishing people over and over again in our minds for the pain they've caused us.

  But we are told by God never to take our own revenge (Romans 12:19). Let God deal with the person. Let him or her off your hook because as long as you refuse to forgive someone, you are still hooked to that person. You are still chained to your past, bound up in your bitterness. By forgiving, you let the other person off your hook—but he or she is not off God's hook. You must trust that *God* will deal with the person justly and fairly, something *you* simply cannot do.

  "But you don't know how much this person hurt me!" you might say. You're right. We don't, but Jesus does, and He tells you to forgive others for your sake. Until you let go of your anger and hatred, the person is still hurting you. You can't turn back the clock and change the past, but you can be free from it. You can stop the pain, but there is only one way to do it—forgive from your heart. Forgive others for *your* sake so you can be free from your past.

- *Forgiveness is agreeing to live with the consequences of another person's sin.* You are going to live with those consequences anyway whether you like it or not, so the only choice you have is whether you will do so in the *bondage of bitterness* or in the *freedom of forgiveness*. No one truly forgives without accepting and suffering the pain of another person's sin. That can seem unfair, and you may wonder, *Where is the justice?* But the cross makes forgiveness legally and morally right. Jesus died once, for *all* our sins.

  Jesus took the *eternal* consequences of sin upon Himself. God "made Him who knew no sin to be sin on our behalf, so that we might become the righteousness of God in Him" (2 Corinthians 5:21). We, however, often suffer the temporary consequences of other people's sins. That is simply a harsh reality of life that all of us have to face.

- *Do not wait for the other person to ask for your forgiveness.* Remember, Jesus did not wait for those who were crucifying Him to apologize before He forgave them. Even while they mocked Him and jeered at Him, He prayed, "Father, forgive them; for they do not know what they are doing" (Luke 23:34).

- *Forgive from your heart.* Allow God to bring the painful memories to the surface; acknowledge how you feel toward those who've hurt you. If your forgiveness doesn't touch the emotional core of your life, it will be incomplete. Too often we're afraid of the pain so we bury our emotions deep down inside us. Let God bring them to the surface so He can begin to heal those damaged emotions.

- *Forgiveness is choosing not to hold someone's sin against him or her anymore.* It is common for bitter people to bring up past issues with those who have hurt them. They want those others to feel as bad as they do! But we must let go of the past and choose to reject any thought of revenge.

This doesn't mean you continue to put up with the future sins of others. God does not tolerate sin, and neither should you. Don't allow yourself to be continually abused by others. Take a stand against sin while continuing to exercise grace and forgiveness toward those who have hurt you. If you need help setting scriptural boundaries to protect yourself from further abuse, talk to a trusted friend, counselor, or pastor.

- *Don't wait until you feel like forgiving.* You will never get there. Make the hard choice to forgive even if you don't feel like it. Once you choose to forgive, Satan will lose his power over you in that area, and God will heal your damaged emotions. *Freedom* is what you will gain right now—not necessarily an immediate change in feelings

Now you are ready to begin. Starting with the first person on your list, make the choice to forgive him or her for every painful memory that comes to your mind. Stay with that individual until you are sure you have dealt with all the remembered pain. Then work your way down the list in the same way.

As you begin forgiving people, God may bring to your mind painful memories you've totally forgotten. Let Him do this even if it hurts. God wants you to be free; forgiving those people is the only way. Don't try to excuse the offender's behavior, even if it is someone you are really close to.

Don't say, "Lord, please help me to forgive." He is already helping you and will be with you all the way through the process. Don't say, "Lord, I want to forgive…" because that bypasses the hard choice we have to make. Say, "Lord, I *choose* to forgive…."

For every painful memory you have about each person on your list, pray aloud,

> *Lord, I choose to forgive (<u>name the person</u>) for (<u>what they did or failed to do</u>), which made me feel (<u>share the painful feelings</u>).*

After you have forgiven each person for all the offenses that came to your mind, and after you have honestly expressed how you felt, conclude this step by praying aloud,

> *Lord, I choose not to hold onto my resentment. I thank You for setting me free from the bondage of my bitterness. I relinquish my right to seek revenge and ask You to heal my damaged emotions. I now ask You to bless those who have hurt me. In Jesus' name, I pray, amen.*

Step 4: Rebellion vs. Submission

We live in a rebellious age. Many people only obey laws and authorities when it is convenient for them. There is a general lack of respect for those in government, and Christians are often as guilty as the rest of society in fostering a critical, rebellious spirit. Certainly, we are not expected to agree with our leaders' policies that are in violation of Scripture, but we are to "honor all people; love the brotherhood, fear God, honor the king" (1 Peter 2:17).

God established all governing authorities and requires us to be submissive (Romans 13:1-5; 1 Peter 2:13-17). Rebelling against God and the authorities He has set up is a very serious sin, for it gives Satan an opportunity to attack. God requires more, however, than just the outward appearance of submission; He wants us to sincerely submit from the heart to those in authority. It is for your spiritual protection that you live under the authority of God and those He has placed over you.

The Bible makes it clear that we have two main responsibilities toward those in authority over us: to pray for them, and to submit to them (Romans 13:1-7; 1 Timothy 2:1-2). To commit yourself to that godly lifestyle, pray the following prayer aloud from your heart:

> *Dear heavenly Father, You have said in the Bible that rebellion is the same thing as witchcraft and as bad as idolatry. I know I have not always been submissive, but instead, I have rebelled in my heart against You and against those You have placed in authority over me. I pray that You would show me all the ways I have been rebellious. I choose now to adopt a submissive spirit and a servant's heart. In Jesus' precious name I pray, amen.*

(See 1 Samuel 15:23.)

Being under authority is clearly an act of faith! By submitting, you are trusting God to work through His established lines of authority even when those who exercise that authority are harsh or unkind or tell you to do something you don't want to do. There may be times when those over you abuse their authority and break the laws that are ordained by God for the protection of innocent people. In those cases, you will need to seek help from a *higher authority* for your protection. The laws in your state may require that such abuse be reported to the police or other governmental agency. If there is continuing abuse (physical, mental, emotional, or sexual) where you live, you may need further counseling help to deal with that situation.

If authorities abuse their position by requiring you to break God's law or compromise your commitment to Him, then you need to obey God rather than man (Acts 4:19-20). Be careful, though. Don't assume that an authority is violating God's Word just because he or she is telling you to do something you don't like. We all need to adopt a humble, submissive spirit to one another in the fear of Christ (Ephesians 5:21). In addition, however, God has set up specific lines of authority to protect us and to give order to our daily lives.

As you prayerfully look over the next list, allow the Lord to show you any *specific* ways in which you have been rebellious to authority. Then, using the prayer of confession that follows the list, specifically confess whatever the Lord brings to your mind.

❑ Civil government (including traffic laws, tax laws, attitude toward government officials) (Romans 13:1-7; 1 Timothy 2:1-4; 1 Peter 2:13-17)

❑ Parents, stepparents, or legal guardians (Ephesians 6:1-3)

❑ Teachers, coaches, school officials (Romans 13:1-4)

❑ Employers, both past and present (1 Peter 2:18-23)

❑ Husband (1 Peter 3:1-4) or wife (Ephesians 5:21; 1 Peter 3:7) [*Note to Husbands:* Take a moment and ask the Lord if your lack of love for your wife could be fostering a rebellious spirit within her. If so, confess that now as a violation of Ephesians 5:22-33.]

❑ Church leaders (Hebrews 13:7)

❑ God (Daniel 9:5,9)

For each way in which the Spirit of God brings to your mind that you have been rebellious, use the following prayer to specifically confess that sin:

> *Lord, I confess that I have been rebellious toward (name) by (say what you did specifically). Thank You for forgiving my rebellion. I choose now to be submissive and obedient to Your Word. By the shed blood of the Lord Jesus Christ, I pray that all ground gained by evil*

spirits in my life due to my rebellion would be canceled.
In Jesus' name I pray, amen.

Step 5: Pride vs. Humility

Pride kills. Pride says, "I don't need God or anyone else's help. I can handle it by myself." Oh no, you can't! We absolutely need God, and we need each other. The apostle Paul wisely wrote, "[we] worship in the Spirit of God and glory in Christ Jesus and put *no confidence in the flesh*" (Philippians 3:3, emphasis added). That is a good definition of humility: putting no confidence in the flesh, that is, in ourselves, but rather being *"strong in the Lord and in the strength of His might"* (Ephesians 6:10, emphasis added). Humility is confidence properly placed in God.

Proverbs 3:5-7 expresses a similar thought: "Trust in the LORD with all your heart and do not lean on your own understanding. In all your ways acknowledge Him, and He will make your paths straight. Do not be wise in your own eyes; fear the LORD and turn away from evil." (James 4:6-10 and 1 Peter 5:1-10 also warn us that serious spiritual problems will result when we are proud.) Use the following prayer to express your commitment to living humbly before God:

> *Dear heavenly Father, You have said that pride goes before destruction and an arrogant spirit before stumbling. I confess that I have been thinking mainly of myself and not of others. I have not denied myself, picked up my cross daily, and followed You. As a result, I have given ground to the devil in my life. I have sinned by believing I could be happy and successful on my own. I confess that I have placed my will before Yours, and I have centered my life around myself instead of You.*
>
> *I repent of my pride and selfishness and pray that all ground gained in my members by the enemies of the Lord Jesus Christ would be canceled. I choose to rely on*

> *the Holy Spirit's power and guidance so that I will do nothing from selfishness or empty conceit. With humility of mind, I will regard others as more important than myself. And I choose to make You, Lord, the center of my life.*
>
> *Please show me now all the specific ways in which I have lived my life in pride. Enable me through love to serve others and in honor to prefer others. I ask all of this in the gentle and humble name of Jesus, my Lord, amen.*

(See Proverbs 16:18; Matthew 6:33; 16:24;
Romans 12:10; Philippians 2:3.)

Having made that commitment to God in prayer, now allow Him to show you any specific ways in which you have lived in a proud manner. The following list may help you. As the Lord brings to your mind areas of pride, use the prayer on the next page to guide you in your confession.

❑ Having a stronger desire to do my will than God's will

❑ Leaning too much on my own understanding and experience rather than seeking God's guidance through prayer and His Word

❑ Relying on my own strengths and abilities instead of depending on the power of the Holy Spirit

❑ Being more concerned about controlling others than about developing self-control

❑ Being too busy doing "important" things to take time to do little things for others

❑ Having a tendency to think that I have no needs

❑ Finding it hard to admit when I am wrong

❑ Being more concerned about pleasing people than pleasing God

❑ Being concerned about getting the credit I feel I deserve

❑ Thinking I am more humble, spiritual, religious, or devoted than others

❑ Being driven to obtain recognition by attaining degrees, titles, or positions

❑ Often feeling that my needs are more important than another person's needs

❑ Considering myself better than others because of my academic, artistic, or athletic abilities and accomplishments

❑ Other ways I have thought more highly of myself than I should (list here):

For each of the above areas that has been true in your life, pray aloud,

> *Lord, I agree I have been proud in (name the area). Thank You for forgiving me for my pride. I choose to humble myself before You and others. I choose to place all my confidence in You and none in my flesh. In Jesus' name, amen.*

Dealing with Prejudice and Bigotry

Prejudice and bigotry are other forms of pride, ones that are all too common. Our first reaction might be to deny that these attitudes could be true of us. But if we have any awareness of prideful attitudes toward others, this would be a good cause for us to prayerfully allow God to search our heart and bring to the surface anything that needs to be dealt with. (See appendix F, page 327.)

Step 6: Bondage vs. Freedom

Many times we feel trapped in a vicious cycle of "sin-confess-sin-confess" that never seems to end. We can become very discouraged and end up just giving up and giving in to the sins of our flesh. To find freedom we must follow James 4:7: "Submit therefore to God. Resist the devil and he will flee from you." We submit to God by confession of sin and repentance (turning away from sin). We resist the devil by rejecting his lies. Instead, we walk in the truth and put on the full armor of God (see Ephesians 6:10-20).

Gaining freedom from sin that has become a habit often requires help from a trusted brother or sister in Christ. James 5:16 says, "Confess your sins to one another and pray for one another so that you may be healed. The effective prayer of a righteous man can accomplish much." Sometimes the assurance of 1 John 1:9 is enough: "If we confess our sins, He is faithful and righteous to forgive us our sins and to cleanse us from all unrighteousness."

Remember, confession is not saying, "I'm sorry"; it is openly admitting, "I did it." Whether you need help from other people or just the accountability of walking in the light before God, pray the following prayer aloud:

> *Dear heavenly Father, You have told me to put on the Lord Jesus Christ and make no provision for the flesh in regard to its lust. I confess that I have given in to fleshly lusts that wage war against my soul. I thank You that in Christ my sins are already forgiven, but I have broken Your holy law and given the devil a chance to wage war in my body. I come to You now to confess and renounce these sins of the flesh so that I might be cleansed and set free from the bondage of sin. Please reveal to my mind all the sins of the flesh I have committed and the ways I have grieved the Holy Spirit. In Jesus' holy name I pray, amen.*

(See Proverbs 28:13 NIV; Romans 6:12-13; 13:14; 2 Corinthians 4:2; James 4:1; 1 Peter 2:11; 5:8.)

The following list contains many sins of the flesh, but a prayerful examination of Mark 7:20-23, Galatians 5:19-21, Ephesians 4:25-31, and other Scripture passages will help you to be even more thorough. Look over the list below and the Scriptures just listed and ask the Holy Spirit to bring to your mind the ones you need to confess. He may reveal to you others as well. For each one the Lord shows you, pray a prayer of confession from your heart. There is a sample prayer following the list. (Note: Sexual sins, divorce, eating disorders, substance abuse, abortion, suicidal tendencies, and perfectionism will be dealt with later in this Step. Further counseling help may be necessary to find complete healing and freedom in these and other areas.)

❑ Stealing

❑ Quarreling or fighting

❑ Jealousy or envy

❑ Complaining or criticism

☐ Sarcasm

☐ Lustful actions

☐ Gossip or slander

☐ Swearing

☐ Apathy or laziness

☐ Lying

☐ Hatred

☐ Anger

☐ Lustful thoughts

☐ Drunkenness

☐ Cheating

☐ Procrastination

☐ Greed or materialism

☐ Others:

Lord, I confess that I have committed the sin of (name the sin). Thank You for Your forgiveness and cleansing. I now turn away from this sin and turn to You, Lord. Strengthen me by Your Holy Spirit to obey You. In Jesus' name, amen.

Wrong Sexual Use of Our Body

It is our responsibility not to allow sin to have control over our bodies. We must not use our bodies or another person's body as an instrument of unrighteousness (see Romans 6:12-13). Sexual immorality is not only sin against God but is sin against your body, the temple of the Holy Spirit (1 Corinthians 6:18-19). To find freedom from sexual bondage, begin by praying the following prayer:

> *Lord, I ask You to bring to my mind every sexual use of my body as an instrument of unrighteousness so that, in Christ, I can renounce these sexual sins and break the bondage of each of them in Christ. In Jesus' name I pray, amen.*

As the Lord brings to your mind every wrong sexual use of your body, whether it was done to you (rape, incest, sexual molestation) or willingly by you (pornography, masturbation, sexual immorality), renounce *every* occasion.

> *Lord, I renounce (<u>name the specific use of your body</u>) with (<u>name any other person involved</u>). I ask You to break that sinful bond with (<u>name</u>).*

After you are finished, commit your body to the Lord by praying,

> *Lord, I renounce all these uses of my body as an instrument of unrighteousness, and I admit to any willful participation. I choose now to present my eyes, mouth, mind, heart, hands, feet, and sexual organs to You as instruments of righteousness. I present my whole body to You as a living sacrifice, holy and acceptable. I choose to reserve the sexual use of my body for marriage only.*
>
> *I reject the devil's lie that my body is not clean or that it is dirty or in any way unacceptable to You as a result of my past sexual experiences. Lord, thank You that You have totally cleansed and forgiven me and that You love and accept me just the way I am. Therefore,*

I choose now to accept myself and my body as clean in
Your eyes. In Jesus' name, amen.

(See Hebrews 13:4)

Special Prayers for Special Needs

Divorce

Lord, I confess to You any part that I played in my
divorce (ask the Lord to show you specifics). Thank You
for Your forgiveness, and I choose not to condemn
myself. I renounce the lie that divorce affects my identity in Christ. I am a child of God, and I reject the lie
that I am a second-class Christian because of the
divorce. I reject the lie that says I am worthless and
unlovable and that my life is empty and meaningless. I
am complete in Christ who loves me and accepts me just
as I am. Lord, I commit the healing of all hurts in my
life to You, as I have chosen to forgive those who have
hurt me. I also place my future into Your hands and
choose to seek human companionship in Your church.
(If married—) I surrender completely to Your presence
and power in my marriage. (If single—) I choose to
trust you, Lord, to provide another spouse if it is Your
will. And if not, I know that Your grace is sufficent for
me. I pray all this in the healing name of Jesus, my
Savior, Lord, and closest friend, amen.

Homosexuality

Lord, I renounce the lie that You have created me or
anyone else to be homosexual, and I agree that in Your
Word You clearly forbid homosexual behavior. I choose
to accept myself as a child of God, and I thank You that
You created me as a man (woman). I renounce all
homosexual thoughts, urges, drives, and acts, and

renounce all ways that Satan has used these things to pervert my relationships. I announce that I am free in Christ to relate to the opposite sex and my own sex in the way that You intended. In Jesus' name, amen.

Abortion

Lord, I confess that I was not a proper guardian and keeper of the life You entrusted to me, and I admit that as sin. Thank You that, because of Your forgiveness, I can forgive myself. I recognize that the child is in Your caring hands for all eternity. In Jesus' name, amen.

Suicidal Tendencies

Lord, I renounce all suicidal thoughts and any attempts I've made to take my own life or in any way injure myself. I renounce the lie that life is hopeless and that I can find peace and freedom by taking my own life. Satan is a thief and comes to steal, kill, and destroy. I choose life in Christ, who said He came to give me life and give it abundantly. Thank You for Your forgiveness that allows me to forgive myself. I choose to believe that there is always hope in Christ. In Jesus' name I pray, amen.

(See John 10:10.)

Drivenness and Perfectionism

Lord, I renounce the lie that my self-worth is dependent upon my ability to perform. I announce the truth that my identity and sense of worth is found in who I am as Your child. I renounce seeking the approval and acceptance of other people, and I choose to believe that I am already approved and accepted in Christ because *of His death and resurrection for me. I choose to believe the truth that I have been saved, not by deeds done in righteousness, but according to Your mercy. I choose to believe that I am no longer under the curse of the law because Christ became a curse for me. I receive the free gift of life in Christ and choose to abide in Him. I renounce striving for perfection by living under the law. By Your grace, heavenly Father, I choose from this day forward to walk by faith in the power of Your Holy Spirit according to what You have said is true. In Jesus' name, amen.*

Eating Disorders or Self-Mutilation

Lord, I renounce the lie that my value as a person is dependent upon my appearance or performance. I renounce cutting or abusing myself, vomiting, using laxatives, or starving myself as a means of being in control, altering my appearance, or trying to cleanse myself of evil. I announce that only the blood of the Lord Jesus cleanses me from sin. I realize I have been bought with a price and my body, the temple of the Holy Spirit, belongs to God. Therefore, I choose to glorify God in my body. I renounce the lie that I am evil or that any part of my body is evil. Thank You that You accept me just the way I am in Christ. In Jesus' name I pray, amen.

Substance Abuse

Lord, I confess that I have misused substances (alcohol, tobacco, food, prescription or street drugs) for the purpose of pleasure, to escape reality, or to cope with difficult problems. I confess that I have abused my body and programmed my mind in a harmful way. I have quenched the Holy Spirit as well. Thank You for forgiving me. I renounce any satanic connection or influence in my life that has come through my misuse of food or chemicals. I cast my anxieties onto Christ, who loves me. I commit myself to yield no longer to substance abuse; instead I choose to allow the Holy Spirit to direct and empower me. In Jesus' name, amen.

Step 7: Curses vs. Blessings

The next step to freedom is to renounce the sins of your ancestors as well as any satanic assignments directed toward you or your ministry. In giving the Ten Commandments, God said,

> You shall not make for yourself an idol, or any likeness of what is in heaven above or on the earth beneath or in the water under the earth. You shall not worship them or serve them; for I, the LORD your God, am a jealous God, visiting the iniquity of the fathers on the children, on the third and the fourth generations of those who hate Me, but showing lovingkindness to thousands, to those who love Me and keep My commandments (Exodus 20:4-6).

Iniquities can be passed on from one generation to the next if you don't renounce the sins of your ancestors and claim your new spiritual heritage in Christ. You are not guilty for the sin of any ancestor, but because of their sin, you may be genetically predisposed to certain strengths or weaknesses and influenced by the physical and spiritual atmosphere in which you were raised. These conditions can contribute toward causing you to struggle with a particular sin. Ask the Lord to show you specifically what sins are characteristic of your family by praying the following prayer:

Dear heavenly Father, I ask You to reveal to my mind now all the sins of my ancestors that are being passed down through family lines. I want to be free from those influences and walk in my new identity as a child of God. In Jesus' name, amen.

As the Lord brings those areas of family sin to your mind, list them here. You will be specifically renouncing them later in this step.

1. _____

2. _____

3. _____

4. _____

5. _____

6. _____

7. _____

8. _____

9. _____

10. _____

In order to walk free from the sins of your ancestors and any assignments targeted against you, read the following declaration and pray the following prayer aloud. Remember, you have all the authority and protection you need in Christ to take your stand against such activity.

Declaration

I here and now reject and disown all the sins of my ancestors. I specifically renounce the sins of (name the areas of family sin the Lord revealed to you). As one who has now been delivered from the domain of darkness into the kingdom of God's Son, I choose to believe that all the sins and iniquities of my ancestors have been confessed and that I now stand forgiven and cleansed in Christ. As one who has been crucified and raised with Jesus Christ and who sits with Him in heavenly places, I renounce all satanic assignments that are directed toward me and my ministry. I choose to believe that Jesus has broken every curse that Satan and his workers have put on me. I announce to Satan and all his forces that Christ became a curse for me when He died for my sins on the cross. I reject any and every way in which Satan may claim ownership of me. I belong to the Lord Jesus Christ, who purchased me with His own blood. I reject all blood sacrifices whereby Satan may claim ownership of me. I declare myself to be fully and eternally signed over and committed to the Lord Jesus Christ. By the authority I have in Christ, I now command every enemy of the Lord Jesus to leave my presence. I commit myself to my heavenly Father to do His will from this day forward.

(See Galatians 3:13.)

Prayer

Dear heavenly Father, I come to You as Your child, bought out of slavery to sin by the blood of the Lord Jesus Christ. You are the Lord of the universe and the Lord of my life. I submit my body to You as an instrument of righteousness, a living and holy sacrifice, that I may glorify You in my body. I now ask You to fill me with the Holy Spirit. I commit myself to the renewing of my mind in order to prove that Your will is good, acceptable, and perfect for me. All this I pray in the name and authority of the risen Lord Jesus Christ, amen.

Maintaining Your Freedom

Even after finding freedom in Christ by going through these seven steps, you may come under attack hours, days, or even weeks later. But you don't have to yield to the world, the flesh, or the devil. As you continue to walk in humble submission to God, you can resist the devil and he *will* flee from you (James 4:7).

The devil is attracted to sin like flies are attracted to garbage. Get rid of the garbage and the flies will depart for smellier places. In the same way, walk in the truth, confessing all sin and forgiving those who hurt you, and the devil will have no place in your life.

Realize that one victory does not mean that the battles are over. Freedom must be maintained. After completing these steps to freedom, one happy lady asked, "Will I always be like this?" The answer is, she will maintain her freedom as long as she remains in a right relationship with God. Even if she slips and falls, she should know how to get right with God again.

One victim of horrible atrocities shared this illustration:

> It's like being forced to play a game with an ugly stranger in my own home. I kept losing and wanting to quit but the ugly stranger wouldn't let me. Finally, I called the police (a higher authority), and they came and escorted the stranger out. He knocked on the door trying to regain entry, but this time I recognized his voice and didn't let him in.

What a beautiful picture of gaining and keeping our freedom in Christ! We call upon Jesus, the ultimate authority, and He escorts the enemy of our souls away from us.

How to Maintain Your Freedom

Your freedom must be maintained. We cannot emphasize that enough. You have won a very important battle in an ongoing war. Freedom will continue to be yours as long as you keep choosing the truth and standing firm in the strength of the Lord. If you become aware of lies you have believed, renounce them and choose the truth. If new, painful memories surface, forgive those who hurt you. If the Lord shows you other areas of sin in your life, confess those promptly. This tool can serve as a constant guide for you in dealing with the things God points out to you. Some people have found it helpful to walk through the Steps to Freedom in Christ again. As you do, read the instructions carefully.

For your encouragement and growth, we recommend these additional books: *Victory Over the Darkness* (or the youth version, *Stomping Out the Darkness*), *Walking in Freedom* (a 21-day follow-up devotional), and *Living Free in Christ*. To maintain your freedom in Christ, we strongly suggest the following as well.

1. Be involved in a loving, caring church fellowship where you can be open and honest with others and where God's truth is taught with grace.

2. Read and meditate on the Bible daily. Memorize key verses from the Steps to Freedom in Christ. You may want to read the "Statement of Truth" (see Step 2) aloud daily and study the verses mentioned.

3. Learn to take every thought captive to the obedience of Christ. Assume responsibility for your thought life. Don't let your mind become passive. Reject all lies, choose to focus on the truth, and stand firm in your true identity as a child of God in Christ.

4. Don't drift back to old patterns of thinking, feeling, and acting. This can happen very easily if you become spiritually and mentally lazy. If you are struggling with walking in the truth, share your battles openly with a trusted friend who will pray for you and encourage you to stand firm.

5. Don't expect other people to fight your battles for you, however. They can help you, but they can't think, pray, read the Bible, or choose the truth for you.

6. Commit yourself to daily prayer. Prayer demonstrates a life of trusting in and depending on God. You can pray the following prayers often and with confidence. Let the words come from your heart as well as your lips and feel free to change them to make them your prayers.

Daily Prayer and Declaration

Dear heavenly Father, I praise You and honor You as my Lord and Savior. You are in control of all things. I thank You that You are always with me and will never leave me nor forsake me. You are the only all-powerful and only wise God. You are kind and loving in all Your ways. I love You and thank You that I am united with Christ and spiritually alive in Him. I choose not to love the world or the things in the world, and I crucify the flesh and all its passions.

Thank You for the life I now have in Christ. I ask You to fill me with the Holy Spirit so I may say no to sin and yes to You. I declare my total dependence upon You, and I take my stand against Satan and all his lying ways. I choose to believe the truth of Your Word despite what my feelings may say. I refuse to be discouraged, because You are the God of all hope. Nothing is too difficult for You. I am confident that You will supply all my needs as I seek to live according to Your Word. I thank You that I can be content and live a responsible life through Christ who strengthens me.

I now take my stand against Satan and command him and all his evil spirits to depart from me. I choose to put on Your full armor, the armor of God, so I may be able to stand firm against all the devil's schemes. I submit my body as a living and holy sacrifice to You, and I choose to renew my mind by Your living Word. By so doing I will be able to prove that Your will is good, acceptable, and perfect for me. In the name of my Lord and Savior, Jesus Christ, amen.

Bedtime Prayer

Thank You, Lord, that You have brought me into Your family and have blessed me with every spiritual blessing in the heavenly places in Christ Jesus. Thank You for this time of renewal and refreshment through sleep. I accept it as one of Your blessings for Your children, and I trust You to guard my mind and my body during my sleep.

As I have thought about You and Your truth during the day, I choose to let those good thoughts continue in my mind while I am asleep. I commit myself to You for Your protection against every attempt of Satan and his demons to attack me during sleep. Guard my mind from nightmares. I renounce all fear and cast every anxiety upon You, Lord. I commit myself to You as my rock, my fortress, and my strong tower. May Your peace be upon this place of rest now. In the strong name of the Lord Jesus Christ I pray, amen.

Prayer for Cleansing Home, Apartment, or Room

After removing and destroying all objects of false worship, pray this prayer aloud in every room if necessary:

Heavenly Father, I acknowledge that You are the Lord of heaven and earth. In Your sovereign power and love, You have given me all things to enjoy. Thank You for this place to live. I claim my home as a place of spiritual safety for me and my family and ask for

Your protection from all the attacks of the enemy. As a child of God, raised up and seated with Christ in the heavenly places, I command every evil spirit claiming ground in this place, based on the activities of past or present occupants, including me, to leave and never return. I renounce all curses and spells directed against this place. I ask You, heavenly Father, to post Your holy, warring angels around this place to guard it from any and all attempts of the enemy to enter and disturb Your purposes for me and my family. I thank You, Lord, for doing this, in the name of the Lord Jesus Christ, amen.

Prayer for Living in a Non-Christian Environment

After removing and destroying all objects of false worship from your possession, pray this aloud in the place where you live:

Thank You, heavenly Father, for a place to live and to be renewed by sleep. I ask You to set aside my room (or portion of this room) as a place of spiritual safety for me. I renounce any allegiance given to false gods or spirits by other occupants. I renounce any claim to this room (space) by Satan based on the activities of past or present occupants, including me. On the basis of my position as a child of God and joint-heir with Christ, who has all authority in heaven and on earth, I command all evil spirits to leave this place and never return. I ask You, heavenly Father, to station Your holy, warring angels to protect me while I live here. In Jesus' mighty name I pray, amen.

Continue to walk in the truth that your identity and sense of worth comes through who you are in Christ. Renew your mind with the truth that your *acceptance, security,* and *significance* are in Christ alone.

We recommend that you meditate on the following truths daily. Try reading the entire list aloud, morning and evening, for the next few weeks. Think about what you are reading and let your heart rejoice in the truth.

In Christ

I renounce the lie that I am rejected, unloved, dirty, or shameful, because in Christ I am completely accepted. God says...

I am His child (John 1:12)

I am Christ's friend (John 15:15)

I have been justified (Romans 5:1)

I am united with the Lord, and I am one spirit with Him (1 Corinthians 6:17)

I have been bought with a price: I belong to God (1 Corinthians 6:19-20)

I am a member of Christ's body (1 Corinthians 12:27)

I am a saint, a holy one (Ephesians 1:1)

I have been adopted as God's child (Ephesians 1:5)

I have direct access to God through the Holy Spirit (Ephesians 2:18)

I have been redeemed and forgiven of all my sins (Colossians 1:14)

I am complete in Christ (Colossians 2:10)

I renounce the lie that I am guilty, unprotected, alone, or abandoned, because in Christ I am totally secure. God says...

I am free forever from condemnation (Romans 8:1-2)

I am assured that all things work together for good
(Romans 8:28)

I am free from any condemning charges against me
(Romans 8:31-34)

I cannot be separated from the love of God (Romans
8:35-39)

I have been established, anointed, and sealed by God
(2 Corinthians 1:21-22)

I am confident that the good work God has begun in
me will be perfected (Philippians 1:6)

I am a citizen of heaven (Philippians 3:20)

I am hidden with Christ in God (Colossians 3:3)

I have not been given a spirit of fear, but of power, love,
and a sound mind (2 Timothy 1:7)

I can find grace and mercy to help in time of need
(Hebrews 4:16)

I am born of God and the evil one cannot touch me
(1 John 5:18)

*I renounce the lie that I am worthless, inadequate, helpless, or
hopeless because in Christ I am deeply significant. God says...*

I am the salt of the earth and the light of the world
(Matthew 5:13-14)

I am a branch of the true vine, Jesus, a channel of His
life (John 15:1,5)

I have been chosen and appointed by God to bear fruit
(John 15:16)

I am a personal, Spirit-empowered witness of Christ's (Acts 1:8)

I am a temple of God (1 Corinthians 3:16)

I am a minister of reconciliation for God (2 Corinthians 5:17-21)

I am God's co-worker (2 Corinthians 6:1)

I am seated with Christ in the heavenly realm (Ephesians 2:6)

I am God's workmanship, created for good works (Ephesians 2:10)

I may approach God with freedom and confidence (Ephesians 3:12)

I can do all things through Christ who strengthens me! (Philippians 4:13)

I am not the great "I Am,"
but by the grace of God I am what I am.

(See Exodus 3:14; John 8:24,28,58; 1 Corinthians 15:10.)

Seeking the Forgiveness of Others

Now that you have found your freedom in Christ, there may be an additional step for you to take. In Step 3 you dealt with the need to forgive others who have offended you, which is the resolution a problem between you and God. You may also need to seek the forgiveness of those you have offended. You need to know if and when to take that further step, and how to do it in a wise and godly manner. (See appendix G, page 329.)

Appendix A
to the Steps to Freedom in Christ

Evaluating Your Priorities

~

Who or what is most important to us becomes that which we worship. Our thoughts, love, devotion, trust, adoration, and obedience are directed to this object above all others. Our worship may end up being directed toward the true God or turned away toward other "gods."

We were created to worship the true and living God. In fact, the Father seeks those who will worship Him in spirit and in truth (John 4:23). As children of God, "we know also that the Son of God has come and has given us understanding, so that we may know him who is true. And we are in him who is true—even in his Son Jesus Christ. He is the true God and eternal life" (1 John 5:20 NIV).

The apostle John follows the above passage with a warning: "Little children, guard yourselves from idols" (1 John 5:21). An idol is a false god, any object of worship other than the true God. Though we may not bow down to statues, it is easy for people and things of this world to subtly become more important to us than our relationship with God. The following prayer expresses the commitment of a heart that chooses to "worship the Lord your God, and serve Him only" (Matthew 4:10).

> *Dear Lord God, I know how easy it is to allow other things and other people to become more important to me than You. I also know that this is offensive to Your holy eyes because You have commanded that I "shall have no other gods" before You.*

I confess to You that I have not loved You with all my heart and soul and mind. As a result, I have sinned against You, violating the first and greatest commandment. I repent of and turn away from this idolatry, and now choose to return to You, Lord Jesus, as my first love.

Please reveal to my mind any and all idols in my life. I choose to renounce every idol that would give Satan any right in my life. In the name of Jesus, the true God, amen.

(See Exodus 20:3; Matthew 22:37;
Revelation 2:4-5.)

The checklist below may help you recognize those areas where things or people have become more important to you than the true God, Jesus Christ. Notice that most (if not all) of the areas listed below are not evil in themselves; but they become idols when they usurp God's rightful place as Lord of our lives.

❑ Ambition

❑ Food or any substance

❑ Money or possessions

❑ Computers, games, or software

❑ Financial security

❑ Rock stars, media celebrities, or athletes

❑ Church activities

❑ TV, movies, music, or other media

❑ Sports or physical fitness

❑ Fun or pleasure

❑ Ministry

❑ Appearance or image

❑ Work or school

❑ Busyness or activity

❑ Friends

❑ Power or control

❑ Boyfriend or girlfriend

❑ Popularity or opinion of others

❑ Spouse

❑ Knowledge or being right

❑ Children

❑ Hobbies

❑ Parents

❑ Others:

Use the following prayer to renounce any areas of idolatry or wrong priority the Holy Spirit brings to your mind.

> *In the name of the Lord Jesus Christ, I confess that I have made (person or thing) more important than You, and I renounce that false worship. I choose to worship only You, Lord. I ask You, Father, to enable me to keep this area of (name the idol) in its proper place in my life.*

Appendix B
to the Steps to Freedom in Christ

Satanic Rituals or Heavy Occult Activity

∾

If you have been involved in satanic rituals or heavy occult activity (or you suspect it because of blocked memories, severe and recurring nightmares, or sexual bondage or dysfunction), we strongly urge you to say aloud the "Special Renunciations for Satanic Ritual Involvement" on the next page. Read across the page, renouncing the first item in the column under "Domain of Darkness" and then announcing the first truth in the column under "Kingdom of Light." Continue down the page in that manner.

In addition to the "Special Renunciations" list, all other satanic rituals, covenants (promises), and assignments must be specifically renounced as the Lord brings them to your mind.

Some people who have been subjected to Satanic Ritual Abuse (SRA) develop multiple or alter personalities in order to cope with their pain. If this is true in your case, you need someone who understands spiritual conflict to help you work through this problem. For now, walk through the rest of the Steps to Freedom in Christ as best you can. It is important that you remove any demonic strongholds in your life *before* trying to integrate the personalities. Every personality that surfaces must be acknowledged and guided into resolving its issues. Then, all true personalities can agree to come together in Christ.

Special Renunciations for Satanic Ritual Involvement

Domain of Darkness	Kingdom of Light
1. I renounce ever signing or having my name signed over to Satan.	1. I announce that my name is now written in the Lamb's Book of Life.
2. I renounce any ritual whereby I was wed to Satan.	2. I announce that I am part of the bride of Christ.
3. I renounce any and all covenants, agreements, or promises that I made to Satan.	3. I announce that I have made a new covenant with Jesus Christ alone that supersedes any previous agreements.
4. I renounce all satanic assignments for my life, including duties, marriage, and children.	4. I announce and commit myself to know and do only the will of God, and I accept only His guidance for my life.
5. I renounce all spirit guides assigned to me.	5. I announce and accept only the leading of the Holy Spirit.
6. I renounce any giving of my blood in the service of Satan.	6. I trust only in the shed blood of my Lord, Jesus Christ.
7. I renounce ever eating flesh or drinking blood in satanic worship.	7. By faith, I take Holy Communion, the body and blood of the Lord Jesus.
8. I renounce all guardians and satanist parents that were assigned to me.	8. I announce that God is my heavenly Father and the Holy Spirit is my guardian by whom I am sealed.
9. I renounce any baptism whereby I am identified with Satan.	9. I announce that I have been baptized into Christ Jesus and my identity is now in Him alone.
10. I renounce any sacrifice made on my behalf by which Satan may claim ownership of me.	10. I announce that only the sacrifice of Christ has any claim on me. I belong to Him. I have been purchased by the blood of the Lamb.

Appendix C
to the Steps to Freedom in Christ

Truth About Your Father God

~

Sometimes we are greatly hindered from walking by faith in our Father God because of lies we have believed about Him. We are to have a healthy fear of God (awe of His holiness, power, and presence), but we no longer need to fear punishment from Him. Romans 8:15 says, "You have not received a spirit of slavery leading to fear again, but you have received a spirit of adoption as sons by which we cry out, 'Abba! Father!'" The following exercise will help break the chains of those lies and enable you to begin to experience that intimate "Abba, Father" relationship with Him.

Work your way down the lists on the next page item by item, left to right. Begin each statement with the heading in bold at the top of that list. Read through the lists *aloud*.

The Truth About Our Heavenly Father

I renounce the lie that my Father God is...	I joyfully accept the truth that my Father God is...
1. distant and uninterested	1. intimate and involved (Psalm 139:1-18)
2. insensitive and uncaring	2. kind and compassionate (Psalm 103:8-14)
3. stern and demanding	3. accepting and filled with joy and love (Zephaniah 3:17; Romans 15:7)
4. passive and cold	4. warm and affectionate (Isaiah 40:11; Hosea 11:3-4)
5. absent or too busy for me	5. always with me and eager to be with me (Jeremiah 31:20; Ezekiel 34:11-16; Hebrews 13:5)
6. never satisfied with what I do; impatient, or angry	6. patient and slow to anger (Exodus 34:6; 2 Peter 3:9)
7. mean, cruel, or abusive	7. loving, gentle, and protective of me (Psalm 18:2; Jeremiah 31:3; Isaiah 42:3)
8. trying to take all the fun out of life	8. trustworthy and wants to give me a full life; His will is good, perfect, and acceptable (Lamentations 3:22-23; John 10:10; Romans 12:1-2)
9. controlling or manipulative	9. full of grace and mercy; He gives me freedom to fail (Luke 15:11-16; Hebrews 4:15-16)
10. condemning or unforgiving	10. tenderhearted and forgiving; His heart and arms are always open to me (Psalm 130:1-4; Luke 15:17-24)
11. nit-picking, exacting, or perfectionistic	11. committed to my growth and proud of me as His growing child (Romans 8:28-29; 2 Corinthians 7:4; Hebrews 12:5-11)

I am the apple of His eye!
(Deuteronomy 32:10 NIV)

Appendix D
to the Steps Freedom in Christ

Resolving Anxiety

≈

Anxiety is different from fear in that it lacks an object or adequate cause. We can become anxious because we are uncertain about a specific outcome or don't know what is going to happen tomorrow. It is normal to be concerned about things we value; to not do so would demonstrate a lack of care. We can be temporarily anxious about an examination to be taken, attendance at a planned function, or the threat of an incoming storm. Such concern is normal, and it should ordinarily move us to responsible action.

For some people, however, the anxiety is more intense and prolonged. They struggle with a large number of worries and spend a lot of time and energy doing so—and the intensity and frequency of the worrying are always out of proportion to the actual problem.

If persistent anxiety is a problem in your life, the "Anxiety Worksheet" on page 319 can help you to cast all your anxieties on Christ because He cares for you (1 Peter 5:7). Below we walk you through this worksheet step-by-step.

1. *Pray.*

   Prayer is the first step in casting all your anxiety on Christ. Remember Paul's word, "Be anxious for nothing, but in everything by prayer and supplication with thanksgiving let your requests be made known to God" (Philippians. 4:6). Ask God to guide you with the following prayer:

Dear heavenly Father, I come to You as your child purchased by the blood of the Lord Jesus Christ. I declare my dependence upon You, and I acknowledge my need of You. I know that apart from Christ I can do nothing. You know the thoughts and intentions of my heart, and You know the situation I am in from the beginning to the end. I feel as though I am double-minded, and I need your peace to guard my heart and my mind. I humble myself before You and choose to trust You to exalt me at the proper time in any way You choose. I place my trust in You to supply all my needs according to Your riches in glory and to guide me into all truth. I ask for Your divine guidance so that I may fulfill my calling to live a responsible life by faith in the power of Your Holy Spirit. "Search me, O God, and know my heart; try me and know my thoughts; and see if there be any hurtful way in me, and lead me in the everlasting way" (Psalm 139:23-24). In Jesus' precious name I pray, amen.

2. *Resolve any personal and spiritual conflicts.*

The purpose of the Steps to Freedom in Christ is to help you get radically right with God and eliminate any possible influences of the devil on your mind. Remember, that "the Spirit clearly says that in later times some will abandon the faith and follow deceiving spirits and things taught by demons" (1 Timothy 4:1 NIV). You will be a double-minded person if you pay attention to a deceiving spirit. You need to have the presence of God in order to have "the peace of God, which surpasses all comprehension, [that] will guard your hearts and your minds in Christ Jesus" (Philippians 4:7).

3. *State the problem.*

A problem well-stated is half-solved. In an anxious state of mind, you typically can't see the forest for the trees. Put the problem in perspective: Will it matter for eternity? Generally speaking, the process of worrying takes a greater toll on people than the negative consequences of what they have been worrying about. Many anxious people find tremendous relief by simply having their problems clarified and put into perspective.

4. *Divide the facts from the assumptions.*

People may be *fearful* of the facts, but not *anxious*. Fear has an *object*. (We'll be dealing with this in the "Steps to Overcoming Phobias" on page 323.) But we become anxious because we *don't know* what is going to happen tomorrow. Since we don't know, we make assumptions—and a peculiar trait of the mind is its tendency to assume the worst. If you accept your mind's assumption as *truth*, this will drive you to the outer limits of anxiety. And if you are prideful and presumptuous about tomorrow, you will end up suffering some negative consequences. "By pride comes nothing but strife" (Proverbs 13:10 NKJV). Therefore, as best as possible, measure your assumptions against the truth.

5. *Determine what you have the right or ability to control.*

You are responsible only for that which you have the right and ability to control. You are not responsible for that which you don't. Your sense of worth is, in reality, tied only to that for which you are responsible. If you *aren't* living a responsible life, you *should* feel anxious! Don't try to cast your responsibility onto Christ—He will throw it back. But do cast your anxiety onto Him, because His integrity is at stake in meeting your needs if you are living a responsible and righteous life.

6. *List everything related to the situation that is your responsibility.*

   Commit yourself to be a responsible person and fulfill your calling and obligations in life.

7. *Rest in the truth that everything else is God's responsibility.*

   Your only remaining responsibility is to continue to pray and focus on the truth according to Philippians 4:6-8. Any remaining anxiety your have probably comes from your assuming responsibilities that God never intended you to have.

Anxiety Worksheet

1. Go to God in prayer.

2. Resolve all known personal and spiritual conflicts.

3. State the problem.

4. Divide the facts from your assumptions.

   a. List the facts relating to the situation.

   b. List your assumptions relating to the situation.

   c. Verify the above assumptions; that is, measure them against the truth.

5. Determine what you have the right or ability to control.

    a. Figure out what you can control as a matter of personal responsibility.

    b. Figure out what you have no right or ability to control.

6. List everything related to the situation that is your responsibility.

7. If you have fulfilled *your* responsibility, the rest is *God's* responsibility, except for you to continue to walk with God in prayer according to Philippians 4:6-8.

Appendix E
to the Steps to Freedom in Christ

Steps to Overcoming Phobias

~

If you have successfully resolved your personal and spiritual conflicts by submitting to God and resisting the devil, then you are ready to analyze your fears and work out a responsible course of action. Below we take you step-by-step through the "Phobia Finder" on page 325.

1. *Analyze your fear under God's authority and guidance.*

Begin by praying the following prayer aloud:

> *Dear heavenly Father, I come to You as Your child. I put myself under Your protective care and acknowledge that You are the only legitimate object of fear in my life. I confess that I have been fearful and anxious because of my lack of trust and my unbelief. I have not always lived by faith in You, and too often I have relied on my own strength and resources. I thank You that I am forgiven in Christ.*
>
> *I choose to believe the truth that You have not given me "a spirit of fear, but of power and of love and of a sound mind" (2 Timothy 1:7 NKJV). Therefore I renounce any spirit of fear. I ask You to reveal to my mind all the fears that have been controlling me. Show me how I have become fearful, and show me the lies I have believed. I desire to live a responsible life in the power of Your Holy Spirit. Show me how these fears have kept me from doing that. I ask this so that I can confess, renounce, and overcome every fear by faith in You. In Jesus' name I pray, amen.*

The following list may help you recognize some of the fears that have been hindering your walk of faith. On a separate sheet, write down the ones that apply to you as well as any others not on the list that the Spirit of God has revealed to you. As you prayerfully recall your past, write a brief description of what happened (and when) to trigger that fear.

❑ Fear of Satan

❑ Fear of death

❑ Fear of not being loved by God

❑ Fear of never being loved

❑ Fear of not being able to love others

❑ Fear of marriage

❑ Fear of never getting married

❑ Fear of divorce

❑ Fear of never having children

❑ Fear of rejection by people

❑ Fear of disapproval

❑ Fear of embarrassment

❑ Fear of confrontation

❑ Fear of failure

❑ Fear of financial problems

❑ Fear of the future

❑ Fear of the death of a loved one

❑ Fear of going crazy

❑ Fear of being a hopeless case

❑ Fear of being or becoming homosexual

❑ Fear of being victimized by crime

❑ Fear of having committed the unpardonable sin

❑ Fear of specific people, animals, or objects

❑ Other specific fears the Lord brings to mind (lists here):

The root of any phobia is a belief that is not based in truth. These false beliefs need to be rooted out and replaced by the truth of God's Word. Take as much time in prayer as you need to discern these lies, because renouncing them and choosing the truth is a critical step toward gaining and maintaining your freedom in Christ. You have to know and choose to believe the truth in order for it to set you free. Write down the lies you have believed for every fear, and then write down the corresponding truth from the Word of God.

2. *Determine the ways you have been living under the control of fear rather than living by faith in God.*

The next step is to determine how fear has prevented you from living a responsible life, compelled you to do that which is irresponsible, or compromised your Christian witness. After you have gained the necessary insights into your fear, it is time to experience God's cleansing through confession and repentance (1 John 1:9; Proverbs 28:13). Confession is agreeing with God that what you did was sinful. Repentance is the choice to turn away from sin and walk by faith in God. Pray the following prayer for each of the controlling fears that you have analyzed above:

Dear Lord, I confess and repent of the fear of (name the fear) I have believed (state the lie). I renounce that lie, and I choose to believe the truth, which is (state the truth). I also confess any and all ways this fear has resulted in my living irresponsibly, or compromising my witness for Christ (name these ways specifically).

I now choose to live by faith in You, Lord, believing Your promise that You will protect me and meet all my needs as I live by faith in You (Psalm 27:1; Matthew 6:33-34). In Jesus' trustworthy name I pray, amen.

After working through every fear the Lord has revealed to you (including their accompanying lies and sinful behavior), then pray the following prayer:

Dear heavenly Father, I thank You that You are indeed trustworthy. I choose to believe You, even when my feelings and circumstances tell me to fear. You have told me not to fear, for You are with me; to not anxiously look about me, for You are my God. You will strengthen me, help me, and surely uphold me with Your righteous right hand (Isaiah 41:10).

3. *Prayerfully work out a plan of responsible behavior.*

The next step is to face the fear and prayerfully work out a plan to overcome it. Someone once said, "Do the thing you fear the most and the death of fear is certain."

Fear is like a mirage in the desert. It seems so real until you move toward it—but then it disappears into thin air. But as long as we back away from fear, it will haunt us and grow in size until it becomes a giant in our life.

4. *Determine in advance what your response will be to any fear object.*

The fear of God is the one fear that can dispel all other fears, because God rules supreme over every other fear object, including Satan. Even though "your enemy the devil prowls around like a roaring lion looking for someone to devour" (1 Peter 5:8 NIV), he has been defeated by Jesus Christ. "Having disarmed the powers and authorities, he made a public spectacle of them, triumphing over them by the cross" (Colossians 2:15 NIV).

The presence of any fear object should prompt us to focus on God, who is both omnipresent (always present) and omnipotent (all-powerful). To worship God is to acknowledge and ascribe to Him His divine attributes. This keeps fresh in our minds the truth that our loving heavenly Father is always with us and is more powerful than any enemy or circumstance.

5. *Commit yourself to carry out your plan of action in the power of the Holy Spirit.*

Remember, you are never alone in the battle. "It is God who is at work in you, both to will and to work for His good pleasure" (Philippians 2:13).

Phobia Finder

1. Analyze your fear under God's authority and guidance.

   a. Identify all fear objects (that is, what you are afraid of).

    b. Determine when you first experienced the fear.

    c. What events preceded the first experience?

    d. Determine the lies behind each phobia.

2. Determine the ways you have been living under the control of fear rather than living by faith in God.

    a. How has fear—

      1) prevented you from doing what is right and responsible?

      2) compelled you to do what is wrong and irresponsible?

      3) prompted you to compromise your witness for Christ?

    b. Confess any active or passive way in which you have allowed fear to control your life.

    c. Commit yourself to God to live a righteous and responsible life.

3. Prayerfully work out a plan of responsible behavior.

4. Determine in advance what your response will be to any fear object.

5. Commit yourself to carry out your plan of action in the power of the Holy Spirit.

Appendix F
to the Steps to Freedom in Christ

Dealing with Prejudice and Bigotry

~

Pride is the original sin of Lucifer. It sets one person or group against another. Satan's strategy is always to divide and conquer, but God has given us a ministry of reconciliation (2 Corinthians 5:19). Consider for a moment the work of Christ in breaking down the long-standing barrier of racial prejudice between Jew and Gentile:

> [Christ] is our peace, who has made the two one and has destroyed the barrier, the dividing wall of hostility, by abolishing in his flesh the law with its commandments and regulations. His purpose was to create in himself one new man out of the two, thus making peace, and in this one body to reconcile both of them to God through the cross, by which he put to death their hostility. He came and preached peace to you who were far away and peace to those who were near. For through him we both have access to the Father by one Spirit (Ephesians 2:14-18 NIV).

Many times we deny that there is prejudice or bigotry in our hearts, yet "nothing in all creation is hidden from God's sight. Everything is uncovered and laid bare before the eyes of him to whom we must give account" (Hebrews 4:13 NIV). The following is a prayer asking God to shine His light upon your heart and reveal any area of proud prejudice.

Dear heavenly Father, I know that You love all people equally and that You do not show favoritism. You accept people from every nation who fear You and do what is right. You do not judge them based on skin color, race, economic standing, ethnic background, gender, denominational preference, or any other worldly matter. I confess that I have too often prejudged others or regarded myself superior. I have not always been a minister of reconciliation, but have been a proud agent of division through my attitudes, words, and deeds. I repent of all hateful bigotry and proud prejudice, and I ask You, Lord, to now reveal to my mind all the specific ways in which this form of pride has corrupted my heart and mind. In Jesus' name, amen.

(See Acts 10:34; 2 Corinthians 5:16.)

For each area of prejudice, superiority, or bigotry that the Lord brings to mind, pray the following prayer aloud from your heart:

I confess and renounce the prideful sin of prejudice against (<u>name the group</u>). I thank You for Your forgiveness, Lord, and ask now that You would change my heart and make me a loving agent of reconciliation with (<u>name the group</u>). In Jesus' name, amen.

Appendix G
to the Steps to Freedom in Christ

Seeking the Forgiveness of Others

~

If you bring your gift to the altar, and there remember that your brother has something against you, leave your gift there before the altar, and go your way. First be reconciled to your brother, and then come and offer your gift. Agree with your adversary quickly, while you are on the way with him, lest your adversary deliver you to the judge, the judge hand you over to the officer, and you are thrown into prison. Assuredly, I say to you, you will by no means get out of there till you have paid the last penny (Matthew 5:23-26 NKJV).

The Motivation for Seeking Forgiveness

Matthew 5:23-26 is the key passage on seeking forgiveness. Several points in these verses bear emphasizing. The worshiper coming before God to offer a gift *remembers* that someone has something against him. The Holy Spirit is the One who brings to his or her mind the wrong that was done.

Only the actions which have hurt other people need to be confessed to them. If you have had jealous, lustful, or angry thoughts toward others, and they don't know about it, these are to be confessed to God alone.

An exception to this principle occurs when restitution needs to be made. If you stole or broke something, damaged someone's reputation, and so on, you need to go to that person and make it right, even if he or she is unaware of what you did.

The Process of Seeking Forgiveness

1. Write out what you did wrong and why you did it.

2. Make sure you have already forgiven the offended person for whatever he or she may have done to you.

3. Think through exactly how you will ask the person to forgive you. Be sure to:

   a. Label your action as "wrong."

   b. Be specific and admit what you did.

   c. Make no defenses or excuses.

   d. Do not blame the other person, and do not expect or demand that he or she ask for your forgiveness.

   e. Your confession should lead to the direct question: "Will you forgive me?"

4. Seek the right place and the right time to approach the offended person.

5. Ask for forgiveness in person with anyone with whom you can talk face-to-face, with the following exception: *Do not go alone* when your safety is in danger.

6. Except where no other means of communication is possible, *do not write a letter* because a letter can be very easily misread or misunderstood; a letter can be read by the wrong people (those having nothing to do with the offense or the confession); a letter can be kept when it should have been destroyed.

7. Once you sincerely seek forgiveness, you are free—whether the other person forgives you or not (Romans 12:18).

8. After seeking forgiveness, fellowship with God in worship (Matthew 5:24).

Notes

~

An Anger Epidemic

1. John Marks, "The American Uncivil Wars," *U.S. News Online*, April 22, 1996, p. 2.

2. National Center for Victims of Crime Web site, "Statistics: Workplace Violence," 1998, p.1. URL: <http://www.ncvc.org/stats/wv.htm>.

3. C. Leslie Charles, *Why Is Everyone So Cranky?* (New York: Hyperion, 1999).

4. Anita Bruzzese, "Why are people so cranky at work?" *Asheville Citizen-Times*, July 23, 2000, p. G1.

5. July 1999 Gallup Poll, as cited in *Access Atlanta* Web site, URL: <http://www.accessatlanta.com>.

6. American Medical Association Web site, "Facts about Family Violence," p. 1. URL: <http://www.ama-assn.org>.

7. AMA Web site, p. 2.

8. AMA Web site, p. 3.

9. Karen S. Peterson, "Why Everyone Is So Short-Tempered," *USA Today*, July 18, 2000, p. 2A.

10. "Did Springer Show Lead to Slaying?" *Asheville Citizen-Times*, July 28, 2000, p. A3.

11. Peterson, p. 1A.

12. Peterson, p. 1A.

13. Alan Sipress, "Raging Drivers Violate Funeral Corteges," *Washington Post*, July 9, 2000.

14. Sipress.

Chapter 1—Anger—A Matter of Life and Death

1. S.I. McMillen, M.D., *None of These Diseases* (Minneapolis: Successful Living, Inc., 1963), p. 69.

2. Meyer Friedman and Ray Rosenman, *Type A Behavior and Your Heart* (New York: Knopf, 1974).

3. Redford and Virginia Williams, *Anger Kills* (New York: Harper Perennial, 1993).

Chapter 2—Goals and Desires

1. J.R. Averill, "Studies of Anger and Aggression: Implications for Theories of Emotion," *American Psychologist* 38 (1983): pp. 1145-1160.

2. W. Doyle Gentry, Ph.D., *Anger-Free* (New York: Quill, 1999), p. 114.

3. David G. Benner, ed., *Baker Encyclopedia of Psychology* (Grand Rapids, MI: Baker Book House, 1990), pp. 58-59.

4. W. E. Vine, *An Expository Dictionary of New Testament Words* (Old Tappan, NJ: Fleming H. Revell Company, 1966), pp. 55-56.

5. Vine, p. 56.

6. Bill Gillham, *Lifetime Guarantee* (Eugene, OR: Harvest House, 1993), p. 38

7. Gillham, pp. 27-33.

8. To see how this relates to anxiety disorders, see our book *Freedom From Fear* (Eugene, OR: Harvest House, 1999). To see how this relates to the problem of depression, see Neil's book *Finding Hope Again* (Ventura, CA: Regal Books), coauthored with Hal Baumchen.

9. Neil T. Anderson, *Victory Over the Darkness*, 2nd ed. (Ventura, CA: Regal Books, 2000), pp. 131-132.

10. Anderson, *Victory Over the Darkness*, p. 132.

11. From the poem "Disappointment—His Appointment," by Edith Lillian Young, date and publisher unknown.

Chapter 3—Be Angry but Don't Sin

1. C.S. Lewis, *Letters to Malcolm, Chiefly on Prayer* (San Diego, CA: Harvest Books, 1983), p. 97.

2. Les Carter and Frank Minirth, *The Anger Workbook* (Nashville, TN: Thomas Nelson, Inc., 1993), p. 34.

3. Gary Chapman, *The Other Side of Love* (Chicago: Moody Press 1999), pp. 18-19.

Chapter 4—Mental Strongholds

1. Steve McVey, *Grace Walk* (Eugene, OR: Harvest House Publishers, 1995), p. 28.

2. James Strong, *Strong's Exhaustive Concordance of the Bible* (Nashville, TN: Abingdon, 1980).

3. Strong.

4. Neil Anderson and Mike and Julia Quarles, *Freedom from Addiction* (Ventura, CA: Regal Books, 1996), pp. 40,39. Used by Permission.

5. Taken from Neil's book *Who I Am in Christ* (Ventura, CA: Regal Books, 2001). Used by permission.

Chapter 5—Flesh Patterns of Anger

1. William R. Moody, *The Life of Dwight L. Moody* (Murfreesboro, TN: Sword of the Lord Publishers, n.d.), pp. 110-111.

2. Ron and Pat Potter-Efron, *Letting Go of Anger* (Oakland, CA: New Harbinger Publications, Inc., 1995), p. 6, emphasis added.

3. Ken Voges and Ron Braund, *Understanding How Others Misunderstand You* (Chicago: Moody Press, 1990), pp. 38-41.

4. Voges and Braund, p. 71.

5. Potter-Efron, p. 104.

6. Potter-Efron, p. 33.

7. Les Carter and Frank Minirth, *The Anger Workbook* (Nashville, TN: Thomas Nelson, Inc., 1993), p. 32.

8. Lee LeFebre, "The Nature of the Flesh," part 1, *The Grace Life Conference* (Aurora, CO: CrossLife, 1997), cassette tape.

9. A.W. Tozer, *The Pursuit of God* (Camp Hill, PA: Christian Publications, Inc., 1982), pp. 29-30.

Chapter 6—Amazing Grace

1. From Bill Hybels's video *Becoming a Contagious Christian* (Willow Creek Association, 1995).

2. Henri Nouwen, *The Return of the Prodigal Son* (New York: Doubleday, 1994), pp. 112-113.

3. J.I. Packer, *Knowing God* (Downers Grove, IL: InterVarsity Press, 1973), p. 120.

Chapter 7—Grace for Life

1. David C. Needham, *Alive for the First Time* (Sisters, OR: Multnomah Publishers, Inc., 1995), p. 141.

2. From Walt Mueller, *Understanding Today's Youth Culture* (Wheaton, IL: Tyndale House Publishers, 1994), p. 316.

3. J.I. Packer, *Knowing God* (Downers Grove, IL: InterVarsity Press, 1973), p. 120.

Chapter 8—The Need to Forgive

1. A version of a story first published in Neil Anderson and Rich Miller, *Leading Teens to Freedom in Christ* (Ventura, CA: Gospel Light Publishers, 1997), pp. 203-204. Used by Permission.

2. James Strong, *Strong's Exhaustive Concordance of the Bible* (Nashville, TN: Abingdon, 1980).

3. W.E. Vine, *Vine's Expository Dictionary of Old and New Testament Words* (Iowa Falls, IA: World Bible Publishers, 1981), p. 257.

4. Strong.

5. Frederick Buechner, *Wishful Thinking*, rev. ed. (San Francisco: Harper San Francisco, 1993), p. 2.

6. Marie Ragghianti, "Every Day I Have to Forgive Again," *Parade Magazine*, April 23, 2000, p. 6.

7. "The Shots Still Echo," *People Magazine*, November 8, 1999, p. 62.

8. "The Shots," p. 60.

9. "The Shots."

10. Tom Bowers, "Someone I Had to Forgive," *Guideposts*, January, 1999, p. 7.

11. Bowers, p. 9.

12. Bowers, p. 9.

13. There are many worthwhile books to read on the subject of the problem of suffering and evil in the world. We would particularly like to recommend Philip Yancey's books *Where Is God When It Hurts?* and *Disappointment with God*.

14. Adapted from a document received from Grace Ministries International. Author unknown.

Chapter 9—Forgiving from the Heart

1. Charles Stanley, *The Gift of Forgiveness* (Nashville, TN: Thomas Nelson, Inc., 1991), p. 16.

2. Stanley, p. 195.

3. Marie Ragghianti, "Every Day I Have to Forgive Again," *Parade*, April 23, 2000, p. 6. Reprinted with permission from *Parade*, © 2000.

4. Author unknown (Honeycomb Publishing, Box 1434, Taylors, SC 29687).

Chapter 10—It's a Mad, Mad World

1. *ASA Connections*, September/October 2000, advertisement on inside front cover.

2. *ASA Connections*, pp. 20-21.

3. Adult suicide rates in rural areas exceed those in urban locales, according to a 1995 (the most recent available) study cited in the *Asheville Citizen-Times*, October 15, 2000, p. A2. The suicide rate per 100,000 people in rural areas was 17.94, contrasted with a rate of 14.91 in urban areas. According to the same survey, the

suicide rate in the western U.S. was nearly 50 percent higher than in the Northeast.

4. Mark Bubeck, *The Adversary* (Chicago: Moody Press, 1975), pp. 46-47.

5. C. Leslie Charles, *Why Is Everyone So Cranky?* (New York: Hyperion, 1999), p. 229.

6. Charles, p. 20-21.

7. A.W. Tozer, *The Pursuit of God* (Camp Hill, PA: Christian Publications, Inc., 1982), p. 21-22.

8. Philip Yancey, *Where Is God When It Hurts?*, first part of double volume with *Disappointment with God* (Grand Rapids, MI: Zondervan Publishing House, 1996), p. 19.

9. Yancey, preface p. 2.

10. Charles, *Why Is Everyone So Cranky?*, p. 60.

11. Elene C. Brown, "Why We're All So Cranky," *Daily Local News* [Philadelphia, Pennsylvania], January 11, 2000, p. D1.

12. Brown, p. D1

Chapter 11—A Peace of Your Mind

1. Donald S. Whitney, *Spiritual Disciplines for the Christian Life* (Colorado Springs, CO: NavPress, 1991), p. 194.

2. Richard J. Foster, *Celebration of Discipline* (Philadelphia: Harper & Row, 1988), p. 106.

3. From Leonard Ravenhill, "Worship," an audiotape message given at the Inn of Last Resort, Franklin, NC.

Chapter 12—Connecting to the Power

1. Bill Gillham, *Lifetime Guarantee* (Eugene, OR: Harvest House Publishers, 1993), pp. 103-104.

2. A.W. Tozer, *How to Be Filled with the Holy Spirit* (Camp Hill, PA: Christian Publications, n.d.), p. 39.

3. Timothy Beougher and Lyle Dorsett, *Accounts of a Campus Revival* (Wheaton, IL: Harold Shaw Publishers, 1995), pp. 95-96.

4. Andrew Murray, *The Believer's Full Blessing of Pentecost* (Minneapolis: Bethany House Publishers, 1984), pp. 89-90.

Chapter 13—Breaking Strongholds of Anger, Part One

1. Jean Peerenboom, "When Anger Strikes," *Asheville Citizen-Times*, August 20, 2000, p. B3.
2. Peerenboom, citing Sue Kelly-Kohlman, *A dANGERous Choice? Help Kids Make Good Decisions Through Anger Control* (Green Bay, WI: Irish Eyes Publishing, 2000).

Chapter 14—Breaking Strongholds of Anger, Part Two

1. The Scripture verses quoted in this prayer are Galatians 5:24; Galatians 6:14; and Colossians 2:15.

Steps to Freedom in Christ

1. Taken from Neil T. Anderson, *Living Free in Christ* (Ventura, CA: Gospel Light Publications, 1995). Used by Permission.

Books and Resources from
Freedom in Christ Ministries
and Neil T. Anderson

Core Message and Resources

- *The Bondage Breaker*® (Harvest House). Study guide and audiobook also available. This book explains spiritual warfare, what your protection is, ways that you are vulnerable, and how you can live a liberated life in Christ. Well over one million copies in print.

- *Victory Over the Darkness* with study guide, audio book, and videos (Regal Books). Explains who you are in Christ, how you walk by faith, how your mind and emotions function, and how to relate to one another in Christ. Well over one million copies in print.

- *Breaking Through to Spiritual Maturity* (Regal Books). A curriculum for teaching the basic message of Freedom in Christ Ministries.

- *Discipleship Counseling* with videos (Regal Books). Discipleship and counseling are integrated practically with theology and psychology to help Christians resolve personal and spiritual conflicts through repentance.

- *Steps to Freedom in Christ* and interactive video (Regal Books). This discipleship counseling tool helps Christians resolve their personal and spiritual conflicts.

The Bondage Breaker® Series (Harvest House). Truth from the Word of God on specific issues—to bring you help and freedom in your life.

- *Praying by the Power of the Spirit*
- *Finding God's Will in Spiritually Deceptive Times*
- *Finding Freedom in a Sex-Obsessed World*

Resources on Specific Issues

- *Getting Anger Under Control* with Rich Miller (Harvest House). Exposes the basis for anger and shows how you can control it.

- *Freedom from Fear* with Rich Miller (Harvest House). Discusses fear, anxiety, and anxiety disorders and reveals how you can be free from them.

- *Daily in Christ* (Harvest House). This popular daily devotional will encourage, motivate, and challenge you to experience the reality of *Christ in you*.

- *Breaking the Bondage of Legalism* with Rich Miller and Paul Travis (Harvest House). An exposure and explanation of legalism, the guilt and shame it brings, and how you can overcome it.
- *God's Power at Work in You* with Dr. Robert Saucy (Harvest House). A thorough analysis of sanctification, along with practical instruction on how you can grow in Christ.
- *A Way of Escape* (Harvest House). Exposes the bondage of sexual strongholds and shows you how they can be torn down in Christ.
- *The Seduction of Our Children* with Steve Russo (Harvest House). Reveals what teenagers are experiencing and how you as a parent can be equipped to help them.
- *Who I Am in Christ* (Regal Books). Thirty-six short chapters on who you are in Christ and how He meets your deepest needs.
- *Freedom from Addiction* with Mike Quarles (Regal Books).
- *One Day at a Time* with Mike Quarles (Regal Books).
- *The Christ-Centered Marriage* with Dr. Charles Mylander (Regal Books).
- *The Spiritual Protection of Our Children* with Peter and Sue Vander Hook (Regal Books).
- *Leading Teens to Freedom in Christ* with Rich Miller (Regal Books).
- *Finding Hope Again* with Hal Baumchen (Regal Books). Depression and how to overcome it.
- *Released from Bondage* with Judy King and Dr. Fernando Garzon (Thomas Nelson).
- *Freedom in Christ Bible* (Zondervan). A one-year discipleship study with notes in the Bible.
- *Blessed Are the Peacemakers* with Dr. Charles Mylander (Regal Books).
- *A Biblical Guide to Alternative Medicine* with Dr. Michael Jacobson (Regal Books).
- *Setting Your Church Free* with Dr. Charles Mylander (Regal Books).
- *Christ-Centered Therapy* with Dr. Terry and Julie Zuehlke (Zondervan).

The Victory Over the Darkness Series (Regal Books)
- *Overcoming a Negative Self-Image* with Dave Park
- *Overcoming Addictive Behavior* with Mike Quarles
- *Overcoming Doubt*
- *Overcoming Depression*

Youth Books

- *The Bondage Breaker*® *Youth Edition* with Dave Park (Harvest House)
- *Stomping Out the Darkness* with Dave Park (Regal Books)
- *Stomping Out Fear* with Dave Park and Rich Miller (Harvest House)
- *Stomping Out Depression* with Dave Park (Regal Books)
- *Radical Image** with Dr. Robert Saucy and Dave Park
- *Sold Out for God** with Dr. Robert Saucy and Dave Park
- *Higher Ground** with Dr. Robert Saucy and Dave Park
- *Extreme Faith* with Dave Park (Harvest House)
- *Reality Check* with Rich Miller (Harvest House)
- *Awesome God* with Rich Miller (Harvest House)
- *Real Life** with Dave Park
- *Ultimate Love** with Dave Park
- *Righteous Pursuit* with Dave Park (Harvest House)
- *Purity Under Pressure* with Dave Park (Harvest House)
  * Available directly from Freedom in Christ Ministries only

Contact information for Freedom in Christ Ministries:
9051 Executive Park Drive, Suite 503
Knoxville, TN 37923
Telephone: (865) 342-4000
E-mail: info@ficm.org
Web site: www.ficm.org